Faith, Reason, and Compassion

Faith, Reason, and Compassion
A Philosophy of the Christian Faith

James Gilman

ROWMAN & LITTLEFIELD PUBLISHERS, INC.
Lanham • Boulder • New York • Toronto • Plymouth, UK

ROWMAN & LITTLEFIELD PUBLISHERS, INC.

Published in the United States of America
by Rowman & Littlefield Publishers, Inc.
A wholly owned subsidiary of The Rowman & Littlefield Publishing Group, Inc.
4501 Forbes Boulevard, Suite 200, Lanham, Maryland 20706
www.rowmanlittlefield.com

Estover Road
Plymouth PL6 7PY
United Kingdom

Copyright © 2007 by Rowman & Littlefield Publishers, Inc.

All rights reserved. No part of this publication may be reproduced, stored in a retrieval system, or transmitted in any form or by any means, electronic, mechanical, photocopying, recording, or otherwise, without the prior permission of the publisher.

British Library Cataloguing in Publication Information Available

Library of Congress Cataloging-in-Publication Data

Gilman, James Earl.
  Faith, reason, and compassion : a philosophy of the Christian faith / James Gilman.
    p. cm.
  ISBN-13: 978-0-7425-5270-8 (alk paper)
  ISBN-10: 0-7425-5270-5 (alk paper)
  ISBN-13: 978-0-7425-5271-5 (alk paper)
  ISBN-10: 0-7425-5271-3 (alk. paper)
  1. Faith and reason. 2. Christianity—Philosophy. 3. Philosophical theology. I. Title.
BT20.G55 2007
231'.042—dc22   2006024245

Printed in the United States of America

∞™ The paper used in this publication meets the minimum requirements of American National Standard for Information Sciences—Permanence of Paper for Printed Library Materials, ANSI/NISO Z39.48-1992.

To my parents
William Harold and Florence Evelyn Gilman
for their Christian love and compassion

Contents

Preface ... ix

PART I REENFRANCHISING THE MIND

Chapter 1 Matters of the Mind ... 3
Chapter 2 Reenfranchising the Mind ... 15

PART II FAITH AND REASON

Chapter 3 Belief in God's Existence ... 39
Chapter 4 Belief in God's Goodness ... 67
Chapter 5 Belief in God's Miracles ... 97

PART III FAITH AND CULTURE

Chapter 6 Christian Faith and Other Faiths ... 123
Chapter 7 Christian Faith and Society ... 159

Bibliography ... 187
Index ... 191
About the Author ... 193

Preface

The writing of this book, whose working title was *Fidelity of Mind*, was disrupted and delayed, gratefully, by the writing of another book titled *Fidelity of Heart: An Ethic of Christian Virtue*. I say gratefully because this book would not be what it is without first writing that earlier book. Both methodologically and substantively this book is different and, I hope, better as a result: methodologically, by discovering how the physics of symmetry, asymmetry, and supersymmetry is useful for framing issues in philosophy of religion; substantively, by seeing how the moral experience of compassion is crucial for solving those issues.

This book employs an innovative methodology drawn from the resources of modern physics. Such innovation is necessary because the mix of ideas in this book is somewhat unusual. It blends ingredient from philosophy of religion and from ethics, and does so in a way that, as far as I know, is unprecedented. Two mentors, both now emeritus from Drew University, I am indebted to, each of whom represents one ingredient in this blend: Charles Courtney tutored me in the discipline of thinking critically and creatively about philosophy of religion, and Edward Long, Jr., in the scope and scale of Christian ethics. Both demonstrate a steadfast commitment to his discipline's historical tradition while encouraging an innovative way of reconceiving it. For their wisdom and guidance I am grateful. Many colleagues and friends at Mary Baldwin College have contributed in various ways to the pattern of ideas in this book, including Roderic Owen, Edward Scott, Pat Hunt, Annette Evans, Ken Beals, Perry Neal, Robert Everett, and Jack Hill. And not least, I am indebted to my brother Roger (philosopher and Dean of Fairhaven Honors College, Western Washington State University) with whom over many years I have had numerous conversations about the important ideas in this book. For the insight and perspective he invested in those conversations, no compensation is adequate. I am grateful to editors at Rowman & Littlefield, especially Marian Haggard and Elaine McGarraugh, for their skilled editing. More than all else, my children, Ian James (who helped develop the index) and Caitrin Marie, inspire me to be better than I am in all that I do.

PART I

REENFRANCHISING THE MIND

> Not
> the serene apostle who knew
> the world at its source,
> but the one who had to press
> his flesh to the wounded
> flesh of a god he had not loved
> enough, breath by breath.
> I hear him stammer, *my God,*
> the way a hand with a match
> shakes striking fire
>
> > Margaret Gibson, *Core*

CHAPTER ONE

Matters of the Mind

Habits of Mind

First the women and then some of the other disciples enter the tomb only to find the body of Jesus gone and the burial linen lying about. Some believe what by all accounts and in any age is unbelievable, that Jesus has risen from the dead. But when Thomas, who had not been with the others, is told by them that the tomb is empty and that they have "seen the Lord," he is understandably skeptical. "Unless I see in his hands the print of the nails, and place my fingers in the mark of the nails, and place my hand in his side, I will not believe." Eight days later, Thomas and other disciples suddenly find Jesus standing with them in a room. Jesus invites Thomas to touch his hands and his side, and then says to him, "Do not be faithless, but believing." Thomas does indeed eventually declare faith in Jesus' resurrection, "My Lord and my God." But for Jesus that is not the end of the matter. He takes the occasion to situate Thomas' evidential belief in relation to that of the others, who by faith believe. Those whose belief is inspired by faith are "blessed," says Jesus, in contrast to Thomas, whose belief requires empirical evidence (John 20:1–29).[1] Jesus does not question the genuineness of Thomas' belief; but he does question the "faithless" way in which Thomas comes to it. The priority that Jesus seems to grant faith may very well today disturb many, especially philosophers of religion, who are generally trained to believe nothing unless on the basis of solid evidence and sound reason. In our advanced, scientific age at least, it would seem sensible enough for Thomas to seek and demand evidence. It is Jesus who seems to articulate what to contemporary ears sounds unreasonable, even irrational: that the "blessed" are those for whom belief is based not on evidence but on simple faith.

What should and can we make of this? Is it simply and solely faith, devoid of all reason, that Jesus extols? And how can we assess the difference between the way the disciples and Thomas come to believe in Jesus' resurrection? How can we assess the difference between believing by faith and believing by reason? How are the two related, if at all? How and why is believing by faith when you "have not seen" more "blessed" than believing "because you have seen"? Whatever Jesus may have had in mind in drawing the distinction as he did (and the argument of this book stands as my interpretation of it), this story provides a catalyst for treating a problem that is most basic for philosophy of religion, namely, What is the relationship between faith and reason? How properly should faith and reason situate themselves in relation to each other? This is the principal problem this book intends to address and seeks to solve. It is the problem with which this book begins and ends. It is the problem underlying specific issues addressed in each chapter. And the solution it offers is based on a particular reading of John's gospel, namely, that implicit in Jesus' comments is the view that faith and reason are mutually interdependent, equally necessary habits of mind. Jesus has been with his disciples for three years, preaching and teaching, feeding the hungry, and healing the sick. He has already a number of times forewarned them of his death and resurrection. So, now, in this moment, on the basis of the trustworthiness of his promise, might he not reasonably expect that his disciples by faith believe?

The pivotal notion by which I articulate the interdependence of the disciples' faith and the evidence demanded by Thomas' doubt is that of "mind." By "mind" I refer specifically to two activities or habits of intellect—faith and reason—which properly operate interdependently. These two activities do not exhaust, of course, the idea of "mind" but explicate the use of "mind" that I make in this book. Although distinguishable, faith and reason are inseparable activities that constitute a single systolic/diastolic motion of intellect so that the activity of the one is always at least implicit in the activity of the other. What I refer to when I use the phrase "fidelity of mind," then, is the commitment philosophers of religion make to both faith and reason—that is, the commitment they properly make in analyzing and interpreting religious experience, showing in their theories the various ways it is a function of both habits of mind. Specifically, I show how faith is that activity by which the mind "apprehends" a dimension of reality that is situated asymmetrically (God, miracles) in relation to the symmetry of the universe. And I show how reason is that activity by which the mind "comprehends" those patterns of physical and moral reality that are systematically and rationally ordered. I show how faith invites or elicits reason's critical activity as the necessary completion of what it apprehends. And I show how reason presupposes faith's activity of apprehending as the necessary and ultimate origination of what it explains and justifies.

I am not unaware of employing terms (e.g., asymmetry, apprehending, symmetry) and assertions that require clarification and explanation, and throughout this book I intend to provide them. To begin to do so, I trace briefly two threads woven into the historical fabric of the Western intellectual tradition, each of which corresponds to one of these two activities of mind. One thread (faith) weaves into that fabric a tradition of religious and metaphysical beliefs, and the other thread (reason) weaves into it a tradition of critical, scientific analysis. Historically these two threads at times have tended to be woven rather loosely and at other times more tightly. What I argue in this book is that neither thread is by itself strong enough to bear the weight of religion's intellectual and practical life. When asked to do so alone each thread frays or snaps. But when securely woven together they are able to sew a single, seamless fabric of sufficient strength to support and sustain the weight and bulk of religious life.

By "fideism" I mean the tendency to favor the role of faith in understanding religion over the role of critical analysis and reason. As a tradition, fideism traces its thread to Christian scriptures and especially to the theology of St. Paul. From this anchor and winding throughout the history of Western thought an assortment of fideistic patterns spin off. The most basic pattern depicts truth in religion as primarily and ultimately based on faith rather than on reason or evidence. It depicts religion as consisting of beliefs that cannot be established by proofs or empirical evidence but must simply be accepted. Some of the more radical forms of fideism promote irrationalism, rejecting (if not reviling), reason, and science quite completely, sometimes insisting not only that they have no value for religious belief but that they are hostile to it. Tertullian, for example, inspired by St. Paul's view that the central beliefs of Christianity are considered foolishness by Greek philosophy, insists *credo quia absurdum*, that religious beliefs are incompatible with reason's demand for justification and evidence. More mystical versions of radical fideism insist that super-rational, mystical experiences transcend categories of reason and are the true and ultimate sources of religion and religious beliefs. The mysticism of St. John of the Cross, for example, claims that the believer can train herself or himself in such a way as to be able to escape the prison of reason and flourish in the dark, mysterious light of the incomprehensible One. In contrast, David Hume, on empirical rather than mystical grounds, famously argues, at the end of his essay "Of Miracles," that miracles, and beliefs based on them, are contrary to reason and evidence. Accordingly, the believer must be moved, if moved at all, by faith; for he must believe what is contrary to custom and experience. Most famously, Kierkegaard, who approved of

Hume's formulation, argues that Christian faith at its core (e.g., the Incarnation, the Resurrection) is incompatible with reason—indeed, that it is paradoxical by all the standards of reason. He argues, for example, that reason and science cannot accommodate the paradoxical belief that the eternal has become a concrete, historical fact. For Kierkegaard, the subjectivity of genuinely Christian truth requires the follower of Christ by faith to leap beyond the horizon of reason and grasp the absurdity of paradox. More recently, Wittgenstein is thought by some to have advocated a form of fideism, especially in his later philosophy. Fideism was one of the earliest criticisms lodged against Wittgenstein's philosophy of religion, by Kai Nielsen.[2] "The Wittgensteinian twist to fideism is the claim that, qua form of life, religion is a *fait accompli* which neither stands in need of justification nor should fear censure from nonreligious forms of life."[3]

More moderate forms of fideism developed in the Western tradition, many of which are rooted in the thought of St. Augustine. Rather than insisting that faith is contrary to reason, this tradition insists only that faith precedes reason, that in religion faith is epistemologically prior to reason, as suggested by Augustine's motto *credo ut intelligam*. But even though for St. Augustine faith and reason are interdependent, faith is nevertheless prior to reason, with the latter playing the role of faith's handmaiden, assisting it in the search for truth, explaining and comprehending beliefs apprehended by faith. This also seems to be the orientation of Pascal in his *Pensées*, for example, when he argues that although by reason atheism can be shown to be unadvisable, the ultimate truths of theism can be approached and accepted only by faith. Pascal also argues, however, that once accepted by faith reason can assist the believer in understanding the force and viability of Christian beliefs. Recently a cadre of philosophers who insist that belief in God is foundational (e.g., Plantinga, Wolterstorff) argue on behalf of a moderate and modified form of fideism or, as others might argue, a moderate or modified form of rationalism. Some, like John Apczynski,[4] deny that Plantinga's approach is fideistic. I would argue, however, that insofar as Plantinga insists that belief in God is properly basic, it is liberated from the kind of justification or evidence demanded of other beliefs that are not properly basic, even though it is still susceptible to being justified, but indirectly on the basis of other beliefs and premises.

Although the thread of fideism is favored by some philosophers, the equally sturdy thread of rationalism, originating in Christian scriptures, also winds its way throughout the fabric of Western thought. The Apostle Peter instructed that Christians should be ready always to give a defense or reason for the hope that is within (I Peter 3:15), and ever since, Christian thinkers have been more than eager to oblige. By "rationalism" I do not refer to a narrower use of this word that marks a specific modern historical movement (Descartes, Spinoza, Leibniz). That movement stressed, in opposition to empiricism, the power of a priori reason to comprehend necessary truths about the world and regarded natural science as primarily an a priori enterprise. Instead I mean to refer to that general tendency and thread throughout Western history that stresses the priority of reason over faith, that for a belief, including religious belief, to be acceptable one must be able to show that it is in some sense reasonable and justifiable. Conceiving it broadly in this way, rationalism includes historical movements such as empiricism and rationalism, as well as thinkers as different as Descartes, Hume, Kant, and Hegel who give primary place and role to reason in all matters religious.

The Enlightenment is a movement to which the word "rationalism" might be fairly but cautiously ascribed, especially to certain thinkers in France (d'Alembert, d'Holbach, Voltaire, Condorcet), England (Locke, Hume), and Germany (Leibniz, Kant) who place a great deal of trust in the power of reason and scientific inquiry and education. As a result of its exceptional faith in reason, enlightened thinkers often, although not always, minimize a positive role for emotions in enlightened human life, and they often, although not always, minimize or eliminate the role of faith and piety in enlightened religion. D'Holbach, for instance, exemplifies a thinker whose philosophy makes little or no space for the role of the emotions or religion in enlightened life. Hume, in contrast, insists on the centrality of emotions, arguing that they are the soil in which reason grows and flourishes. Yet, he denies quite completely any place for faith and religion in the life of the enlightened mind. Kant, in contrast, makes room for both the emotions and faith, but only by cramping them within the boundaries of critical, rational inquiry.[5] This more radical version of rationalism generally rejects the classic arguments for the existence of God,[6] insisting that they are rationally unpersuasive and hinder progress toward a scientific interpretation of religion.

A more moderate version of rationalism treats the arguments for the existence of God favorably, insisting that on the basis of a priori reason (Aquinas, Descartes) or a posteriori reason (Paley, Swinburne) God's existence can be proven. Its assumption is that reason, as a gift from God, functions as a kind of prolegommena to religious faith, leading the person who earnestly follows the dictates of reason to faith in God. Aquinas certainly set forth his famous "five proofs" partly to show that Christian faith and revelation are rooted in the soil of reason. Descartes' methodical doubt, initially situating the self skeptically in relation to belief in the world and God, finds an a priori, ontological way to prove God's existence and clear a space for a rational version of Christian faith. Similarly, William Paley, even after Hume's criticism of such an argument in *Dialogues Concerning Natural Religion* (posthumously, 1779), set forth in *Natural Theology* (1802) his classic a posteriori "watch" version of the teleological argument, an argument that continues to attract attention. In 1995, for example, the physicist Charles Townes, a Nobel laureate, stated that "physicists are running into stone walls of things that seem to reflect intelligence at work in natural law."[7] More recently, philosophers like John Hick and Richard Swinburne perpetuate this moderate version of rationalism and manage to attract as co-participants in such endeavors a great many contemporary philosophers of religion. These efforts by rationalists to ground faith in reason are more "moderate" than those efforts of the "radical" rationalists discussed above. For their explicit aim is not to undermine or restrict religious faith but to ground it more firmly in a capacity of human mind without which, they believe, a respectable, viable, and scientific version of a theistic worldview is quite impossible.

The particular challenge of this book lies in its attempt to weave into a single cloth these two threads (fideism and rationalism) and activities of mind (faith and reason) and to show how only by enfranchising both can the mind satisfy the demands made on it by religion and religious experience. What, then, can we make of Jesus' declaration that those who believe God's promises by faith are more blessed than those who believe on the evidence of reason? First, by saying this, Jesus does not reject the evidence of reason demanded by Thomas. Indeed, he shows Thomas evidence of his resurrection and Thomas believes. Second, those disciples who believe in Christ's resurrection by faith believe on the basis of the testimony of those who witnessed the empty tomb. Their faith apprehends the significance of the empty tomb without needing or demanding direct evidence, as did Thomas. Christians today tend toward one of these groups or the other. Some, like many of the disciples, are satisfied with the witness of personal experience and the Bible independent of evidence and arguments; others, like Thomas, require evidence and arguments to bolster faith. In either case, faith and reason, as activities of mind, are operative in some sense, even though perhaps not equally. My presumption is that in accounting for religion neither faith nor reason possess independent, privileged status; they should be treated as internally interdependent activities. The challenge of this book, in other words, is partly its scope. All the relevant sources and materials from these two intellectual traditions (fideism and rationalism), diverse and copious as they are, cannot be treated, and I shall not try to do so. A sampling from each tradition, as we progress, will suffice. Fortunately, there are a few sources that manage to integrate both habits of mind. The largely ignored work of R. G. Collingwood is one of these sources, and I draw on it at various pivotal places throughout the book to help show how faith and reason, as interdependent habits of mind, work together. Separately these habits are feeble and frail but together they form a kind of organic habit whereby the mind is able to satisfy the demands made by the complexities and simplicities of religious life.

Fidelity of Mind

What are we to make, then, of philosophers of religion who tend to marginalize one (faith) or the other (reason) of these two habits of mind? First of all, we can be sure that their philosophies will fail to fairly and fully articulate the rich and varied patterns of religion as practiced by faith communities. Indeed, by favoring one of these habits over the other a philosophy drifts toward one of two fallacies, what I shall refer to as the fallacy of rationalism or the fallacy of fideism. Both fallacies suffer in common one thing, namely, a corruption of consciousness in which the mind suppresses, disowns, or disenfranchises what it considers to be certain repugnant features of religious experience in order to accentuate more clearly certain other attractive features. What results in both cases is not only a distorted picture of the nature of religion but also a vulnerable condition that, as we shall see, renders religion and society susceptible to corrupting forces that they are not likely to survive.

Consider the fallacy of fideism, for example. Fideists tend to suppress and disown the vital and indispensable role reason plays in the life of religious belief and practice. They reject reason's efforts to explain, justify, or criticize the beliefs and practices of religion. Religion is simply an expression of the human spirit, is not based on rational grounds, and thus is not susceptible to explanation and justification. Rather, religion is a phenomenon that we can describe and appreciate as a profound expression of the human spirit's quest for meaning and direction. No matter how strange or bizzare religious beliefs and practices may seem to minds nurtured on scientific reason, when it comes to "forms of life" such as religion, we must, as Wittgenstein says, "leave everything as it is"[8] without yielding to the temptation to explain, justify, or criticize it. It does not require a great deal of reflection to see the danger in such a fallacious way of thinking. We shall see (in chapter 7), for example, that by rendering religious faith impervious to critical scrutiny, such a fallacious habit of mind has the potential to justify to itself even extreme forms of irrationality and brutality; indeed, it has the potential to crush the very foundations of civilized life, as in fact was the case when the irrationality of a neo-pagan religion emerged in the midst of twentieth-century Europe and threatened to extinguish the flame of civilization.

Or consider the fallacy of rationalism. In committing this fallacy, rationalists are inclined to suppress and disown the vital and indispensable role faith plays in the life of those who practice religion. They reject as superstitious what they consider to be irrational features of religion, such as belief in miracles or a personal God, and practices that smack of ritual magic, such as the Eucharist or exorcisms and religious emotions (enthusiasm). Since scientific reason is the touchstone of advanced, civilized life, religion is viable only insofar as its beliefs are liable to rational formulation and justification. That is why it is important to the rationalist that religious beliefs, like belief in God's existence, or incarnation, or miracles, be capable of rational explanation, and if they are not, that philosophy (at least) abandon them. Only then will religion be respected as a genuinely intelligible enterprise that contributes to civilizing society. This is precisely why Kant eagerly purged from Christianity and Christian morality all elements, like emotion and superstitious belief (incarnation), not liable to rational formulation. Only then could there be established, he insisted, a truly scientific, liberal way of civilized life. Again, it does not require a great deal of reflection to envision the danger to which such a fallacy exposes religion and society. By distilling from religion only those elements capable of rational formulation, and by disenfranchising from religion and society those powerful emotions, invoked by ritual practice, that inspire human activity, civil society becomes a dry, withered stalk unable to withstand the powerful winds of sublimated emotion that reappear and avenge themselves on the scientific culture that suppressed them in the first place. As indeed was the case when, in response to Enlightenment rationalism (chapter 7), a brutal, irrational form of neo-pagan fascism arose and threatened the survival of a civilized way of life based on scientific reason and liberal politics.

My impression is that many philosophers of religion today tend toward rationalism more than fideism, acknowledging at the same time that many aim at striking a balance between faith and reason. But since a fair number favor a form of rationalism that tends to minimize faith and the particularity and local dialect of specific faith traditions, it might be well to bear in mind insightful comments by Kierkegaard, who, in a poignant metaphor, refers to rationalism as the practice of ventriloquism. The rationalist contrives to speak "in such a way that it cannot be determined who the speaker is; the words are heard all right, but as if they were not localized, as if no one were speaking them." The philosophical ventriloquist "means to speak in such a way that the speaker cannot be recognized: it is a mystification in which the I is disguised as a third person, or as an abstract, [disembodied] I." There are advantages to the philosopher in assuming the role of ventriloquist. As ventriloquist, he need not bear responsibility for his voice, or for the distortion his disembodied voice gives to speech: "This is the voice of scientific reason speaking." Nor must the philosopher as ventriloquist bear responsibility for what Kierkegaard calls "the situation." By "the situation" he means "the decisive factor in determining whether the speaker is or is not in character regarding what he is saying; for the situation decides whether what is being said is airy nonsense, speech without real roots, which . . . is true of all speech which is devoid of situation."[9]

To practice philosophy of religion as an occasion for ventriloquism, as an occasion to speak in a disembodied voice, independently of the local dialects of particular faith traditions, disadvantages both philosophy and religion, and throughout this book I hope to show how and why. Suffice to say here that my commitment is to "fidelity of mind," to examining some of the issues typically treated by philosophy of religion but to treating them as a Christian philosopher who is passionately and equally committed to exercising both habits of mind, both faith and reason. That is why as subtitle to this book I have consciously and deliberately chosen "A Philosophy of Christian Faith" and not "A Philosophy of Religion." This is not to suggest that those who commit themselves to executing a traditional philosophy of religion are any less dedicated to practicing the faith of their choice, but only that their philosophies of religion are not informed by the practice of their local faith dialect. By approaching issues in philosophy of religion from the particularity of a local faith dialect, I reenfranchise the activity of mind sometimes neglected by philosophers of religion, namely, faith. At the same time, I am submitting that faith tradition to the critical scrutiny and analysis of reason. I hope to show in this book the generous rewards a balance of these two activities of mind promises and in so doing persuade the reader that the distinction between being a philosopher of religion and a Christian (or Jewish, or Buddhist) philosopher is significant and terribly consequential. It is a matter of some urgency that philosophers of religion make an intentional transition to, say, a Christian, or Jewish, or Buddhist, or humanist philosophy of religion.

The Plan of This Book

A word about the book's plan and organization: It treats both substantive and methodological issues and demonstrates throughout the mutual interaction of the two. Much of my inspiration for writing it arises from doubts I have about certain assumptions implicit in philosophy of religion. First, I doubt that substantive issues, like the existence of God, evil and suffering, and miracles, can be addressed candidly and effectively by a methodology presupposing that the muscles of rational thought can be exercised independent of the distinctive beliefs and practices that a particular local faith tradition provides. Second, I have doubts that a discipline, like philosophy of religion, that disenfranchises almost completely the role religious emotions play in the life of religious communities is likely to find its way to solutions that are satisfying to those who practice religion, let alone those who are alienated from it.

That is why I treat the problems typical of philosophy of religion in an untypical way, with a methodology that presupposes a particular religious tradition, in this case Christianity, and that reenfranchises emotions (e.g., compassion) as crucial to shaping solutions to philosophical problems. The question chapter 2 seeks to answer, accordingly, is, On what basis can we develop a philosophical method that draws on the substantive beliefs and practices of a particular religious tradition, that reenfranchises the role of religious emotions in intellectual life? I develop such a methodology on the basis of three principles: symmetry, asymmetry, and supersymmetry. I confiscate these three terms from physics and deploy them collectively as a metaphor in service to a method whereby, it seems to me at least, the problems belonging to philosophy of religion can be critically and constructively treated. I explain and illustrate each of these principles to establish a framework for constructing a philosophy of Christian faith of sufficient strength to bear the weight demanded of it by problems philosophy raises regarding religion. I am not aware of a philosophical method employing the approach I execute here. I hope that it contributes constructively to the continuing conversation between philosophy and religion and that its use will point in a direction that others will feel inspired to pursue.

Applying this methodology to basic problems ordinarily addressed by philosophy of religion is the aim of part II, "Faith and Reason." Since these problems (God, evil and suffering, and miracles) are internal to the Christian tradition and manifest distinctively Christian dimensions, I believe they must be solved internally in terms of Christian beliefs and practices. In each chapter (3–5) I engage a substantive problem and subject it to the critical scrutiny and constructive tools provided by my methodology. My procedure in each chapter is similar. I discuss each problem first in terms of symmetry, a principle favored by rationalism, and then in terms of asymmetry, a principle favored by fideism. I show how each of these principles is situated in relation to each other, how each enhances our understanding of the problem and contributes to its solution. But I also show how separately, or even jointly, these two principles are ultimately unable to adequately address and solve the philosophical problem. Finally, then, I show how for each problem the Christian idea and experience of compassion functions as a kind of supersymmetrical principle whereby the discrepancy between symmetry (reason) and asymmetry (faith) is overcome and transformed. Questions linger at the end of part II, however: "external" questions regarding the relation of Christianity to other religions and to society.

Part III, "Faith and Culture," dedicates itself to these and related questions. Chapter 6 focuses on the relationships between religions. Does shared territory exist between religions? How is it possible to protect and preserve religious particularity and diversity while promoting conversation and cooperation? How can we affirm the distinctive particularity of each religious tradition while affirming a universal criterion for making interreligious judgments? How can we profess devotion to the uniqueness of our local narrative tradition while also propounding a metanarrative to which all traditions can subscribe? And what is the status of truth in and among religious traditions? By drawing on the three methodological principles (symmetry, asymmetry, and supersymmetry) I am able to address these perennial questions. I argue that although different local religious traditions find themselves situated asymmetrically in relation to each other there is nevertheless a way of traversing these differences and finding common territory where conversation and cooperation can and should take place. Compassion, not some common core of belief or practice, I argue, constitutes the shared territory and public space between religions and constitutes the way both particularity and universality are preserved and promoted. Compassion is the moral practice by which the truth claimed by devotees of one tradition is justified to devotees of other traditions.

Finally, in chapter 7, I address a question that follows from chapter 6 and is especially urgent today, namely, What can and should be the role of religion in society? How should a religion, in this case Christianity, situate itself in relation to any society in which it finds itself? Contemporary philosophers of religion have tended to ignore this question, leaving it to be treated by social ethicists and theologians. Christian philosophers (e.g., Augustine, Aquinas, Hobbes, Locke, Kant, Hegel, and Kierkegaard), however, treat this issue as one of the most important and urgent, as an issue requiring not only the moral vision of theology but also the critical scrutiny of philosophy. I argue that even though religions and societies properly stand asymmetrically in relation to each other, compassion can and should be the common ground on which they meet. Indeed, compassion inspires religious communities in general and Christian communities in particular to play in society two compassionate roles, prophetic and pastoral, gadfly and midwife. By practicing these roles in any society, Christianity, or any religion, plays a vital role in promoting and preserving civility.

A word about the general approach that I take toward each philosophical issue: I begin each chapter with a story taken from the biblical tradition and use that story as a touchstone and guide for treating each issue. Doing so encapsulates what is distinctive and significant about the approach I have chosen to develop in this book. Beginning with a local narrative establishes a starting point within a faith tradition from which I then draw theological and spiritual resources that I submit to the critical analysis and scrutiny of reason in the task of resolving issues treated by philosophy of religion.

The question this book addresses, then, is What does it mean for a philosopher, who examines religion and religious experience, to practice "fidelity of mind"? What does it mean to enfranchise fairly and fully into one organic habit the mind's activities of faith and reason? My hope is that the approach that I deploy to answer this question will prove itself a bridge of strength sufficient to support the weight and bulk of faith and reason together. What is required of the philosopher, I think, is to practice simultaneously and equally both the believing faith of the disciples and the critical scrutiny of Thomas' doubt. My sense is that unless philosophers think about religious matters in such a way as this (as Christians or Jews or Buddhists instead of as disembodied philosophers of religion), solutions to the problems they typically treat will remain elusive.

Notes

1. All biblical quotations are from the Revised Standard Version of the Bible.
2. Kai Nielsen, "Wittgenstein's Fideism," *Philosophy* 42 (July 1967): 205–206.
3. Brian R. Clack, *An Introduction to Wittgenstein's Philosophy of Religion* (Edinburgh, Scotland: Edinburgh University Press, 1999), 84.
4. John Apczynski, "Belief in God, Proper Basicality, and Rationality," *Journal of the American Academy of Religion* LX, 2 (Summer 1992): 305.
5. Disciples often traduce the teachings of the master, as when the followers of Kant cultivate the role of reason in his thought without granting equal attention to the role of emotion. In his *Lectures on Ethics*, for example, Kant argues that the emotions have a vital role in ethics, in shaping a character able to fulfill his rational duty. Scholars are beginning to compensate for this oversight. See my discussion of Kant, love, and emotion in *Fidelity of Heart: An Ethic of Christian Virtue*, especially 42–45.
6. However, Kant does offer an argument for God's existence based on practical reason.
7. Charles Townes, *Making Waves* (New York: American Institute of Physics, 1995), quoted in Max Jammer, *Einstein and Religion* (Princeton, N.J.: Princeton University Press, 1999), 158.
8. Ludwig Wittgenstein, *Philosophical Investigations*, trans. G. E. M. Anscombe (New York: Macmillan, 1958), 124. See Brian Clack's discussion of this issue in *An Introduction to Wittgenstein's Philosophy of Religion*, esp. 82–89.
9. Søren Kierkegaard, *Søren Kierkegaard's Journals and Papers* 4, ed. and trans. H. Hong and E. Hong (Indianapolis: Indiana University Press, 1975), 124–125.

CHAPTER TWO

Reenfranchising the Mind

While waiting for friends in Athens, the Apostle Paul begins to wonder about the great cultural and religious heritage represented by statues of gods and goddesses scattered throughout the city. As was his inclination, Paul found reason to converse with local philosophers and theologians, in this case Epicurean and Stoic, comparing and contrasting Christianity with Greek religion and philosophy. On the one hand, he compares his beliefs favorably with Greek thought. He agrees that no human is far from God, for, quoting a Stoic philosopher, "in him we live and move and have our being;" and, quoting a poet, "we are indeed his offspring" (Acts 17: 28). On the other hand, Paul contrasts his Christian beliefs with Greek thought, proclaiming that the unknown god to whom the Greeks have erected an altar is not only the God who created the universe but also the God who raised Jesus from the dead. The response of the Greeks to Paul's gospel was, as you might expect, mixed. Some mock, some want to hear more, and some believe (Acts 17: 16–34). Much has been made of this encounter between Paul and contemporary philosophers. My interest is first in the way Paul connects with ideas that are current and compelling in his day and in his skill at employing those ideas in service to his own philosophy; second, I am interested in the boldness with which he preaches a new and unique message, one so rich and provocative as to generate from his audience a wide range of reactions. Similarly, throughout this book, I show how certain current and compelling ideas in physics might be employed in constructing a unique and provocative philosophy of Christian faith.

At least two forces, modernism/rationalism and postmodernism/fideism, shape the intellectual terrain today and compete for dominance. With scientific reason as model, rationalists tend to assume that human reason can discover and justify objective, universal, ahistorical, and eternal religious truths quite apart from faith. With literary criticism as model, fideists tend to assume that religious belief must be rooted in the soil of faith and the particularity of historical faith traditions and that faith is largely impervious to the critical scrutiny of reason. Many philosophers, of course, embrace both reason and faith as essential to the work of the philosopher of religion. My aim in this book is to draw on the latter tradition and in doing so provide an alternative to the disjunction between rationalism and fideism. I intend to do so partly by avoiding their pitfalls and advancing their strengths and partly by constructing, with help from physics, an innovative methodology whereby philosophy, and in this particular case a philosophy of Christian faith, might profit and progress beyond the suspended intellectual animation resulting from the high tide of modernism (rationalism) and the undertow of postmodernism (fideism).

A recent variation of this rationalist/fideist dichotomy involves a familiar dilemma posed for philosophers by the new physics: How can the mind affirm both the universal order and symmetry of the world and at the same time its particular anomalies and asymmetries? How can the mind simultaneously accommodate a reality that is orderly and rational on the one hand and random and irrational on the other? By what activity of mind is reality's symmetry comprehended, and by what activity of mind is reality's asymmetry apprehended? The version of this dilemma specific to philosophy of religion is classic and more familiar to us. How can the mind accommodate both the rationality of God's creation and the irrationality of God's revelation? What habits of mind are suited to comprehending the symmetry of natural law and apprehending the asymmetry of miracles? I hope to address these questions by employing a method that viewed from one perspective is conventional and classic and viewed from another is unique and creative. My hope is that its classic dimension will educate and nurture the new, like the solera system of winemaking in which older sherry has the power to educate and improve younger ones.

I set forth in this chapter, and sustain throughout the book, a philosophical method anchored by three principles derived from contemporary physics. These principles seem capable of liberating philosophy of religion from the rationalism/fideism stalemate and launching it toward horizons that are wide and open. Physicist Frank Close, in his intriguing book *Lucifer's Legacy: The Meaning of Asymmetry*,[1] speaks of symmetry, asymmetry, and supersymmetry as three principles whereby physicists interpret the subatomic reality described by the new physics. These three familiar principles, taken analogically, provide a method by which philosophers might creatively and constructively interpret and resolve classic problems belonging to religion. Understanding subatomic events in terms of symmetry, asymmetry, and supersymmetry provides analogical clues for comprehending certain metaphysical events and resolving certain problems addressed by philosophy of religion. Such analogies between science and philosophy are not unprecedented. Descartes searches for an indubitable starting point of philosophy analogous to Archimedes' search for an immovable point from which to explain astronomical phenomena. Inspired by Copernicus' cosmological revolution Kant propagates an analogous metaphysical revolution of his own. Similarly, the threefold way physicists interpret the subatomic world provides, analogously, cues and clues that helpfully guide philosophers through the sometimes bewildering terrain of religion. By co-opting these three principles from physics, I am not suggesting that philosophy must subjugate itself to the tyranny of scientific reasoning, as philosophers sometimes have insisted. Nor do I suggest that the nature of the physical universe is a window into the nature of the spiritual universe or that the latter merely mirrors the former. Rather, what I suggest is that these categories that are helpful to physicists in understanding the subatomic world are analogously helpful to philosophers of religion in their efforts to understand the world of religion. What, then, can we make philosophically of these three principles—symmetry, asymmetry, and supersymmetry? How do they help address and solve those problems perennial to the philosophy of religion?

Reason and Symmetry

To experience most fully the symmetry of Paris' Tuileries Gardens, says physicist Frank Close, you should stand in the Place de la Concorde and look toward the Louvre at the far end of the gardens.[2] As you enter the park you will find that what you see when you look to your left is the mirror image of what you see when you look to your right. If on your left you see a stone wall with its curved, concave side toward you, you can be sure that you will see on your right a stone wall with its curved, concave side toward you. If on your left there is a statue or flower garden or tree, you can be sure that on your right will be carefully arranged identical objects and patterns. If you sit and rest on a bench along the left side of the axis path you will see directly across the path from you on its opposite side an identical bench. And so it goes throughout the entire length of the gardens until you arrive at the Louvre at its eastern edge. For Close, the symmetry of the Tuileries Gardens is a metaphor for the natural symmetry and order of the universe. "Symmetry is fascinating and appealing," he says: "Scientists seek it in their data and incorporate it in their theories, ironically even when there is no immediate evidence for it."[3] Perhaps the most fundamental example of the appeal of such symmetry involves matter, which is "the stuff of which we are made" and "half of a symmetric whole," and antimatter, "the faithful opposite of matter."[4] Experiments at CERN (the European Council for Nuclear Research in Geneva) recreating conditions at the origin of the universe show "that particles of matter and antimatter emerged in equal amounts, perfectly balanced.... [T]he perfect symmetrical emergence of the primeval particles of matter and antimatter."[5] Indeed, such symmetrical order and reason's search for it establish the possibility of a scientific and mathematical interpretation of the universe.

Symmetry

In mathematics and the sciences "symmetry" refers to a characteristic of shapes, equations, and objects. An object is symmetric when a given operation is applied to an object and the object does not appear to change. Customarily three such operations are identified—reflection, rotation, and translation. Reflection symmetry, which is the most familiar, inverts an object into its mirror image (matter/antimatter). Rotation revolves an object around a central axis; rotate an equilateral triangle around its central axis and it remains the same in respect to its angle of 120 degrees. Translation symmetry refers to the movement of an object from one area to another or in one direction or another by a vector. The simplest example of a vector is a line connecting two points AB. AB represents the vector in the direction from point A to point B, whereas BA represents the vector of equal magnitude from point B to point A.

In particle physics reflection symmetry establishes what physicists refer to as the "standard model,"[6] which is a theory of fundamental particles and how they interact. It describes the strong, weak, and electromagnetic fundamental forces, as well as the fundamental particles of which all matter consists, and is consistent with both quantum mechanics and special relativity. In the standard model, the theory of the electroweak interaction is combined with the theory of quantum chromodynamics, both of which are gauge field theories; they model the forces between fermions by coupling them with bosons which mediate the forces. So far, almost all experimental tests of the three forces described by the standard model agree with its predictions. It is not, however, a complete or comprehensive model, primarily because it does not describe gravity. What is important for the purposes of my thesis is that the standard model both describes fundamental symmetries in the universe as well as points toward asymmetries, most notably the asymmetries associated with antimatter. On the basis of the standard model as a description of symmetry, physicists are able to make predictions that are relatively certain and reliable.

The generalization of symmetry in the universe has become one of the most powerful tools of theoretical physics, as applied not only to particle physics but also to cosmology, the universe as a whole. It is in this generalization and application that the idea of symmetry functions analogically as a method for executing a philosophy of religion, in this case from the perspective of the Christian tradition. Scientists are not the only ones who find the uniformity and symmetry of the universe fascinating and appealing. Philosophers and theologians search with equal passion for a rational, uniform understanding of the order and symmetry of the universe. One does not have to read far in the works of great thinkers like Plato and Aristotle, Augustine and Aquinas, Descartes and Spinoza, Locke and Hume, Kant and Hegel, Einstein and Wittgenstein to feel with them a profound passion for order and symmetry. Their common philosophical and theological assumptions parallel the assumptions of science: first, by assuming that the universe as a whole, taken metaphysically, manifests an order and symmetry; and second, that the task of human reason is to discover and articulate theoretically an account of this uniform and symmetrical totality. The difference between science and metaphysics is that scientific reason investigates the universe's physical symmetries whereas metaphysics investigates the totality of its uniformity and order; science investigates the myriad, particular instances of symmetry by developing specific laws and theories that describe and interpret the particular patterns of physical events; metaphysics investigates the idea of the universe's uniformity and symmetry as a whole, as a totality of multiple symmetries and uniformities that together constitute a cosmos, a pattern and order of everything collectively. It is the aim of metaphysical reason to discover, interpret, and articulate this totality. Thus, for example, just as science searches for the cause of each particular, natural event, metaphysics searches for the cause of the cosmos as a whole, of all events collectively. In this way, as I have suggested, scientific reason's search for natural uniformities and symmetries provides an analogy and model by which metaphysical reason might execute its search for the universe's uniformity and symmetry as a whole.

By metaphysical "symmetry," then, I generalize from particle physics and refer to a metaphysical "standard model" or theory that describes the universe as a whole insofar as it manifests an intelligible order, pattern, and design. Reason discovers, interprets, and develops from this order a comprehensive metaphysical theory, in this case, a coherent philosophy of religion from the perspective of Christian faith. The principle of cause and effect, for example, describes a uniformity or symmetry of order that governs not only all physical events in the universe but the universe as a whole. Physicists speak of converting the symmetry of one group (particle physics) into that of another (cosmology). Just as all natural events in the universe have causes, so the universe as a whole, as a natural event, has a cause. In this way there is a kind of translational symmetry from the particular to the universal, from the causes of particular physical events to the cause of the totality of physical events taken together. There is, as we shall see, a difference in the causes of these two kinds of events, but insofar as both have causes, the symmetry of the one can be translated into the symmetry of the other. Accordingly, "metaphysical reason" refers to that activity of mind devoted to discovering and interpreting the symmetry of the whole into a comprehensive version of the world in its totality, a version within which phenomena can be predicted with relative certainty. Thus, for example, if God is identified as the cause of the universe as a whole, and if God is all-good and powerful, then metaphysical reason will infer that God is not the cause of horrendous evil in the world and will provide an explanation of that inference. In short, by "metaphysical symmetry" I refer to a general uniformity, beauty, and harmony constituting the universe as a whole. The desire and drive to discover this symmetry, this "blessed rage for order,"[7] seems to belong uniquely to human creatures and is their special blessing and burden. We shall see below that in order for the mind to provide a comprehensive description and explanation of the world in its complexity and totality the mind must develop a "cumulative case." When it comes to articulating the metaphysical and religious dimension of that order, the role of reason, the task of Christian (or any) philosophy is finally to develop a "cumulative case" on the basis of "retrospective reason."

Symmetry and Cumulative Case

What Basil Mitchell refers to as a "cumulative case"[8] provides in metaphysics and religion an alternative to scientific rationalism and its approach to discovering and defending the universe's order. Any attempt to make a case for or against a particular metaphysical point of view, or what Nelson Goodman calls a "world-version"[9] (e.g., Christianity, Marxism, humanism), must be made cumulatively. That is, the way a reasonable case can and must be made, if made at all, for a comprehensive, metaphysical interpretation of the universe's symmetry (world-version) is by means of a cumulative case. A cumulative case can be reasonable, but, as Mitchell argues, "it does not take the form of a strict proof or argument from probability."[10] Rather, a persuasive, successful cumulative case, such as the case for Christian theism, "makes better sense of all the evidence available than does any alternative on offer. . . ." Indeed, cumulative case concerns "what Gilbert Ryle calls 'the plausibility of theories' rather than proof or probability in any strict sense."[11] To show that a world-version is rational, devotees must develop a plausible and persuasive case based on the accumulated weight of a vast and varied pattern of ideas and experiences. This is in contrast to "coercive attempts" to compel skeptics to believe the truth of a theistic world-version by means of simple prospective proofs and probabilities (e.g., the ontological or teleological arguments for the existence of God). Mitchell subscribes, as do I, to the legacy of Hume, that "it is not possible to prove traditional Christian theism or to render it probable in any strict sense of the word." But neither can theism "be shown to be necessarily false or logically incoherent." Either "there can be no rational case for or against Christianity," argues Mitchell, and we must settle for simple fideism or simple skepticism, or the case for Christian theism "must be a cumulative one which is rational, but does not take the form of a strict proof or argument from probability."[12] In agreement with Mitchell, I argue that the case for a Christian, or any, world-version can persuasively be made only in terms of a cumulative case. Such a case will embrace both faith's apprehension of certain absolute presuppositions and reason's comprehension of a vast network of empirical evidence and logical inferences.

The nature of cumulative case, then, involves answering the questions, What is the meaning of "faith's apprehension of absolute presuppositions" and What is the meaning of "reason's comprehension of empirical evidence and logical implications"? To answer, I draw on R. G. Collingwood's presuppositional approach to metaphysics, especially as developed in his *Essay on Metaphysics*. There he argues that any comprehensive metaphysical system, any world-version, is a function of a constellation of historically rooted absolute presuppositions, and that any rational case that is to be made for it must be made in a way that amounts to developing a cumulative case. In part III of that *Essay* he sketches what such a case for Christian theism might look like and how that world-version is related to natural science and the symmetry of the natural world. Collingwood goes so far as to argue that the set of presuppositions that make up Christian theism form a world-version that has "as a matter of historical fact been the main or fundamental presuppositions of natural science ever since."[13] Whether this claim can be substantiated is a historical question and not within the scope of this book. What is within its scope is whether for the set of absolute presuppositions that anchor Christianity's world-version a cumulative case can be made that is rational and persuasive, whether a reliable and compelling cumulative case can be made for a Christian version of the world. In chapter 3 I set forth a full explanation of Collingwood's theory of absolute presuppositions and how a cumulative case is the function of retrospective reason.

Reason as Prospective and Retrospective

The preference in metaphysics for constructing a "cumulative case" implies also a preference for "retrospective" as distinguished from "prospective" reason. David Burrell distinguishes these two forms of reason, even though they both share a common object, namely, the order and symmetry of the world. Prospective reason and justification, he says, seeks to answer the questions, Why should I accept this belief? or Why should I undertake this activity?, questions that no doubt were in the mind of doubting Thomas. In contrast, retrospective reason and justification asks, What is persuasive about this belief I hold? or What am I doing engaged in this activity?[14] Prospective reason, on the one hand, assumes that we should not believe until by means of proof and probability we are forced to accept a belief as rational. It is thus the kind of reasoning the sciences rightly employ to determine, by means of coercive proofs and probabilities, what beliefs regarding the complex order and operations of the empirical world we can rationally and justifiably commit ourselves to. Retrospective reason, on the other hand, assumes that in assessing metaphysical beliefs one must first presuppose them; only then is one in a position to discover the nature of those beliefs and the extent to which they are symmetrically patterned and rational. Furthermore, one must first accept them in order to develop as far as is possible and on the basis of a selected set of presuppositions a persuasive cumulative case for a particular world-version. Hence, *credo ut intelligam*. Retrospective reason employs presuppositional thinking and does so to construct a persuasive and plausible case for the rationality of a particular metaphysical world-version to which one already stands committed. Both forms of reason take as their object the order and symmetry of the world. But whereas prospective scientific reason attempts to decipher the symmetry of a vast array of facts and logical relationships, retrospective reason attempts to decipher what metaphysical world-version is presupposed by and best accounts for that vast array. Especially in chapter 3, I elaborate this distinction between prospective and retrospective reason and show how retrospective reason constructs a cumulative case for a Christian version of the world.

But uniformity and symmetry do not account for all there is of the universe. It is common knowledge that the new physics has undermined and discredited the Newtonian view of a perfectly symmetrical, deterministic universe. Analogously, I argue that the metaphysical dimension of reality is not entirely symmetrical and uniform. Physical and metaphysical reality is constituted by asymmetries as well as symmetries. Although asymmetries emerge as a deviation from the standard model, and although scientific reason can measure them as asymmetries, reason cannot comprehend and justify them. The fallacy of rationalism is committed when philosophers disavow and suppress the asymmetrical dimension of reality (e.g., Kant's *Religion within the Limits of Reason*) and the asymmetrical activity of mind (e.g., faith) by which it attempts to apprehend metaphysical reality in its asymmetry.

Faith and Asymmetry

Symmetry, we now know, does not tell us the whole story of the universe, physical or metaphysical. "The world is an asymmetrical place full of asymmetrical beings," insists Close.[15] Indeed, as he continues his stroll through the Tuileries Gardens, he suddenly comes across, on a side path, a statue of Lucifer whose head has broken off its pedestal and lies on the ground. Immediately Close expects and predicts that were he to turn around and walk to the other side of the gardens he would find "a correspondingly positioned plinth and fiendish statue. I half expected that this too would be broken, so preserving the symmetry of the park." When Close turns around and looks to the other side of the gardens, he does indeed find there a mirror statue of Lucifer, but he sees that the head of the "diabolical twin grin[s] from its plinth as it had done since its creation. In the entire gardens," Close observes, "the designer symmetry was perfect with the sole exception of headless Lucifer."[16] What is notable and noteworthy about the headless Lucifer is that and how it deviates from the symmetry that the observer would otherwise expect. The alert visitor would rightly expect and predict that the Lucifer on the left would have his head just like the Lucifer on the right; that it does not situates it asymmetrically in relation to the garden's design and is apprehended by the visitor insofar as it deviates from the expected symmetry. As with symmetry, Close finds that the asymmetry of "the Tuileries Gardens and its interruptions by the disfigured devil are metaphors for our grander perceptions of the natural world."[17] The universe is not simply a place of simple symmetry, but, like the Tuileries, a place of asymmetrical beings and events; and as we shall see, the universe's asymmetry is apprehended by the mind insofar as it deviates from its symmetry as predicted by the standard model.

Asymmetry

By "asymmetry" I refer to two characteristics: incommensurability and uncertainty/unpredictability. First, incommensurability in physics refers to certain events that are ill-proportioned and incongruent with predictions based on the standard model; analogously, in metaphysics, it refers to certain events that are ill-proportioned and incongruent with predictions based on scientific reason and the laws of nature. More generally "asymmetry" refers to a dimension of the physical and metaphysical universe that is not proportioned and congruent with the symmetry and uniformity of the world; it refers to events and phenomena that do not cohere with the standard, intelligible order of things discovered by scientific reason; it refers to events that deviate from the laws of nature and reason in terms of which the mind makes sense of the order of the universe and on the basis of which metaphysical certainty is established and predictions are made.

Close notes numerous examples of asymmetry, including the familiar example of the relation of matter and antimatter during the big bang. "A perfect Creation," he says,

> with its symmetry untainted, would have led to matter and antimatter in precise balance and a mutual annihilation when in the very next instant they recombined: a precisely symmetrical universe would have vanished as soon as it had appeared. . . . Creation was barely completed before something interceded; the perfection where the essence of every atom of substance had been counterbalanced by a precise

antipartner was lost forever. This act degraded the symmetry between matter and antimatter, with the result that after the great annihilation, a small proportion of the matter was left over. Those remnants are what have formed us and everything around us as far as we can see.[18]

This primitive disruption of symmetry, Close goes on to argue, engendered throughout the universe "multitudes of natural asymmetries that seem to have been necessary for human life to have emerged."[19] For biological life to emerge, for example, "asymmetry has been necessary." The sun has been burning hydrogen for millions of years and radiating the light and heat necessary for producing the biological and chemical processes of life. The magnificent electromagnetic force that radiates warmth from the sun to the earth is much stronger than the weak force that transmutes the hydrogen in the atomic particles of the sun and makes it possible for the sun to conserve its fuel and survive long enough for life on earth to develop. "Had it not been like this, had the force driving the solar furnace been as powerful as the electromagnetic force, all of the solar fuel would have been exhausted within five hundred thousand years—far too brief a time for life on earth, or anywhere, to have emerged."[20] Throughout *Lucifer's Legacy* Close enumerates dozens of examples of asymmetry in the natural world to demonstrate what he and other physicists take as incontrovertible, that asymmetry is a *conditio sine qua non* of the natural world as we know it. Taken analogically, the asymmetry of the natural world provides the philosopher with clues for detecting the metaphysical asymmetry of the spiritual world. Just as in physics so analogously in philosophy, substantial progress is not likely to be made unless philosophers are willing to accept and accommodate in their theories the metaphysical asymmetry of the moral and spiritual universe. In each chapter I introduce specific beings (e.g., Satan) and events (e.g., miracles) that situate themselves asymmetrically in relation to reality's symmetry.

Second, "asymmetry" also refers to the uncertainty and unpredictability of the behavior of incommensurate events, in both the physical and metaphysical universes. Thus, for example, miracles stand to the laws of nature (principle of causality) as antimatter stands to matter and the standard model. The unpredictability of the behavior of miraculous events in relation to the laws of nature is analogous to the unpredictability of the behavior of antimatter in relation to matter and the standard model. The new physics discovered in the microworld of quanta two interrelated principles, uncertainty and unpredictability, that manifest themselves analogously in the macroworld of metaphysics and contribute to the shape of a philosophy of Christian faith. By "quantum factor" I refer to the fact that there belongs to the subatomic world of electrons and photons such a degree of chaos, randomness, and chance as to persuade physicists to positively declare, with Paul Davies, that "the uncertainty of the microworld is intrinsic."[21] It is widely known that awareness of this quantum factor emerged from the investigations of physicists like Werner Heisenberg and Niels Bohr. In Heisenberg's celebrated principle of uncertainty or indeterminacy, "uncertainty" refers to the stunning fact that in the subatomic world of nature certain events occur that have no causes, that the chain of cause and effect is broken "by allowing effects to occur that have no cause."[22] Previously the atomic world was thought to be governed by laws roughly parallel to the Newtonian laws of mechanics governing the solar system, a kind of micromechanical subatomic world paralleling the macromechanical astronomical world. Several discoveries in the 1920s brought about the astonishing discovery that this was not so. For example, it was discovered that in the subatomic world a particle, such as an electron, would appear in a particular place without any identifiable occurrence acting on that particle to explain its presence in its new place. This quantum jump, leap, or gap, as scientists sometimes refer to it, is intrinsic to the subatomic world. For, as Davies explains, "No matter how much information is available about the forces and influences acting on the particle, there is no way that its arrival at the designated place can be regarded as 'fixed' by anything else. The outcome is intrinsically random. The particle just pops up in that place with no rhyme or reason."[23] Hence, quantum events are uncertain; no causal relation can be known by which to explain why and how these particles appear in the particular place they do.

Because of their causal uncertainty, accordingly, quantum events are also said by scientists to be unpredictable. Indeed the unpredictability of their behavior is directly linked to their causal uncertainty. Whereas the causal uncertainty of subatomic events has metaphysical implications for the philosopher, their unpredictability holds epistemological implications, in that "we cannot know in detail," as Polkinghorne puts its, "the future of quantum or chaotic systems,"[24] let alone the future behavior of individual particles like electrons. The classic example of unpredictability has to do with the position of a particle on the one hand and its motion or momentum on the other. We cannot know where an electron is (its position) and simultaneously know how it is moving (its momentum). When position is known, then momentum is unpredictable; and when momentum is known, then position is unpredictable. As Davies explains,

> the very concept of an atom with a definite location and motion is meaningless. You can ask where an atom is and get a sensible answer. Or you can ask how it is moving and get a sensible answer. But there is no answer to a question of the sort 'Where is it and how fast is it going?' Position and motion (strictly momentum) form two mutually incompatible aspects of reality for the microscopic particle.[25]

By locating position, the scientist cannot know momentum; by measuring momentum, the scientist cannot know position.

What then can be made analogically of the incommensurability and uncertainty of asymmetries, of what Paul Davies calls "nature's rebelliousness,"[26] as a method for developing a philosophy of Christian faith? Whatever else might be made of them, we might concede Wittgenstein (toward the end of the *Tractatus*) at least on one point, that such asymmetries lie *at* and *not within* (as Kant wished it) the limits of science and reason, and hence are grasped by faith and not scientific reason.

Faith

By "faith" I refer to the mind's capacity to "apprehend" asymmetrical phenomena directly and immediately. Although "faith" is a word we properly use to refer to an activity of the religious mind, it parallels in certain ways the apprehension of asymmetries in physics. In both physics and religion, faith apprehends immediately and directly those asymmetries that, in their incommensurability and uncertainty, deviate from the predictions of the standard model: for example, antimatter in physics and miracles in metaphysics. The role of scientific reason is to comprehend and explain the universe's symmetry and order, to identify natural causes, provide rational explanations, determine relative certainty, and make predictions. Since asymmetries deviate from the standard model and laws of nature by which order and uniformity is identified, they do not lend themselves to rational, scientific comprehension. Rather, asymmetries are apprehended by faith; faith grasps them immediately in their incommensurability, uncertainty, and unpredictability. The issue is not whether asymmetries exist so much as whether and how their behavior can be explained and predicted. To scientific reason and the standard model they are at the same time undeniable and inscrutable. Apprehending them instead of comprehending them scientifically is the activity of mind which in religion is called "faith."

By "apprehend," accordingly, I do not mean what Kierkegaard means when he insists that faith "leaps" beyond the limits of reason and science to grasp paradoxes or irrationalities. Nor do I mean what Tertullian meant when he said that what he believed by faith was absurd or contrary to reason. Rather by "apprehend" I refer to that activity by which the mind grasps asymmetrical phenomena that deviate from standards of order and uniformity established by scientific reason. Faith is the noetic activity of mind that grasps incommensurable, metaphysical events; it grasps, as Collingwood might put it, those absolute presuppositions that express in language metaphysical phenomena that deviate from the norm established by reason; it grasps metaphysical beliefs (e.g., God as uncaused cause) that stand asymmetrically in relation to reason's standard model of order and symmetry.

I will have a great deal more to say in subsequent chapters about asymmetries and faith as the activity of mind by which they are apprehended. For now I will illustrate the role of "asymmetry" and "faith" in physics and how their use there provides by way of analogy a model and method for understanding their role in metaphysics and for executing a philosophy of Christian faith.

A familiar example of asymmetry in physics, as already suggested, is the behavior of matter and antimatter. Several research teams[27] have obtained measurements that show to a very high degree an asymmetry in the behavior of matter and antimatter, so that the difference in their respective behaviors is consistent with the standard model theory of particle physics. The standard model predicts an asymmetry or difference in the decay rates of certain subatomic particles called beauty or B-mesons (matter) and anti-beauty mesons (antimatter). It also predicts the residual matter from the big bang, matter that forms humans, galaxies, and all else. The Belle experiment in particular corroborates asymmetry and uncertainty. On the basis of the big bang theory one would expect and predict that the universe should be equal quantities of matter and antimatter, whereas in reality the universe seems to be made almost entirely of matter. Because of this asymmetry, all but one part in a billion of the matter and antimatter particles are combined into light. The remainder is matter of which we are made.

Two recent research projects, the Belle (KEK) and Stanford experiments, acquired measurements consistent with each other and with the standard model prediction. In the KEK experiment, for example, in order to measure asymmetry and uncertainty, researchers looked at a B-meson that disintegrates in one-trillionth of a second into two particles, a J/y and a K-short meson. The J/y then decays instantaneously into two particles, a positive and a negative muon. The K-short meson decays in roughly one ten-billionth of a second into a positive and a negative pion. Both studies garnered similar results in terms of measuring asymmetry and uncertainties. What about the sin2fl quantity?

- For the Belle research the values are: 0.99 +/− 0.14 +/− 0.06
- For the Stanford research the values are: 0.59 +/− 0.14 +/− 0.05

The first number is the asymmetry, the second is the statistical uncertainty, and the third is the systematic uncertainty. Given their uncertainties, both measurements are inconsistent with a value of zero (symmetry), therefore indicating a matter/antimatter asymmetry. The mind apprehends directly and immediately the sin2fl quantity in its deviation from the value of 0 without scientific reason being able to substantiate and justify its occurrence, or make predictions based on its incommensurability. About its occurrence there is no doubt, but why and how it occurs scientific reason cannot comprehend or say. The mind must directly apprehend its incommensurability in its deviation from 0. Just as scientific reason and research (such as the studies referred to here) measure asymmetries and uncertainties in the physical universe, so too investigations into the nature of the metaphysical universe indicate the presence of asymmetries (e.g., God, miracles). Just as the Belle and Stanford experiments indicate that the behavior of antimatter situates itself asymmetrically and with relative uncertainty in relation to matter, so too analogously does the behavior of God, as Creator and miracle worker, situate itself asymmetrically and unpredictably in relation to the natural standard model of symmetry (e.g., the principle of causality) in the universe as a whole. God as non-natural, nonhuman uncaused cause of the universe and of miracles is situated asymmetrically in relation to scientific principle of causality which predicts with relative certainty that all physical events will uniformly be caused by natural, physical events. A miracle then reflects behavior that is both asymmetrical and uncertain—asymmetrical in that a non-natural instead of a natural event is identified as its cause, and uncertain in that the occurrence of a miracle cannot be predicted with the same certainty that natural events can, cannot be predicated on the presence of some known natural, causal condition. In other words, events such as God, Satan, and miracles stand in relationship to scientific reason and the universe's order as anti-beauty mesons (antimatter) stand to matter.

In religion, faith is that activity whereby the mind apprehends the asymmetrical dimension of moral and spiritual reality. Faith and not reason is equipped to apprehend in the metaphysical universe events and beings that are situated asymmetrically in relation to the order and uniformity of the natural universe. God, for example, is situated asymmetrically in relation to the symmetry of the laws of nature, for God is an uncreated or uncaused Creator, for whom there is no natural material cause; miracles are situated asymmetrically to the universe's symmetry as events for which no natural cause can be identified, and so on. Reason simply is not equipped to justify such incommensurable beings or events. It can only acknowledge them as deviations from the standard model of cause and effect, as incommensurable events situated asymmetrically in relation to the symmetry of the universe.

Throughout the book, I will have a great deal more to say about faith and the asymmetrical reality it apprehends and about its relation to reason and symmetry. Suffice it to say here that just as it is troubling for scientists to admit and accommodate quantum realities in the physical world, it is equally disturbing for some philosophers to face up to the asymmetries in the moral/spiritual universe. How may philosophers, when treating the problem of evil, for example, account for gratuitous evil and suffering in terms of the religiously common asymmetrical being of Lucifer? Those who don't, do so, I presume, in deference either to scholarly propriety or to a kind of rationalism (Kant) that disowns the asymmetrical nature of metaphysical reality. Fideists (Tertullian), on the other hand, are susceptible to committing a fallacy when they preoccupy themselves with the asymmetrical realities and beliefs of faith and disown the world's symmetry and rationality in relation to which those beliefs stand asymmetrically. Philosophers of religion who tend to neglect one or the other of these activities of mind usually develop theories that suffer what R. G. Collingwood refers to as a "corruption of consciousness."

Corruption of Consciousnes

Most physicists, including Niels Bohr, "accepted [the fact] that atomic uncertainty is truly intrinsic to nature,"[28] that when it comes to the atomic and subatomic world, the uniform laws of nature do not universally apply. There were several dissenting voices, however, the most renowned of which is Albert Einstein, who disputed with Bohr regarding the alleged uncertainty and unpredictability implicit in quantum mechanics. Einstein's famous remark, "God does not play dice," encapsulated his view that the allegation of uncertainty and unpredictability was based not on scientific evidence but on human ignorance of the full nature of atomic reality. "Many ordinary systems, such as the stock market or the weather, are also unpredictable," as Paul Davies explains it, "but that is only because of our ignorance. If we had complete knowledge of all the forces concerned, we could (in principle at least) anticipate every twist and turn."[29] In the 1930s Einstein proposed an experiment which he thought would expose the error of Bohr's way. The experiment tried to show that the apparent uncertainty of the atomic microworld is not intrinsic. Bohr disputed the conclusion Einstein tried to draw, but it was not until John Bell's experiments in the 1960s along with other experiments in the 1970s that physicists were able to demonstrate conclusively "that the uncertainty of the microworld is intrinsic."[30]

The tenacity with which Einstein clung to his belief in a wholly symmetrical, rational universe and to his belief that in it can lay no asymmetry or unpredictability reflects what Collingwood calls a "corruption of consciousness" or an "untruthful consciousness." A corrupt consciousness, says Collingwood, is one that deceives itself by assuming that some aspect of its experience, otherwise known to be so, could not possibly be. As corrupt it is a consciousness that dogmatically disowns, suppresses, or disenfranchises "certain features of its own experience," that shrinks from "something which it is its business to face." It thereby fails to discharge its proper function of "domesticating" and interpreting that aspect of its experience.[31] Collingwood charges the Enlightenment with a corrupt consciousness, for example, arguing that in order to further the cause of scientific reason, it disowned certain features of human experience (e.g., religion, emotions) that seemed incorrigible to rational formulation.

It is easy, of course, to see the splinter in another's eye (the Enlightenment or Einstein) while ignoring the log in one's own. Not only do the Enlightenment and Einstein suffer a corruption of consciousness, philosophers of religion, among whose company I include myself, not infrequently neglect certain features of religious experience that seem to them unpredictable, asymmetrical, and impervious to rational formulation. Kant went to great lengths to cramp faith within the rather narrow confines of Enlightenment reason. Indeed, a primary point of my argument is that the limited success philosophers of religion have had in even their most sophisticated and technical endeavors to solve the problems for which they are responsible is partly due to such a corruption of consciousness, to disowning certain indispensable features of religious experience (e.g., religious affections, miracles, Satan), and to preoccupying themselves almost exclusively with the world's symmetry, with reason and rational explanation. By presupposing, with Einstein, that the world must surely be entirely symmetrical and rational, by presupposing that God does not play dice, philosophers labor, futilely at times, to construct a world more symmetrical and less asymmetrical than it is. In so doing, they disown certain asymmetrical features of reality whose truth is otherwise crucial and compelling if problems treated by philosophy of religion are to be properly and persuasively addressed. The contemporary version of this corruption of consciousness arises, I think, from the fact that philosophers do not fully know what to make of the nature and role of faith as an activity of mind that apprehends the asymmetrical features of metaphysical phenomena. It is fortuitous, perhaps, that the single asymmetrical event that Close discovers in the Tuileries Gardens is a dislodged bust of Lucifer (and yet, perhaps not so fortuitous). For Lucifer, as a mythological figure, symbolizes in the spiritual realm not only a quantum being situated asymmetrically in relation to moral symmetry but symbolizes also a deceiver who seduces humans. Many philosophers affirm the reasonableness of belief in God, fewer believe in miracles, and even fewer are able to bring themselves to speak of Lucifer. Lucifer represents for them, as he does for physicist Close, a being so inscrutable to scientific and metaphysical reason as to defy all propriety and protocol expected of those who fancy themselves careful, critical thinkers. One less magnanimous than I might even suggest that it is Lucifer himself who seduces philosophers into the lair of suppressing belief in Lucifer in particular and in the reality of metaphysical asymmetry in general. Close, however, is willing to accept for physicists the challenge represented by Lucifer. My aim in this book is likewise to accept the challenge represented by Lucifer, and to accept by faith the asymmetrical dimension of the moral and spiritual sphere.

Compassion and Supersymmetry

Three years after his first visit to the Tuileries Gardens, Frank Close returns, "walking along its symmetrical paths.... But something was different: the headless Lucifer was no more—two identical, complete, diabolic twins now faced one another across the centre line of the park. The devilish asymmetry had been repaired."[32] How it was repaired we can easily imagine; skilled workmen carefully reattached the broken head of Lucifer to its pedestal. But how to repair the asymmetry of the universe is something else, difficult even for theoretical physicists to imagine (although no shortage exists of those who try). Some physicists believe that there may be a further dimension of symmetry at work in the subatomic universe and that this dimension could be crucial to reconciling at a more profound and fundamental level the symmetry and asymmetry otherwise characterizing our universe. Physicists refer to this "final link" as a "fifth dimension" or as "supersymmetry," or SUSY.[33] SUSY presupposes that there are as yet unknown, underlying "families of particles of fermions and bosons awaiting discovery." These unknown particles and the particles we know "originally, at the start of time . . . were united" and are capable, at least on paper, of reconciling the universe's asymmetries and providing a "theory of everything."[34] Thus the ongoing quest of some theoretical physicists for a "unified field theory."

Paul Davies, for example, argues that quantum physics introduces a "strong holistic element" into the world "by blurring the distinction between subject and object, cause and effect."[35] How so? Scientists conducted certain experiments in which the experimenters were themselves involved in the construction of reality, in the construction of what actually occurs at the subatomic level. Imagine an electron that strikes an object and then careens off. It could careen either left or right. In fact, as a wave the electron produces ripples that travel both to the left and to the right of the object and each set of ripples coexist in a kind of ghostlike hybrid unreality until an observer, an experimenter, actually "peeks," at which instance one of the ghostly unrealities vanishes while the other observed ripple solidifies into concrete reality. As Davies concludes, "the electron keeps its options open until you actually peek. Both possible worlds coexist in a hybrid, ghostly superposition."[36] Scientists do not yet understand what and how the observer contributes to the sudden transformation of one ghostly unreality into concrete reality, but they are certain of its occurrence. Because of such astounding findings Heisenberg himself admitted that "the common division of the world into subject and object, inner world and outer world, body and soul is no longer adequate."[37] What is suggested by quantum physics is a more holistic view of physical reality in which physicists, by "peeking" participate in the construction of a kind of supersymmetry (SUSY) that overcomes the simple dualisms like subject/object, cause/effect, symmetry/asymmetry. An analogous process, I am suggesting, transpires in the moral/spiritual dimension of reality, a process in which God and humans participate in constructing a supersymmetrical harmony that similarly supercedes the simple dualism (spirit/matter, God/human, self/other, grace/law, faith/reason) otherwise characteristic of the metaphysical/spiritual world. My premise throughout this book is that compassion is a common experience of sufficient power to overcome these discrepancies (i.e., between symmetries and asymmetries) and construct a kind of supersymmetrical harmony.

Compassion

Whether in the near or distant future physicists can identify SUSY remains to be seen. The prospect of seeing for the first time the ultimate foundations of physical reality excites many theoretical physicists. And no less does it excite philosophers and theologians who for centuries have passionately and single-mindedly sought to envision the ultimate unity of spiritual reality. Using SUSY as an analogical clue, I argue throughout this book that there is indeed in the spiritual realm a supersymmetrical "fifth dimension" with the power to overcome the world's symmetrical/asymmetrical dichotomies and establish harmony and wholeness. Given modernity's preference for reason over emotion, philosophers tend to assume that philosophical problems can and ought to be properly resolved, if resolved at all, rationally, theoretically, abstractly. Most philosophers, like Thomas of the gospel story, are given to doubting, and will surely wonder how compassion, as an experience of shared emotions, could possibly have anything to do with comprehending let alone constructing reality. Yet, the argument of this book presupposes and demonstrates what I have argued elsewhere,[38] that emotions, including those that constitute compassion, involve cognitive, intellectual activity of the highest order. Practicing compassion is analogous to the experimenter peeking and thereby determining the direction of the careening electron. By practicing compassion a person or community actually "peeks" at and contributes to the construction of spiritual/moral reality. Just as quantum events undermine our most profound assumption about the subatomic world as existing independently of human influence and manipulation, so practicing compassion undermines our assumption about the spiritual world as monolithic and impervious to human construction.

Compassion is a force as mysterious as it is magnificent. Loaded within it are powers capable of reconciling those dichotomies of metaphysical and spiritual reality. More specifically, I argue that compassion is analogous to SUSY, an activity of such fundamental depth as to be able to resolve and unify dilemmas that typically concern philosophers of religion. I am well aware that virtually all contemporary philosophies of religion, at least by default, are partial to modernity and its preference for reason over emotion and compassion, that the model they are trained to imitate is one of dispassionate ventriloquists. The legacy of Descartes, Locke, and Kant looms large, insisting that matters of religion be subjected to the critical scrutiny of reason alone. By thus disenfranchising the role of religious affections in philosophy of religion, they tend toward the fallacy of rationalism. Although Hume treats emotions more favorably and rightly identifies them as the soil from which reason grows, and although he insists that moral life is a function of natural sympathy (compassion), when it comes to religion, he tends to ignore the power of religious emotions and favor the dictates of scientific reason alone. This rationalist tendency in favor of reason is rapidly being undermined, however. Indeed, the time is long since past when we can isolate reason from emotion and pretend that the latter is irrational, unreliable, and irrelevant to solving problems addressed by philosophy of religion. How then does practicing compassion construct a supersymmetry or spiritual unified field theory? And how does practicing compassion provide answers to questions raised by philosophy in regards to religion?

To say that compassion is the human capacity for emotional intersubjectivity is another way of referring to the common human experience of shared emotions. My friend is sad and so I feel something of his sadness. My daughter is elated at being admitted to the college of her choice, and I feel happy with and for her. Such experiences of emotional intersubjectivity are so common and commonly suffused throughout human experience that philosophers often have failed to notice them and their relevance to solving problems treated by philosophy of religion. Elsewhere I have analyzed the specific structure of emotions and the nature of compassion as the intersubjectivity of a wide range of emotions.[39]

For the immediate purposes of the approach I take in this book, I will examine the philosophical and theological nature and function of compassion as interpreted by a Christian version of the world. Specifically, three forms of compassion are important for realizing the vision of this book: ontological, existential, and spiritual. Ontological compassion refers to the Christian belief that in Christ God became human, that in Christ the being of God shares something of the being of humans and that fundamentally this is an act of compassion. Existential compassion refers to the Christian belief that in Christ God shares something of the human experience of evil and suffering, even the despair and pain of horrendous evil and gratuitous suffering. And spiritual compassion refers to the Christian belief that in Christ God redeems humanity by healing human wounds and by transforming all creation into the promise of God's peaceable kingdom. These forms of compassion, in which God is situated intersubjectively with humans, are essential to executing the vision of a philosophy of Christian faith set forth here. My suspicion and assumption is that unless we reenfranchise compassion in its ontological, existential, and spiritual dimensions, solutions to the problems treated by philosophy of religion will remain relatively elusive, and the hope for discovering a philosophical SUSY will remain an illusion.

Practical Truth

Important to the argument in this book is a principle unique to religion, namely, that in religion practicing compassion is the primary way of justifying truth and truth-claims. Virtually all religions presuppose that religious claims to truth are ultimately compelling and persuasive only insofar as they are put into practice, only if the community to whom that tradition belongs actually lives according to those truths to which it claims devotion. For the Christian community, practical truth, the practice of loving compassion, situates itself at the center of its cumulative case and accounts most completely and convincingly for all of its claims to truth. To disown and suppress compassion as a central fact of religious life, as philosophy of religion does, not only distorts the nature of the form of human experience (i.e., religion) that is at issue but also surrenders use of that tool at which it is perhaps most critical for philosophers to be skilled if they are to reliably reckon with religion. That practicing compassion plays a vital role in justifying religious truth-claims and in solving philosophical problems arising from religious experience is an assertion that begs for justification. That is a task that I shall gladly take up in each chapter. My hope is that throughout the book there will emerge a pattern in which compassion's supersymmetrical power to treat philosophical problems and reconcile spiritual dichotomies progressively manifests itself. Each chapter begins with a problem addressed by philosophers of religion, and each chapter culminates with an analysis of compassion's power to solve that problem.

Regarding the Plan of This Book

From the method I have sketched above the reader can easily see why I have subtitled this book "A Philosophy of the Christian Faith" instead of "A Philosophy of Religion" and why I think (Buddhist, Jewish, Christian, humanist, rationalist) philosophers should prefer the former model to the later. As stepchild of the Enlightenment, philosophy of religion manifests all of its strengths and weaknesses. One of its strengths is a commitment to submit all relevant religious and metaphysical issues to the scrutiny of critical reason. One of its weaknesses is its assumption that such scrutiny can and should be executed from some abstract, ahistorical Archimedean point positioned mysteriously outside traditions and the communities that practice them. I have already suggested why and how I think this is a bad idea, why and how I think philosophers, when treating religion, must operate from within a particular religious (or secular) world-version to which they at least tentatively stand committed. I have chosen to do so from within the Christian tradition. Kant does so as a Christian from within the Enlightenment tradition. Others (e.g., Marxists, Buddhists) have, will, and should continue to do so from within theirs. In so doing genuine progress, I think, is made. But little if any progress is likely to be made by treating problems of religion as if they can be addressed, in the voice of a ventriloquist, independently of the particularity of local traditions that give rise to them in the first place. Instead, like Paul at the Acropolis in Athens, philosophers should interact and converse with other philosophies by acknowledging candidly to themselves and to others the world-version to which they are committed and from which they speak and reason. Perhaps, then, philosophers of religion will with St. Paul feel honored when, in response to their message, some sneer, some wish to hear more, and others believe. My hope is that the three principles—symmetry, asymmetry, and supersymmetry—set forth above will function as a kind of methodological compass by which to navigate the tumultuous and hazardous waters of philosophy of religion.

My aim in part II of this book is to show how these three methodological principles might be employed as a compass through the treacherous waters of three substantive issues that philosophy of religion traditionally treats—the existence of God, the existence of evil and a good God, and the possibility of miracles. In part III I employ these three principles in treating two substantive problems for which finding solutions today is, it seems to me, increasingly urgent. Can we find among the religions of the world a common space for conversation and cooperation (chapter 6)? And can we identify a specific role a religion might profitably play in whatever society and culture it happens to find itself today (chapter 7)? My thesis is that even for these difficult questions the principles of symmetry, asymmetry, and supersymmetry can provide answers that are at once provocative and persuasive.

Notes

1. Frank Close, *Lucifer's Legacy: The Meaning of Asymmetry* (London: Oxford University Press, 2000).
2. Ibid., 1–3.
3. Ibid., 4.
4. Ibid.
5. Ibid., 206.
6. The standard model was the result of research into particle physics in the 1970s. It incorporated all that was known in this field at the time and has since successfully predicted the outcome of a wide variety of experiments; today it is considered well established. However, one part of this model is not yet well established: what causes the fundamental particle to have masses? This one aspect of the standard model is addressed by the Higgs hypothesis, called the Higgs mechanism, that includes the addition of a particle (Higgs boson) as well as one additional force type mediated by exchanges of this boson. The Higgs mechanism does not yet have the status of theory but remains as a hypothesis.
7. This phrase is from Wallace Stevens' poem "The Idea of Order at Key West" and the title of a widely read and discussed book, *The Blessed Rage for Order*, by David Tracy.
8. See chapter 3 of Basil Mitchell's *The Justification of Religious Belief* (New York: Seabury Press, 1973).
9. I borrow the term "world-version" from Nelson Goodman and use it throughout this book to mean roughly what Goodman means by it: symbol systems which attempt to provide a comprehensive interpretation of the world. They are formed, he tells us, through the transformation of previous symbol systems and are subject to critical discussions of

their rightness. See, especially, Goodman's *Ways of Worldmaking* (Indianapolis, Ind.: Hackett Publishing, 1978), chapter 1, section 4.

10. Mitchell, *The Justification of Religious Belief*, 39.
11. Ibid., 40.
12. Ibid., 39.
13. R. G. Collingwood, *An Essay on Metaphysics* (Chicago: Henry Regnery, 1972), 227.
14. David Burrell, "Religious Belief and Rationality," in *Rationality and Religious Belief*, ed. C. F. Delaney (Notre Dame, Ind.: University of Notre Dame Press, 1979), 107–112.
15. Close, *Lucifer's Legacy*, 1.
16. Ibid., 4.
17. Ibid.
18. Ibid., 5–6.
19. Ibid., 6.
20. Ibid., 6–7.
21. Paul Davies, *God and the New Physics* (New York: Simon and Schuster, 1984), 106.
22. Ibid., 102.
23. Ibid., 34–35.
24. John Polkinghorne, *Belief in God in an Age of Science* (New Haven, Conn.: Yale University Press, 1998), 52.
25. Davies, *God and the New Physics*, 102–103.
26. Ibid., 107.
27. For example, a collaboration of several teams of scientists in the Belle experiment at the Japanese National Laboratory for High Energy Physics (KEK); also, researchers at the Stanford Linear Accelerator Center; also, finds of the Hyper CP experiment and CKM sponsored by the High Energy Physics group at the University of Virginia. See K. Abe et al. (Belle Collaboration), "Observation of Large CP Violation in the Neutral B Meson System," *Physical Review Letters* 87, 091802, Issue 9-27, 14 August, 2001; and B. Aubert et al. (BARBAR Collaboration), "Observation of CP Violation in the B 0 Meson System," *Physical Review Letters*, 87, 091801, Issue 9-27, 14 August, 2001.
28. Davies, *God and the New Physics*, 102.
29. Ibid.
30. Ibid., 106. For a fuller explanation of Einstein's, Bohr's, and Bell's experiments see Davies' *God and the New Physics*, 103–107.
31. R. G. Collingwood, *The Principles of Art* (Oxford: Clarendon Press, 1938), 216. See also pp. 216–221, 282–285.
32. Close, *Lucifer's Legacy*, 252–253.
33. Ibid., 248.
34. Ibid., 249–250.
35. Ibid., 111.
36. Ibid., 112–113.
37. Quoted in Davies, *God and the New Physics*, 112.
38. James E. Gilman, *Fidelity of Heart: An Ethic of Christian Virtue* (New York: Oxford University Press, 2001), especially chapters 2 and 6.
39. Gilman, *Fidelity of Heart*.

PART II

FAITH AND REASON

> Efficient,
> I summon St. John, who saw arise
> new heaven and new earth. I bow
> to brother Lawrence, Paracelsus,
> and the physicist who put God
> where God belongs,
> in the detail of the universe—
> albeit a universe randomly
> holy, discontinuous, unevenly
> plucky with photons and stars,
> spontaneous.
>
> Margaret Gibson, *Rings of Fire*

CHAPTER THREE

Belief in God's Existence

The exchange in the praetorium is intense and terse. Frustrated with the predicament in which he finds himself, Pilate asks Jesus, "Are you the King of the Jews?" Jesus replies, "My kingship is not of this world...." Pilate says to him, "So, you are a king," to which Jesus replies, "You say that I am a king. For this I was born, and for this I have come into the world, to bear witness to the truth. Everyone who is of the truth hears my voice." And, so, "What is truth?" asks Pilate, who, before Jesus can answer, promptly leaves (John 18:33–37). How do you suppose Jesus would have answered, if he had? Kierkegaard notes that Pilate's question was in a sense a wise one and yet entirely foolish. It was wise in that "Christ was the truth, and so the question was perfectly in place." But it was also a foolish question. "The fact that at that instant it could occur to Pilate to put such a question to Christ is precise proof that he had absolutely no eye for the truth" and that he was confused: for "Christ's life upon earth, every instant of his life, was the truth... [So] in asking such a question he denounces himself, he reveals that Christ's life has not made clear to him what truth is."[1] No doubt Pilate was simply being cavalier and saucy in asking his questions. And yet, for Christian philosophers it is an earnest and provocative question, worthy of careful consideration. The aim of this chapter, and indeed of this book, is to advance a distinctively Christian way of answering Pilate's question, even though I do not think it is a way of answering exclusive to Christianity.

In this chapter I examine the way Christianity's belief in God is determined to be true or not. I do not make a case trying to justify the truth of that belief, although I think a persuasive one can be made. I only examine on what terms such a case should be made.

I will show how justifying belief in God requires philosophers to "reenfranchise the mind," to recommit themselves in fidelity to the mind's habit of faith as well as its habit of reason. Some Christian philosophers, whether by design or default, tend to speak as ventriloquists, tend to develop theories that favor reason over faith, even though typically they affirm both. This is partly because most presuppose that God and God's creation are constituted by symmetry, which reason, if persistent, can trace and articulate. As a result, the habit and beliefs of faith tend to get marginalized in one of two ways. Either faith becomes a simple act of assent by which the mind initiates a process and pattern whereby religious beliefs are shown to be rational (*credo ut intelligam*), or faith is a kind of receptacle designed to accommodate beliefs that are disclosed rather than discovered, revealed rather than reasoned (*credo quia absurdum*). When the former is the case philosophers tend toward the fallacy of rationalism, and when the latter is the case they tend toward fideism. In either case, faith and reason are situated rather tenuously in relation to each other. My aim in this chapter is to show how faith and reason are mutually interdependent activities without both of which the mind is unable to come to a belief in God. That is what I mean by the phrase "reenfranchising the mind," that faith and reason as interdependent activities constitute a single organic habit by which the mind affirms belief in God.

Philosophers of religion typically begin their inquiries by asking some version of the question, What is required for belief in God to be considered true, rational, and justifiable? What *is* required was, throughout the history of Western thought, for the most part simply assumed. Belief in God, "classical foundationalism" assumed, requires some sort of justification for it to be considered rational. Theists and nontheists alike, from Anselm and Hume to Swinburne and Nielsen, take for granted that justifying religious belief is a compulsory exercise without which rationality could not be claimed, take for granted the notion that any claim to symmetry between the world and God requires rational explanation and justification. Belief in God, accordingly, is denied the status of proper basicality because, as one proponent, Stewart Goetz, insists, it must be inferred.[2] This approach tends toward rationalism although it does not deny that faith plays an important role. In contrast, a number of philosophers (e.g., Plantinga, Wolterstorff, et al.) argue that belief in God, like certain other beliefs, is properly basic and as such its rationality, and belief in its rationality, does not lend itself to direct, prospective justification. It is a belief, as Plantinga puts it, "I accept but don't accept on the basis of any other beliefs. It is a belief grounded in certain conditions for which we claim rationality even though no evidence to support it is forthcoming."[3] Philosophers, like Plantinga, insist that belief in God is rational but as properly basic it is not susceptible to prospective justification. It is susceptible, however, to retrospective justification, justification on the grounds of other beliefs and premises.

What I wish to establish in this chapter is a third line of thought lying somewhere between these two horns, classical foundationalism (CF) and proper basicality (PB). This line of thought acknowledges that asymmetry is an undeniable dimension of God and God's creation and that accounting for this fact requires that we reenfranchise fully all powers of mind, both faith and reason. I try to develop this line of thinking by agreeing with elements belonging to both CF and PB. Specifically, I argue with PB against CF that belief in God is indeed both properly basic and rational. But I also argue with CF against PB that the rationality of belief in God, like parallel metaphysical beliefs, requires and is subject to a certain kind of justification. The pivotal phrase, of course, is "a certain kind of justification"—my reading of this phrase allows me to grasp both horns of the dilemma without, I am hopeful, impaling myself on either. My approach, however, differs in ways from both CF and PB: first, in the fact that God and God's creation are in significant ways asymmetrical, and second, in that I show how justifying religious truth is a matter of retrospective reasoning and constructing a cumulative case. I draw especially on the later philosophy of R. G. Collingwood, whose theory of absolute presuppositions provides, with some modification, a conceptual framework within which this project, I believe, can be achieved.

My procedure is as follows. First, I place belief in God in the context of symmetry and asymmetry, reason and faith. Next, I argue that belief in God is analogous to belief in the self, and that as metaphysical both are properly understood as properly basic, or what Collingwood calls absolute presuppositions. Third, I examine the nature of these beliefs (God and self) in their logical status as absolute presuppositions. Fourth, I show how such kinds of beliefs are justified and, fifth, how our knowledge of such beliefs is a function of a continuous coincidence of both faith and reason. Finally, I show how "ontological compassion," as a convergence of faith and reason, establishes in Christian philosophy a culminating and persuasive belief in God.

Symmetry and Asymmetry

"The world is an asymmetrical place, full of asymmetrical beings. If the Creation had been perfect, and its symmetry had remained unblemished, nothing that we know would ever have been."[4] Frank Close notes a fact that is common belief among contemporary physicists. What should and can philosophers make of it, of the fact that the world is not only asymmetrical but an asymmetrical place? What are its implications for believing in God? for justifying belief in God? Most philosophers and theologians are well aware of this scientific fact, but curiously most continue to develop theories and theologies about God and creation that maximize the world's symmetry and minimize its asymmetry. To the extent that theories tend to disown and minimize the fact and significance of asymmetry, they suffer a corrupt consciousness. When justifying belief in God, for example, they tend to presuppose a universe that is rational and symmetrical and presuppose that reason, if it perseveres, can and must comprehend and articulate that symmetry. One aim of this chapter and book is to show how accounting for the world's asymmetry reshapes our notion of rationality and belief in God, reshapes whether and how we justify belief in God. Our immediate question, then, is, How are God and belief in God asymmetrical and how can we account for this?

I have already indicated that physicists apprehend the universe's asymmetry in terms of its deviation from the symmetry of the standard model. You will recall from our discussion in chapter 2 that in the subatomic microworld certain irregular events or quanta occur which deviate from the standard model and for which motion and place cannot simultaneously be predicted. Using quantum physics as analogy for understanding the universe metaphysically, how does asymmetry, including the two features of incommensurability and uncertainty/unpredictability, manifest itself metaphysically? It does so in two ways: objectively and subjectively.

Objectively, asymmetry is embedded in the Christian belief about God, if we assume, as most Christians do, that God is an uncaused cause or being, as Aristotle and Aquinas insist, or an uncreated creator, as Athanasius argues against Arius in defending the second member of the Trinity.[5] Just as quanta constitute incommensurable events in the subatomic world that deviate from the standard model, so analogously and metaphysically does God, as uncreated creator, constitute an asymmetrical being that deviates from the standard principle of causality that establishes the uniformity and symmetry of the universe. In relation to the world's symmetry and its laws of nature (causation), the reality of God as uncaused or self-caused being is as uncertain metaphysically as quanta are uncertain scientifically, in relation to the standard model and predictions based on it. The existence of God, as a kind of uniquely divine, uncaused quantum, situates itself asymmetrically in relation to the symmetry of creation as a whole. God's indeterminacy or self-determinacy appears to all the principles of reason just as irrational and uncertain as quanta do to scientific reason. Just as physics apprehends the deviation of particles from the standard model without being able to explain and comprehend it, so also metaphysics apprehends (by faith) the deviation of God as uncreated, uncaused cause without being able to explain and justify it prospectively. This means that just as belief in quantum events defies scientific analysis and rationality, so too does belief in God as uncaused creator defy critical and scientific analysis. God, as an uncaused being situated incommensurably in relation to the universe's uniformity, will therefore not lend itself to those ordinary ways of explaining and predicting based on the symmetrical model of the universe. An uncaused cause is an idea that deviates from standard ways of inductively demonstrating or deductively inferring the existence and cause of beings and events. One of the ordinary, scientific ways of comprehending and explaining an event is to identify its cause or causal conditions and make predictions based on that analysis. But since God is a self-determining being that deviates from the principle of causality, "God" will seem to reason to be a being whose existence is relatively uncertain and elusive to ordinary, rational ways of analyzing and explaining the existence of beings. This does not mean that God as self- or uncaused cause has no explanation, but, as we shall see, only that its cause and explanation must be apprehended by faith and explained in terms of a retrospective, cumulative case.

A scientist might object, as indeed Stephen Hawking does, that a quantum-gravitational cosmological model eliminates the need for God as *creatio originans*, that the causal contingency of the universe requires only that we posit the existence of an uncaused universe rather than the existence of an uncaused deity, and that this explanation, as Davies suggests, is simpler than postulating God as its uncaused cause.[6] A theist might rejoin, as indeed W. L. Craig does, that there would still be a need for God as *creatio continuans*, or, as does Richard Swinburne, that God as the uncaused cause of the universe provides "a simpler beginning of explanation than does the supposition of the existence of an uncaused universe, and that is grounds for believing the former supposition to be true."[7] The point to which I want to draw attention here is that, in either case, since the notion of uncaused cause is situated asymmetrically in relation to the symmetry of the physical universe and in relation to scientific reason and laws, no clearer or keener execution of such reasoning will resolve the issue one way (deity) or the other (universe). Since belief in God as uncreated creator situates itself asymmetrically by deviating from the standard uniformity of the universe, it must first be apprehended by faith. Philosophers trying to prove the existence of an uncaused cause in the macroworld of metaphysics is as futile as physicists trying to prove and justify the existence of uncaused quanta in the microworld of physics. Asymmetry and unpredictability can be explained, but not by scientific reasoning. The most we can hope for, as I show in this chapter, is for faith and reason, acting in concert with one another, to "account for"[8] this metaphysical fact retrospectively and cumulatively.

The power of reason is suited for comprehending the world's symmetry. To reason an uncaused cause appears as "a light shining in darkness, which the darkness cannot comprehend" (John 1:5). Rather, faith is that activity of mind suited for apprehending an uncaused cause in its deviation from the uniformity of creation. Directly and immediately faith grasps metaphysical asymmetries, like an uncaused cause, which prospective, scientific reason cannot prove. This does not mean, for physicist or philosopher, *credo quia absurdum* but only *credo ut intelligam*, if we take the former as believing what is irrational and the latter as believing what must be grasped, if we are to grasp it at all, first by faith. Thus, although not irrational, belief in a God as self- or uncaused creator of the universe is incommensurable with reason's standard model, in terms of which certain events are caused by certain other events. The mind's habit of faith is required to apprehend God's asymmetrical way of existing; it can be accounted for only retrospectively and cumulatively. By faith the human mind apprehends the mysterious asymmetries of the metaphysical world; by retrospective reason a cumulative case comprehends and explains the nature of their deviation.

Subjectively, asymmetry is embedded in Christian belief insofar as God is considered by Christians to be a free, self-determining being whose creative acts are freely undertaken. What makes these free acts asymmetrical is not that they are without sufficient cause and explanation but that their cause and explanation deviate from the uniformity of the universe, that their cause is supernatural and not natural, a free act of divine agency. Miracles are an example of this agency and of the incommensurability and unpredictability of God's freedom. They are asymmetrical, as we shall see in chapter 5, not because they are irrational and inconsistent with the nature of God but because subjectively, as acts of divine agency, they are incommensurate with the uniformity of the standard model's principle of causality in which material events infer material causes, not divine, supernatural causes. Furthermore, miracles are uncertain in that their occurrence cannot be predicated on any standard model, on the basis of which from certain causal conditions certain effects are predictable.

Objectively and subjectively, then, God's existence and belief in God's existence manifest the incommensurability and uncertainty of the spiritual/metaphysical universe. My present aim is to suggest what exactly this claim means and its significance for developing a philosophy of Christian faith.

Asymmetry and Presupposing God

Belief in God, as a belief about the incommensurability of ultimate reality, is similar to other metaphysical beliefs, such as beliefs about the ultimate nature of human beings (e.g., the self, freedom, immortality). One way to determine whether belief in God is properly basic is to determine whether metaphysical beliefs as a species are properly basic. Following the suggestion of McCleod I will ". . . generate an analogical argument about the proper basicality of beliefs about God by using second-order properly basic beliefs about persons."[9] This I intend to do by drawing an analogy between two metaphysical beliefs, belief in the existence of the self and belief in the existence of God.

Undertaking to reject "as absolutely false all opinion in regard to which [he] could suppose the least ground of doubt," Descartes' quest led to the discovery of a single belief, "I think, therefore I am," which "was wholly indubitable."[10] Ever since, philosophers have subjected Descartes' discovery to careful analysis, asking, for example, What is the logical status of "therefore"? and, What kind of certainty belongs to this indubitable belief? Not surprisingly, a variety of interpretations have been offered. Detractors, such as Gassendi, Arnauld, and Reid, fastened on the term "therefore" and thought that they detected a step of inductive inference.[11] Kant, in contrast, insisted that the *cogito* is tautological, that "I am" or "I exist" add nothing new to "I think." In either case, it is assumed that to the world there belongs a simple and unqualified symmetry and rationality, free of asymmetry and irrationality and therefore free of the need for faith as an activity of mind whereby the world in its metaphysical dimension is apprehended.

Descartes, in replying to his critics, tries to clarify exactly what kind of indubitability belonged to his argument. "But when we become aware that we are thinking beings, this is a primitive act of knowledge derived from no syllogistic [inferential] reasoning. He who says 'I think, hence I am or exist' does not deduce existence from thought by a syllogism but, 'by a simple act of mental vision recognizes it as if it were a thing that is known per se.'" Descartes goes on to argue that if the indubitability of the self's existence were a matter of deductive inference, "the major premise, 'that everything that thinks is, or exists,' would have to be known previously; but yet that has rather been learned from the experience of the individual—that unless he exists he cannot think."[12] Although Descartes is more decided about what kind of indubitability does not belong to his argument than he is clear about what kind does, he is correct, nonetheless, in rejecting an inferential understanding of "therefore"; "I am" is indeed a precondition of, and not a deduction from, "I think." But what kind of indubitability, then, belongs to this "primitive act of knowledge"? How are we to interpret Descartes' metaphor, "by a simple act of mental vision recognizes it as if it were a thing that is known per se"? I submit that the indubitability of the self's existence is of a kind of certainty belonging to what R. G. Collingwood calls absolute presuppositions, which beliefs are apprehended by faith.[13] Absolute presuppositions, as I show in the next section, are not only basic beliefs upon which all human thought and practice are conditioned but are also asymmetrical beliefs that, like quantum events, do not lend themselves to the kinds of explanation and justification to which nonmetaphysical beliefs lend themselves. We can account for these beliefs, I think, but we cannot account for them in ways (scientific and philosophical reasoning) developed for explaining symmetrical patterns of the world. Of the indubitability of the self's existence in particular, Collingwood states, "Its certainty does not depend on proof, not even, like that of the Aristotelian first principles, on indirect proof, but on the fact that it cannot be denied," that it must be presupposed.[14] "I am," in other words, is the logical and ontological precondition for declaring "I think." Hume's attempt to verify empirically the existence of the self, for example, not only leads to skepticism but, ironically, requires that we presuppose from the start the existence of a unified self capable of undertaking (as Hume does) such an inquiry, a self capable of questioning its own existence. We are compelled to conclude that our knowledge of "I am," even when consciously held or internalized, is a necessary and absolute presupposition without which "I think" is impossible.

Before proceeding to a discussion of the nature of presuppositional thinking, however, I want to show how belief in God is analogous to belief in the self's existence. Descartes' *cogito*, Collingwood suggests, indicates a path that, if followed, would lead to a new understanding of the kind of belief that belief in God is and a new way of accounting for that belief. Descartes himself did not pursue this path. His quest was for simple rational symmetry, unencumbered by faith; and so he still felt compelled, as do many of his offspring, to invent a proof by which God's existence is inferred. Kant, however, was able at least partly to follow this path; he understood better than most that the true nature of metaphysical belief—God, freedom, and immortality—is compelling not because of any proof or evidence but because it establishes the possibility of thinking rationally at all. Collingwood's view is that Kant was rightly "trying to treat God, freedom, and immortality as certainties of the same kind as Descartes' *cogito ergo sum*: that is, as universal and necessary, and so far rational, but indemonstrable [and directly intuitive], and so far matters of faith."[15] Whether this was indeed what Kant was attempting to do is unimportant. What is important is whether the claim is compelling: namely, whether belief in God, as an asymmetrical, metaphysical belief, is analogous to belief in the self, as an asymmetrical, metaphysical belief, whether it is a properly basic belief whose indubitability is of the same sort as "I think, therefore I am."

Consider first an attempt by Stewart Goetz to show, independent of faith, that belief in God's existence is inferred and thus not properly basic. Goetz argues that from two propositions, "I exist" and "I am a contingent being," we make an inference to a third, "A necessary being exists."[16] Goetz is arguing, "I am a contingent being, therefore a necessary being (God) exists." Motivated by a quest for simple, rational symmetry, Goetz goes on to argue that "one can only maintain that belief in God is properly basic by ignoring one's own contingency. I contend that anyone who believes in God must acknowledge his contingency and that his knowledge of his contingent nature enables him to infer the existence of a necessary being or beings."[17] Now, is it true that we actually infer "a necessary being exists" from "I am a contingent being"? What is the status of "therefore" in this argument and what kind of certainty does it entail? Goetz, and mutatis mutandis all attempts to infer the existence of God, commits the same mistake Descartes' critics commit in trying to interpret the "therefore" of his *cogito*. The use of the "therefore" lures one into thinking a simple deduction has occurred. But to say "I am a contingent being, therefore a necessary being exists" does not infer necessary from contingent being any more than Descartes' *cogito* infers "I am" from "I think." Rather "a necessary being exists" holds logical and ontological priority over "I am a contingent being." Just as "I am" is a precondition for my being aware of "I think," so also "the existence of a necessary being," however internalized and unconscious my awareness of it may be, is a precondition for, and not a deduction from, my awareness of my own existence as contingent. The indubitability in Goetz's argument is precisely of the same kind as "therefore" in Descartes' "I think, therefore I am." Unless "a necessary being exists" there is no "I am a contingent being"; unless I first have an idea of a necessary being, I can have no idea of a contingent being. Just as "I exist" is a presupposition of "I think," so also "the existence of a necessary being" is a presupposition of "I am a contingent being" and similarly functions as a properly basic belief. Understanding "therefore" in this same way permits Collingwood to reinterpret, for example, Anselm's ontological argument, insisting that what it demonstrates "is not that because our idea of God is an idea of *id quo maius cogitari nequit* therefore God exists, but that because our idea of God is of *id quo maius cogitari nequit* we stand committed [already] to belief in God's existence."[18] By failing to recognize the asymmetrical relation in which God as uncaused cause situates itself in relation to reason and symmetry, Goetz and like-minded theists commit the fallacy of rationalism.

The classical arguments for God's existence, properly reinterpreted, then, are not attempts to prove that God exists by establishing something not previously known. Rather, as David Burrell argues, they are "concerned to show that the coherent exercise of reason—to understand whatever presents itself to be understood—itself presupposes a [belief in a] first principle, which is what Jesus and Christians affirm to be God."[19] When once it is recognized that the "proofs" of the existence of God are instances of presuppositional thinking, it can no longer be regarded as a weakness that the existence of God cannot be proven. Indeed, the quest to prove God's existence inferentially is a misguided quest for simple symmetry in a world to which God is related asymmetrically. Such attempts emerge from a corrupt consciousness, committing the fallacy of rationalism by disowning the asymmetrical dimension of creation and creation's uncreated creator. We shall see that faith is the activity of mind by which humans apprehend the world's asymmetry (God, self), the activity by which humans apprehend those absolute presuppositions that reason by itself cannot account for but which reason must be accountable to if it is to articulate the world's symmetry.

Asymmetry: God as Absolute Presupposition

But what does it mean to call a belief an absolute presupposition? What is the logical status of such a belief and how is it situated in relation to indubitability and truth? Every statement of science, history, or ordinary conversation, explains Collingwood, rests upon other statements and beliefs ("relative presuppositions") that may or may not be articulated. These beliefs in turn are based on or presuppose other beliefs that themselves presuppose yet other beliefs, and so on, each belief functioning relative to other beliefs either as presupposing or being presupposed by them. Hence, the acceptance of any statement or belief can be shown to imply a rather lengthy procession of rational beliefs about the pattern of the world's symmetry. Philosophy helps science analyze and organize this vast network of relative presuppositions so that our understanding of them will be coherent and life will be meaningful. For example, the belief that "the choices humans make are not free but are determined by a combination of factors outside their control" (D) situates itself in relation to a number of other beliefs about the universe (B) (e.g., principle of cause and effect, the inevitability of the causal relationship, a mechanistic model of the universe, the sense of freedom as illusory) in such a way that we say that D presupposes those B. Hence, other beliefs (B) are preconditions for accepting and making sense of D. Collingwood insists, however, that this symmetrical procession of relative presuppositions does not recede ad infinitum. Ultimately our inquiry will encounter *a terminus a quo*, a "constellation" of absolute presuppositions or metaphysical beliefs of which, in contrast to relative presuppositions, it is impossible to ask what prior beliefs they presuppose. For absolute presuppositions are properly basic and establish the ultimate incommensurability of an asymmetrical horizon (God as uncaused cause) within which, and only within which, the symmetrical, rational beliefs and principles of all the sciences and of ordinary life arise and make sense.[20] What exactly is the sense and force of "presupposition" and of "absolute" in Collingwood's theory?

"Presupposition" must be distinguished from assumptions and hypotheses. The latter two have to do with our understanding of the world's symmetry. They are suppositions that are optional and belong to the sphere of scientific propositions. One who makes a supposition is aware that he might, if he likes, make instead another one.[21] He can assume that X = 9 but just as easily can assume that X = 17 or nothing at all. A scientist may assume the existence of Euclidian space or Newtonian space and carry out his or her investigation. Absolute presuppositions are not optional in this sense; they cannot be merely supposed but must be presupposed. For example, although interpretations of them may differ, we cannot presuppose that there are no laws of nature if rational, scientific inquiry is to continue. Similarly, the existence of the self cannot be a hypothesis to be tested;

as indicated above, even the attempt to empirically verify the existence of the self requires that we presuppose from the start a unified self capable of carrying out such an inquiry and drawing, for example, a skeptical Humean conclusion. Analogously, neither can the existence of God be treated as a hypothesis; for the very attempt to verify hypotheses, argues Collingwood, presupposes a belief that there belongs to the world of experience an absolute objective unity of reality, a *"totum in toto it totum in qualibet parte,"* and the whole performing a function for the parts without which the parts simply would cease to exist.[22] This then is what "presuppose" means here: that, as Burrell states it, "the activities ingredient to rational inquiry can be shown [to be based on] an operative belief in some overarching unity."[23] That one traditional name for this "unity" or "whole" is God does not mean, of course, that belief in God's existence is a presupposition we are compelled to make but only that those who hold such a belief must treat it as a presupposition and not as an inference from a more basic belief.

By "absolute" Collingwood refers to a dimension of presupposition that is incommensurable with distinctions ordinarily drawn between justifiable and unjustifiable, between truth and falsity. "Absolute" ordinarily means "subject to no conditions." It is the term Collingwood employs to indicate that certain kinds of second-level beliefs are not subject to ordinary conditions of justification but reflect "knowledge of ultimate truth which, owing to its intuitive or imaginative form, cannot justify itself under criticism."[24] This fact reflects that asymmetrical nature of the world and rational thinking about the world: absolute presuppositions (as metaphysical or as religious), although necessary, are not justifiable by any ordinary standards of justifiability. They simply "pop up" like quantum events without any cause or reason to justify them; accordingly, they must be apprehended, if apprehended at all, by faith. So, "unless we have [these absolute presuppositions by faith] already arguing is impossible for us," insists Collingwood. "Nor can we change them by arguing; unless they remain constant all our arguments would fall to pieces; it is proof that depends on them, not they on proof."[25] Further, as absolute a presupposition is neither "derived from experience" nor "undermined" by it; it is, rather, the yardstick by which experience is "judged."[26] A. J. Ayer's principle of verification—that only those propositions are meaningful that can be empirically verified—sustained critical blows for being a belief that by its own standard is unverifiable and therefore meaningless. But this is not surprising; for such second-level metaphysical beliefs as absolute presuppositions, Collingwood is insisting, are situated asymmetrically to scientific rationality and are not subject to its conditions of verification or justification. They transcend those conditions as a precondition of their possibility. Accordingly, we must treat "the existence of God [as] a presupposition, and an absolute one, of all the thinking done by Christians," including thinking about what counts as justifiable and rational.[27]

Take as an example the question of the miraculous, which we shall address in some detail in chapter 4. Why and how is belief in the miraculous perfectly acceptable for the theist, while for the nontheist it is irrational superstition? The answer, it seems, must be in terms of what one permits from the beginning to count as possible; and what one permits to count as possible is a direct function of one's set of absolute presuppositions. Properly understood, Hume's conclusion, in *Essay on Miracles*—that it could never be reasonable to believe in a miracle—is based not merely on the fact that a miracle is something that violates a law of nature but more fundamentally on an absolute belief that he presupposes, namely, that all rationally possible events will always without exception conform uniformly to laws of nature and will not deviate from the standard model on the basis of which possible events can be possibly predicted. This basic presupposition determines what is and is not empirically possible, as well as the patterns of thought that will and will not count as rationally possible. Thus, evidence of two thousand miracles no more than of one will convince Hume of the historical, miraculous activity of a supernatural being; from the start they are inadmissible, because the set of absolute beliefs that he presupposes compels him a fortiori to regard miracles as irrational, superstitious, and impossible. Nor will any argument, no matter how convincing, compel the theist to jettison his belief in the miraculous, so long as her or his set of basic beliefs presuppose a being for whom "all things are possible." The evidence for miracles can be compelling only to one whose set of presuppositions already apprehends the possibility of asymmetrical, incommensurable events. The point to which Collingwood wants to draw attention is that the absolute beliefs (e.g., belief in God, or not) by which a person determines what will and will not count as possible (e.g., miracles, or not) are beliefs that are first apprehended, if apprehended at all, by faith.

It is not uncommon among humans that they mistakenly apotheosize relative presuppositions, treating one or another of them as if they were absolute. All the forms of reductionism (e.g., psychologism, behaviorism, perhaps even process philosophy) falter in this way. One relative detail (e.g., the human psyche, causality, motion/process) of the universe itself is mistakenly exalted as if it were a belief that deserves and serves the status of an absolute presupposition. What is needed to avoid the self-deception of reductionism, argues Walter Wink, is a set of beliefs, like theism, that constitute a genuinely absolute constellation of presuppositions. "The whole history of modern science demonstrates time and again the tendency of scientists [and philosophers and theologians] to absolutize one immanent aspect of creation after another. Science, it now appears, cannot dispense with God after all. It needs God, not as an 'explanation,' but as a grounding presupposition of reality that transcends every theorem, principle, or created component. Acknowledging God is the sole check against idolizing the elements"[28] or the process of which they are a part. Not only do absolute presuppositions possess explanatory power, they are interpretive grounds that properly situate scientific beliefs symmetrically in relation to each other and in relation to an ultimate horizon. But absolute presuppositions themselves are incommensurable and asymmetrically situated in relation to the world's symmetry and reason. Therefore, they cannot be justified in the ways that we ordinarily justify beliefs (relative presuppositions) we hold about the world's symmetry.

Symmetry: Justifying Belief in God

My promise to grasp one horn of the dilemma—that belief in God is properly basic—has now been fulfilled. Absolute presuppositions, such as the existence of the self as free and of God as uncaused cause, are both properly basic beliefs. My promise to grasp the other horn of the dilemma—that belief in God as a properly basic, asymmetrical belief nevertheless lends itself "to a certain kind of justification"—is yet to be fulfilled.

Although an asymmetrical and properly basic belief in God is not justified by any particular argument or evidence, we are still tempted, I think, to regard belief in God, and other second-order metaphysical beliefs, as rational and subject to conditions of justification. We are still inclined to want somehow to justify those crucial, core beliefs that regulate the world and regale it with a symmetry that astonishes. This is a temptation to which I think we should yield. For although not justified in the ordinary ways we justify beliefs about the world's symmetry, not justified by any particular deductive proof or empirical evidence or any mere collection of proofs or evidences, nevertheless asymmetrical, metaphysical beliefs, in their status as absolute presuppositions are subject, Collingwood rightly insist, to a certain kind of justification. They are justifiable by virtue of the rightness, truthfulness, or persuasiveness of the "world-version"[29] that they have the power to produce, by the extent to which that world-version accounts not only for the symmetry embedded in the universe but its asymmetry as well. Indeed, justifying world-versions entails a process of two interrelated activities—reasoning retrospectively and constructing a cumulative case. Since any world-version is basic and comprehensive, its justification must be equally basic and comprehensive and must employ retrospective reason in developing a comprehensive, cumulative case. How so?

First, the process of justification to which metaphysics' asymmetrical, absolute presuppositions (like belief in God or self) lend themselves is "cumulative." Basil Mitchell, in *The Justification of Religious Belief*, argues that if a case can be made for Christian theism at all it must be on the basis of a "cumulative case."[30] Because world-versions are by their nature cumulative (that is, since they attempt to comprehend the universe in its totality), the case made for it must be comprehensive, which kind of case is cumulative, comprehensive of all possible explanations, including explanations for incommensurability and unpredictability. Such a case is grounded and shaped by a set of absolute presuppositions, and because absolute presuppositions situate themselves asymmetrically in relation to the world's symmetry, the case for or against them cannot be based on simple prospective reason, which assumes the universe is uniform and symmetrical, but must be based on retrospective reason which can apprehend even the universe's incommensurability and thereby establish the basis for a cumulative case. So, if theism's world-version is justifiable, Mitchell argues, it is because it makes a more persuasive cumulative case; that is, it "makes better sense of all the evidence available than does any alternative on offer."[31] The constellation of absolute presupposition anchored by belief in God, in other words, gives rise to an intricate network of beliefs, principles, and practices that "cumulated" together form a version of the world that is arguably more persuasive than other world-versions. And of course atheists and humanists dispute this claim. The implication of cumulative case is not that taken individually and separately theistic arguments, such as the cosmological and teleological arguments, are weak and defective but that somehow together they magically acquire strength and health. Not at all. Instead, cumulative case suggests that individual arguments and evidences on their own possess some minimal prospective and explanatory power, but that by accumulating and weaving all of them together a strong and durable fabric is created whose explanatory and persuasive force and vision exceed the simple summation of the individual parts. Just as each ingredient of a sauce possesses culinary delights of its own, blending them together yields a culinary delicacy that far exceeds the delight one takes in tasting each of its ingredients individually. Of any world-version, then, "it can reasonably be demanded, insists Mitchell, . . . that it deal adequately with the phenomenon in its fullest and most impressive forms," including the phenomenon that "has been so strong and so pervasive of a man's entire life that he himself, at least, could scarcely doubt the reality of his encounter with God."[32]

Put differently, making a cumulative case for a particular world-version is analogous on a large scale to the way we determine the justifiability of truth-functional propositions on a small scale, namely, by the relative justifiability of their component parts—by the network of the beliefs, values, propositions, practices, experiences, facts, and interpretation of facts to which a set of absolute presuppositions give rise. In short, the justifiability of a world-version is a function of the truth and persuasiveness of all possible knowledge that a person determines a set of beliefs (e.g., theism, atheism) to yield. The justifiability and rationality of asymmetrical, properly basic, metaphysical beliefs (God, self) are determined by the relative reliability of the world-version they produce, the reliability with which that world-version accounts for the asymmetry as well as the symmetry embedded in the universe. The extent to which a world-version is reliable, in other words, is a function of the extent to which the interdependence of its ideas, beliefs, values, and practices measure up to the totality of ways of making critical judgments: including its coherence, correspondence, practicality, comprehensiveness, resilience, and elasticity as well as its precision and clarity, its explanatory and predictive power, and its edifying, existential, and practical power. No one of these ways or any combination short of all of them together is capable of doing justice to and providing justification for a belief as properly basic and asymmetrical as belief in God. Nor can any one world-version, whether religious or secular, yield total and complete justification; for the reliability of any world-version is always in the process of being worked out, of being reassessed and revised, in light of new discoveries and in competition or cooperation with other world-versions.

This fact will surely be a source of great disappointment for those who prefer short, easy "drive through" ways of justifying metaphysical beliefs preferred by some theist and nontheist rationalists. But there are no shortcuts, it seems to me, nor a point at which absolute justifiability is achieved. We must be satisfied with the prospect that one world-version is more reliable than other world-versions, and then only when it is judged to measure up to all the available ways of making critical judgements better than other world-versions. The asymmetry belonging to belief in God and other metaphysical beliefs, in short, is settled by no single proof or evidence, nor even by a series of proofs or evidences. Instead, it is and should be a matter of seemingly interminable critical attention, discussion, and revision.

Second, constructing a cumulative case for any metaphysical world-version requires what David Burrell calls "retrospective," as distinguished from "prospective," justification. Prospective reason properly occupies itself with the symmetry of the world, with explaining and justifying the relative details of that symmetry. It "seeks to answer: Why should I undertake this activity?" Retrospective reason, in contrast, presupposing already a set of asymmetrical, metaphysical beliefs, asks "What am I doing engaged in it?"[33] Both forms of justification are valid and assist the mind in its attempt to discover the symmetry and asymmetry of the universe. Prospective reason presupposes that I should not believe until I understand. It draws on all the principles of logic and critical thinking in order to demonstrate and justify those relative presuppositions (as Collingwood sometimes calls them) that can be reasonably and reliably believed and practiced. Such beliefs and practices are those constituting the sciences (natural and social) and humanities and arts as well as those that make up the structure of ordinary life and thought. Ideally, these relative beliefs are not to be held unless and until they are shown to be justifiable by all the criteria guiding rational judgments about the world's symmetry. Retrospective thinking, in contrast, is the way a constellation of asymmetrical, absolute presuppositions or metaphysical beliefs are shown to be compelling and justifiable. It presupposes a version of *credo ut intelligam*, that unless I first assent to this constellation of metaphysical beliefs (e.g., Christianity, Marxism) I shall not be able to determine whether a cumulative case can be made for it, or whether the world-version to which it gives rise is persuasive, or more persuasive than another.

Classical foundationalism has always sought prospective justification for belief in God. It assumes that a set of metaphysical beliefs, like Christianity, can be prospectively and coercively justified. I have already argued that I do not think belief in God, insofar as it is an asymmetrical, metaphysical belief, is justifiable in this prospective way. But I have also argued that that does not mean we must resign ourselves to radical fideism or to the view that belief in God, if not justifiable prospectively, is not justifiable at all. If we take retrospective justification as paradigmatic for asymmetrical, metaphysical beliefs we establish a way in which belief in God "earns" a certain persuasive force: "earns" because the persuasive force of which it is capable is won by the hard work of cultivating a cumulative case, is won by the work of explanatory reason sketching a world-version that traces and accounts for us as far as possible the complex symmetry and asymmetry of the world in which we live and move and have our being. Classical foundationalism presupposes a symmetry and rationality to the world that is more simple and more simply symmetrical and transparent than (as we shall see in subsequent chapters) the complexities and asymmetries of the world permit. It commits the "fallacy of misplaced argument" by pretending that the metaphysical status of asymmetrical, absolute presuppositions can be justified by simple, coercive prospective arguments properly employed in justifying symmetrical beliefs of the sciences and ordinary life. Although this prospective way of arguing is legitimate, it is legitimate only when treating the relative and symmetrical presuppositions of the natural and social and human sciences, not when treating the asymmetrical, metaphysical beliefs in their status and role as absolute presuppositions. Retrospective thinking presupposes that humans have already committed themselves by faith to a world-version, even when that world-version is nontheistic. With retrospective reason, as Burrell puts it, "we already find ourselves engaged, at least in part, [so we must] then look back to determine how the [world-version] extends our own past coherently as well as opens us into a promising future."[34] This retrospective sense of justification is perhaps analogous to lovers whose initial intuition of love is or is not vindicated by its power to grow and mature through the engagements of daily life, helping them to interpret their past and open themselves to a promising future. Similarly, justifying belief in God retrospectively involves us in an open and ongoing process of discovering how that belief's interpretive power is able to account for the world's complex symmetry and asymmetry, including the rich diversity of human experience, past, present, and future.

Faith and Reason

Presupposed in the argument above is a particular relation between faith and reason, the two activities of mind for which philosophers of religion are responsible. My present aim is to make that relationship explicit.

Whatever role faith may play in practicing religion, rationalists, who advocate some form of foundationalism, assume that reason is sufficient to establish at least a primitive belief in God's existence. And whatever explanatory role reason may play in understanding belief in God, fideists, who advocate proper basicality, assume that faith, independent of prospective justification, is sufficient for apprehending God's existence. The position I am arguing, in contrast, requires a different, more integrated organic sense of faith and reason as inseparable habits of mind, a sense in which both are simultaneously and interdependently engaged in the act of believing in God.

Anselm's ontological proof of God's existence seems to assume a point at which reason takes priority over faith. But when Gaunilo points out to him that his proof is persuasive only to someone who already believes in God, Anselm, seeming not in the least perturbed, replies that his argument was an instance of "faith seeking understanding," thereby assuming a point at which faith takes priority over reason. So, is it by faith or by reason that we apprehend God's existence, or is it either one or both? Anselm seems to submit two incompatible answers. But if what I have argued above is correct, Anselm's apparent ambivalence should not surprise us; for it suggests to us that somehow asymmetrical, metaphysical beliefs, in their role as absolute presuppositions, involve the simultaneous and mutual activity of both faith and reason. The reason why metaphysical beliefs necessarily activate both faith and reason, it seems to me, is because embedded in the structure of the world is not only symmetry (rationality) but asymmetry (faith, irrationality) as well. Accordingly, both faith and reason are required if we are to properly and fully comprehend the world. How so?

Collingwood provides several clues. In his earlier essays on faith and reason, for example, he says that metaphysical beliefs (belief in the self's and God's existence) establish "a common point in the spheres of faith and reason,"[35] a unique "point at which faith and reason absolutely coincide."[36] How are we to grasp these rather slippery claims? Partly by recognizing that the "common point" at which faith and reason "absolutely coincide" entails the unique kind of asymmetrical, metaphysical beliefs (i.e., absolute presuppositions) discussed above and partly by conceiving of the activities of faith and reason in a certain way. Collingwood conceives of them as "habits of mind" or "attitudes which we take toward reality." His guiding premise is that "faith is our attitude toward reality as a whole, and reason our attitude toward its details as distinct and separate from each other."[37]

Faith is the activity by which the mind apprehends asymmetrical, metaphysical realities (absolute presuppositions, properly basic beliefs) like God, freedom, and immortality. It apprehends, that is, those metaphysical events that are incommensurable with the standard model of a uniform, symmetrical universe and unpredictable by scientific reason. Belief in an uncaused cause, for example, is grasped by faith, whether that cause be conceived of as an eternal being or eternal energy. Reason, which is the kind of thinking the mind does about the world's symmetry, itself cannot comprehend and explain but only acknowledge the reality of metaphysical asymmetries. Faith is required to apprehend directly and immediately properly basic asymmetrical, metaphysical realities. These asymmetrical realities are incommensurable in relation to the universe's uniformity and uncertain and unpredictable in relation to the prospective operations of scientific reason. And yet these asymmetrical, metaphysical beliefs, as absolute presuppositions, establish the possibility of thinking rationally about the world's uniformity and symmetry as well as establish the possibility of a comprehensive, cumulative case. So the object faith apprehends (e.g., God) is asymmetrical, metaphysical reality or "everything in the collective sense—everything as a whole," and the activity of faith is the habit whereby the mind immediately and intuitively apprehends this asymmetrical horizon (i.e., God) that establishes the possibility of rationally understanding the world's symmetry. It apprehends a totality as the infinite, asymmetrical horizon of all reality, a horizon within which the totality of finite things are distinguished.[38] Faith apprehends asymmetrical, metaphysical realities in order that reason might make sense of the world's symmetry and rationality. Religious world-versions name this rationality "creation" and the asymmetrical originator of the universe's rationality "God," while nonreligious world-versions name it "cosmos" and its originator any number of things, including energy, big bang, world soul, absolute mind, and so on. In any case, "our use of reason to explain," notes Burrell, "takes its impetus from a unity more comprehensive than any scheme can account for, much as a particular discussion of justice invariably reflects a cosmic sense of justice. Since that more comprehensive unity cannot be forced into an explanatory scheme, one can only believe it to be the case. Yet our continued use of particular explanatory frameworks would be pointless without such a belief."[39] Faith, in short, is that habit of mind that apprehends asymmetrical, metaphysical realities in order that reason as a habit of mind might grasp the universe's symmetry.

In contrast to faith, the object of reason, states Collingwood, is "everything in the distributive sense—every separate thing," and the network of interrelationships of these separate things. As the scientific habit of mind, reason "is the attitude which we take up toward things as parts of a whole, as finite things distinct from one another and connected with one another by a network of relations which it is the business of thought to trace out in detail. . . . There is no fact or class of facts which can be withdrawn from its analysis or spared its criticism."[40] Thinking rationally about the world's symmetry cannot account *for* the asymmetry of faith's metaphysical beliefs; but reason is in a sense accountable *to* these beliefs, for they make possible the activity of thinking rationally about the world's symmetry. Indeed, the discoveries of reason always fall within the horizon marked off by the symmetrical, metaphysical beliefs that the activity of faith presupposes and apprehends.

How then do these two habits of mind "coincide" in beliefs like the existence of the self and of God? Although Collingwood's explanation sometimes lacks precision and clarity at this point, he does suggest, at least, a way of answering.

Since reason's role in relation to the beliefs of faith is explanatory, reason is always implicit in the act of faith; faith is not an act completed "unless it develops into a rational, self-explanatory system of thought"[41] or world-version; unless it can be shown to be cumulatively and retrospectively persuasive. In other words, "by reason we are making explicit the steps by which faith leaps intuitively to its beliefs"[42] about the universe as a whole. The metaphor Collingwood uses, "reason is faith cultivating itself," pictures a relationship in which the activity of skillful labor (reason) is necessary to bring to fruition the seed (faith) that otherwise lies dormant in the earth, in the heart. Without the seed of faith, on the one hand, reason would not have a garden to cultivate. The world-version implicit in the faith's set of asymmetrical, metaphysical beliefs is brought to natural fruition by the skill and care of reason. And without reason's skillful care, on the other hand, the seed of faith dies a dark and lonely death. "A faith unaccompanied by reason, therefore, is not true faith. The spirit of faith is shown to be a real spirit by embodying itself in reason. . . ." Conversely, the attitude of reason toward reality presupposes at all times the attitude of faith. "Reason builds on a foundation of faith, and moves within a system whose general nature must be determined by faith before reason can deal with it in detail."[43] Reason's power and role is not that it is equipped to produce the attitude of faith but that, given the attitude of faith, it can cultivate patterns of rationality that it finds telescoped within the absolute presuppositions of faith.

Consider, by way of an analogy suggested by Werner Schaaffs,[44] a photon as both wave and particle. As a wave imagine a photon extending through space away from its point of origin. Then imagine the photon absorbed by an atom, "suddenly contracted into a minute dot." What physicists are asking us to imagine is analogous, says Schaaffs, to an express train (light wave) "with several hundred compartments (i.e., wavelengths). The express train enters a railroad station (i.e., an atom) on a vacant track (i.e., electron orbit). However, the entry takes place instantaneously, and the railroad station itself is no bigger than a model toy." Incredible. Impossible for rational minds to grasp, and yet true. This analogy, Schaaffs goes on to explain, "is intended to show what is demanded of our power of intuition when, on the basis of numerous experiments, we sometimes attribute the traditional wave nature to light and, on the basis of numerous other experiments, we at other times attribute a particle nature to it." Schaaffs concludes that not only are our minds "unable to grasp this wave-corpuscle duality . . . ; it is also that to consider both characteristics *simultaneously* present in a single photon *in one and the same experiment* is absurd." And so likewise are metaphysical beliefs as absolute presuppositions. They are situated in relation to the mind's reason and the world's symmetry asymmetrically, at the limits of reason's capacity to comprehend. Accordingly, they must be grasped by the power of faith. But simultaneously with grasping these asymmetries by faith, reason is actively engaged in showing how they help us make sense of the world's symmetry, just as photons jointly and simultaneously in their wave-corpuscle duality make sense of our microworld.

What I am arguing, that philosophers always operate within and not independently of some presupposed world-version, may perhaps be summarized in terms of another analogy. The constellation of absolute presuppositions that define the metaphysical horizon of a world-version is analogous to what physicists call the "event horizon" of a black hole. Any light that happens to wander into a black hole is trapped and cannot escape from it. Looking at the event horizon from the outside in, no events can be seen beyond it. And looking at it from the inside out, no events can be seen beyond it. Any reason looking at the metaphysical "event horizon" of a world-version from the outside in sees nothing beyond it. And reason looking at this same horizon from the inside out sees nothing beyond it. Of course, black holes do share characteristics in common. What I find in one I may very well find in another. And of course, in the sphere of philosophy, unlike the physics of black holes, a person may transpose himself if he chooses from one black hole to another. But once one has "fallen" into a world-version there is no escape, until and unless one chooses an entirely different "event horizon" in which to live and move and think. This is to say by way of analogy that in retrieving the interdependence of faith and reason for the sphere of religious beliefs, I am in agreement with John Smith's view that there is but one avenue of approach: namely, "a revised and strengthened form of the ancient enterprise which went by the name of 'faith seeking understanding.'"[45] Hence, belief in God, and all metaphysical beliefs of its kind, should be seen as engaging two roles simultaneously: as a *terminus ad quo*, an ultimate horizon of reality to which all acts of faith intuitively leap, and as a *terminus a quo*, an ultimate epistemological ground from which all possible acts of reason proceed. Accordingly, in apprehending God's asymmetrical existence, faith, on the one hand, is the explicit, dominant habit of mind, while reason is implicit and recessive. As "the assurance of things hoped for, the conviction of things not seen" (Hebrews 11:1), faith is itself incapable of pursuing the rational implications of those metaphysical beliefs that it apprehends intuitively and immediately. On the other hand, in pursuing as best it can a symmetrical pattern of ideas implied by the horizon of God's existence, reason is the explicit, dominant habit of mind; faith is now implicit and recessive but always an activity presupposed in and underwriting all rational activity. In this way, I think, sense can be made of Collingwood's claim that belief in self and God, and all similar metaphysical beliefs, are such that in them faith and reason "absolutely coincide."

Compassion and Supersymmetry

The typical philosophical analysis of faith and reason ends here. But, from the perspective of a philosophy of Christian faith, this is premature. For the relation of faith and reason, asymmetry and symmetry, God and nature, is for the Christian much more profound and personal. This relationship ultimately and properly culminates in a "supersymmetrical" act of what I refer to as *ontological compassion*. For Christianity, at least, compassion is constituted most fundamentally by a historical act of ontological intersubjectivity, of incarnation, an act in which the being of God shares something of the being of humanity, and vice versa. Whether rationalist (e.g., Kant), which presupposes reason and the world's simple symmetry, or fideist (e.g., Kierkegaard), which presupposes the irrationality and asymmetry of religious beliefs, any such belief in ontological intersubjectivity will appear absurd and contradictory. But for Christian theists who presuppose, along with reason and symmetry, the reality of faith and asymmetry, ontological compassion is a truth they must account for and be accountable to.

One way Christians account for (in contrast to justify) ontological compassion is to apprehend by faith the truth of *imago Dei*. This belief, that humans are created in the image and likeness of God, has proven susceptible to a wide variety of meanings and interpretations. The human capacities for rationality, free will, creativity, and faith are just a few of the interpretations suggested by theologians, all of which seem plausible enough. But very few have suggested the interpretation that seems to me to also make good sense and at the same time account for the ontological intersubjectivity constituting the compassion essential to incarnation. Simply put, *imago Dei* establishes the possibility of the being of God becoming intersubjective with the being of humans, the possibility that God's being can share in the human way of being and human being can share in God's way of being. The Apostle Paul's magnificent discourse in Philippians 2 declares that the ontological intersubjectivity of compassion lies at the very heart of incarnation. Most Christians are familiar with the idea that God in Christ in some sense enters human flesh, shares in the sorrows and joys, poverty and prosperity of human life, for the sake of human salvation. But Paul's discourse makes clear that the incarnation of God in Christ entails not merely a compassionate intersubjectivity of shared emotional and existential experiences but also the compassionate intersubjectivity of shared being. Paul refers to such an ontological intersubjectivity, I think, when he speaks of Jesus as one "who, though he was in the form of God, did not count equality with God a thing to be grasped, but emptied himself, taking the form of a servant, being born in the likeness of men. And being found in human form he humbled himself and became obedient unto death, even death on a cross" (Philippians 2:2–8). Just as the being of humans is created in the image and likeness of God, so the being of God is in Christ incarnated in the image and likeness of humans.

Ontological compassion, in short, is an astonishing asymmetrical Christian belief that must be apprehended by faith if the mind is to make sense of and account for it. The belief that a single being could be constituted by both divinity and humanity, infinitude and finitude, eternity and temporality is incommensurable with the universe's symmetry and deviates from the predictions of scientific reason about human creatures. Reason by itself can make no sense of it, and rationalists (Kant) and fideists (Kierkegaard) eagerly remind Christians of this. It is a belief that situates itself asymmetrically in relation to the symmetry of creaturely being that scientific reason is equipped to decipher. But by reenfranchising faith, the mind apprehends incarnation as a presupposition of the ways Christians think about and live morally in the world. Indeed, the ontological intersubjectivity of compassion, represented by the incarnation, supercedes the metaphysical dichotomies otherwise evident, between the world's asymmetry and symmetry, uncaused cause and laws of nature, divine being and human being, faith and reason. The ontological compassion of incarnation establishes a kind of supersymmetrical wholeness and harmony that overcomes these simple dualisms. Recall how physicists now surmise that a fifth dimension or SUSY introduces into the world not only a profound holistic element but also an active participation by experimenters in the construction of a supersymmetrical reality, a unified field theory. Analogously, compassionate, ontological intersubjectivity with humans is the way God, as chief experimenter, participates in creation and thereby determines, out of all the possibilities, in which specific direction humans can and should live their lives. God, the uncaused asymmetrical creator of creation, in humility becomes subject to the symmetrical laws of creation and in so doing reconciles the disparity, the hostility, between divine being and human being, between creator and creation. The uncaused cause, on this view, voluntarily submits to physical laws of causation and to social laws of custom, and in so doing participates in the construction and reconstruction of creation, reconciling and superceding the ontological dichotomy otherwise obtaining between uncaused cause and cause, between divine and human being. And yet among some rationalists, vestiges of Newton's closed, mechanistic world persist in a remote, aloof God whom the deists insist cannot and must not participate in the physical universe, cannot and must not participate, like a grand experimenter, in constructing and reconstructing the direction reality, especially human reality, shall take.

For philosophers and theoretical physicists, of course, questions follow. How is it possible that the being of God as uncaused cause could enter into and participate in the causally conditioned being of humanity? How can the "force field" specific to divine being interact with the "force field" specific to human being? How is simultaneity between the eternal and temporal possible? Put theologically, how can we account for the possibility of the incarnation, if at all? I cannot hope to answer these questions here. There exists quite an extensive literature by physicists, philosophers, and theologians addressing these questions, but I know of no single theory that, for me, does so adequately.[46] What I want to suggest here is a general direction in which I think the discussion can and should proceed.

First, it is now clear, as Max Jammer suggests, that "the introduction of the field concept into physics . . . opens the possibility of a new conception of the relation between physics and theology."[47] Why and how? "Field" or "force field" in physics refers to the "contextual framework" within which forms of energy (e.g., gravity, electricity, magnetism, nuclear energy) operate.[48] A fundamental question physicists address is, Can energy change or transfer from one field to another? Can the form of energy characteristic of one field (e.g., electricity) transform itself into the form of energy characteristic of another field (e.g., magnetism)? As is well known, Einstein's answer to this question is No. Based on his "locality principle" he argues for the segregation of "force fields" between which fields of energy are not transferable. "But on one supposition we should, in my opinion, absolutely hold fast: the real factual situation of the system S2 is independent of what is done with the system S1, which is spatially separated from, the former."[49] More recently, physicists have disproved Einstein's locality principle and proved in contrast that "local realism leads inescapably to certain mathematical consequences, the so-called Bell inequalities, which are violated by the predictions of quantum mechanics."[50] Further experiments have confirmed these results so that today nonlocality theories (theories based on the fact that energy is changeable and transferable from one force field to another) among physicists are abundant.

Not surprisingly, there is no shortage of theoretical physicists and theologians who speculate on the analogical implications of this fact (the nonlocality of energy) for theology in general and belief in the incarnation in particular. The analogy goes something like this: just as different forms of physical energy are transferable between the framework of various fields, so also different forms of spiritual energy or being are transferable between one field (e.g., divine) and another (e.g., human). Even though physicists do not fully understand all the details of the nonlocality of energy and how it transfers between fields, they are certain of its nonlocality and base further inquiries on that assumption. Analogously, Christian theologians do not fully understand the details of the nonlocality of divine being (or energy), but by faith they presuppose that in the incarnation such a transfer of being occurs and that inquiry should proceed on the basis of that belief. Jammer, in his book *Einstein and Religion*, surveys and critiques several of the efforts by theologians (T. F. Torrence, W. Pannenberg) to explain this transfer of spiritual being from one form (divine) to another (human).[51] And physicist/Anglican priest John Polkinghorne argues for his particular version.[52] Even though there is no agreement as to how, analogously, compassionate ontological intersubjectivity or the transferability of being occurs through incarnation, there is general agreement that the dualisms of the old Newtonian version of the world are shattered and superceded. This has resulted, argues Frank Schubert, "in the establishment of a new paradigm of field theory in which the traditional barrier between God and man . . . is replaced by an essential relatedness."[53]

There are two points to which I wish to draw attention here. First, however, retrospective reason may or may not try to account for the possibility of incarnation cumulatively, it is an event that is situated asymmetrically in relation to the world's symmetry and prospective rationality, and thus an event Christians apprehend by faith. Second, the fundamental significance of incarnation lies in its intersubjectivity, in its status as ontological compassion. For Christian philosophy compassion establishes not merely a moral principle but an ontology whereby traditional dualisms (subject/object, self-cause/cause, divine/human, asymmetry/symmetry, faith/reason) are overcome and a supersymmetrical harmony and wholeness envisioned as a real historical and eschatological possibility. Unlike physicists who still search for SUSY, Christians by faith believe that the mystery of incarnation establishes analogously in the spiritual realm a "unified field theory," a supersymmetry rooted in the soil of an ontological compassion that heals and harmonizes. Humans, moreover, are not mere independent observers but experimenters who help in constructing this supersymmetry by participating in projects of compassion. For Christian philosophers the incarnation's ontological intersubjectivity of compassion is ultimately the answer to Pilate's question "What is truth?," an answer that Pilate was not prepared to hear or accept.

In chapters 2 and 3 I have tried to establish a methodology for developing a philosophy of Christian faith and have begun to apply that methodology to the foundation of theistic belief, namely, belief in God and God's existence. In the remainder of this book I further apply this methodology to issues pertinent and perennial to philosophy of religion. By doing so I contribute to the ongoing construction of a cumulative case on behalf of Christian faith. But although I contribute to such a case I do not complete it. Since a completed cumulative case is comprehensive, no one work and at no one time can ever be completed and closed. It is a continuing and continuous task to which a multitude of philosophers interested in doing so must contribute. But what I hope to establish is a clear and compelling method and a clear and compelling application of that method to several substantial issues that will point philosophers in the right direction, whereby they might collectively and collaboratively contribute to constructing a more complete and comprehensive cumulative case. In other words, I am sketching a part of the map of a cumulative case and establishing the criteria by which others, if they choose, may sketch the remainder of that map.

In the next two chapters, accordingly, I extend the method to two provocative issues, evil/suffering and miracles. We shall find that in both instances, questions are ultimately answered for Christian philosophers in terms of symmetry and reason, asymmetry and faith, and by pursuing the practical implications of ontological compassion (supersymmetry): for the problem of gratuitous evil/suffering, existential compassion; for the problem of miracles, spiritual compassion. It is to the first of these problems that I now turn.

Notes

1. Søren Kierkegaard, *Training in Christianity*, trans. Walter Lowrie (Princeton, N.J.: Princeton University Press, 1952), 199.

2. Stewart C. Goetz, "Belief in God Is Not Properly Basic," *Religious Studies* 19 (1983): 475.

3. Alan Plantinga, "The Reformed Objection to Natural Theology," *Philosophical Knowledge* 54 (1981).

4. Frank Close, *Lucifer's Legacy: The Meaning of Asymmetry* (London: Oxford University Press, 2000), 1.

5. The distinction between created and uncreated being, argues Arthur Peacocke, and not the distinction between natural and supernatural, is fundamental to thinking clearly about the relationship between science and Christianity and is the "stance" he takes "as a result of exploring the implications of the sciences for our understanding of

God's relation to the world." See Arthur Peacocke, *Paths from Science Towards God: The End of All Our Exploring* (Oxford: Oneworld Publications, 2002), 161.

6. Paul Davies, *God and the New Physics* (New York: Simon and Schuster, 1984), 48–49.

7. Richard Swinburne, *The Existence of God* (Oxford: Clarendon Press, 1979), 131–132. For a concise summary of the debate on this issue between W. L. Craig and Quentin Smith, see Max Jammer, *Einstein and Religion* (Princeton, N.J.: Princeton University Press, 1999), 261–265; for the debate itself, see Craig and Smith's *Theism, Atheism, and Big Bang Cosmology* (Oxford: Clarendon Press, 1993).

8. "Account for" does not mean "explain" or "justify" but the capacity of mind to recognize the reality of asymmetries in the universe and how they are situated asymmetrically in relation to the world's symmetry. See in chapter 2 the section on faith and asymmetry.

9. Mark McCleod, "The Analogy Argument for the Proper Basicality of Belief in God," *International Journal for the Philosophy of Religion* 21 (1987): 19. Plantinga seems to follow McLeod's strategy by drawing an analogy between belief in persons and in God. For example, he draws an analogy between the basicality of first-order empirical beliefs, such as "That person is angry," and first-order metaphysical beliefs, such as "God is angry." See Alvin Plantinga, "Is Belief in God Rational?" in *Rationality and Religious Belief*, ed. C. F. Delaney (Notre Dame, Ind.: University of Notre Dame Press, 1979), and "Is Belief in God Properly Basic?" *Nous* 25 (1981): 41–51.

10. Rene Descartes, *Discourse on Method*, trans. John Veitch (La Salle, Ill.: Open Court, 1962), 34.

11. M. Arnauld, *Philosophical Works of Descartes* II, trans. E. S. Haldane and G. R. T. Ross (New York: Dover, 1934), 84. Arnauld says, for example, "And certainly, some one will say that it is no marvel if, in deducing my existence from the fact that I think, the idea that I form of the self, which is in this way an object of thought, represents me to my mind as merely a thinking being, since it has been derived from my thinking alone."

12. Ibid., 38.

13. In attributing this view to Collingwood, I take the liberty of interpreting his earlier essays on faith and reason (1927 and 1928) in terms of his more fully developed theory of absolute presuppositions set forth in *An Essay on Metaphysics* (Oxford: Clarendon Press, 1940). The two earlier essays are "Reason Is Faith Cultivating Itself," *Hibbert Journal* 26, and "Faith and Reason," a pamphlet in the Affirmation Series (London: Ernest Benn), both of which are reprinted in *Faith and Reason: Essays in the Philosophy of Religion by R. G. Collingwood*, ed. Lionel Rubinoff (Chicago, Ill.: Quadrangle Books, 1968), 108–121 and 122–147, respectively.

14. R. G. Collingwood, "Reason Is Faith Cultivating Itself," in *Faith and Reason: Essays in the Philosophy of Religion by R. G. Collingwood*, ed. Lionel Rubinoff (Chicago, Ill.: Quadrangle Books, 1968), 114.

15. R. G. Collingwood, "Faith and Reason," in *Faith and Reason: Essays in the Philosophy of Religion by R. G. Collingwood*, ed. Lionel Rubinoff (Chicago, Ill.: Quadrangle Books, 1968), 137. Following Kant, Collingwood explains how these three beliefs are presuppositions of human experience: "God, because God stands for the rationality, the trustwor-

thiness of the objective world; freedom, because freedom means our own power of determining our own actions, which certainly cannot be tested by scientific inquiry into this or that type of action; immortality, because immortality means the ultimate harmony between human purpose and the destiny of the universe" (139–140).

16. Goetz, "Belief in God Is Not Properly Basic," 482.

17. Ibid., 484.

18. R. G. Collingwood, *An Essay on Metaphysics* (Oxford: Clarendon Press, 1940), 190.

19. David Burrell, "Religious Belief and Rationality;" in *Rationality and Religious Belief*, ed. C. F. Delaney (Notre Dame, Ind.: University of Notre Dame Press, 1979), 98.

20. See part I of *An Essay on Metaphysics*, where Collingwood discusses the details of this theory.

21. Collingwood, *Essay on Metaphysics*, 27–28, 155–161. See also Collingwood's *Religion and Philosophy* (London: Macmillan, 1916), 138.

22. R. G. Collingwood, *Speculum Mentis* (Oxford: Clarendon Press, 1924), 300.

23. Burrell, "Religious Belief and Rationality," 101.

24. Collingwood, *Speculum Mentis*, 132.

25. Collingwood, *Essay on Metaphysics*, 173. See also his "Reason Is Faith Cultivating Itself," 115.

26. Ibid., 193–194.

27. Ibid., 186.

28. Walter Wink, *Unmasking the Powers: The Invisible Forces that Determine Human Existence* (Philadelphia, Pa.: Fortress Press, 1986), 143.

29. See note 9 in chapter 2 regarding my borrowing of the phrase "world-version" from Nelson Goodman.

30. Basil Mitchell, *The Justification of Religious Belief* (New York: Seabury Press, 1973), especially chapter 3.

31. Ibid., 40.

32. Ibid., 41. The skeptic or atheist may of course rejoin that the existence and nature of the universe need not be explained at all, that there is really no need to develop a world-version. And yet there is an obligation, I think, for the skeptic to (1) give a fair and reasonable explanation why no world-version is needed, (2) give a fair and reasonable explanation of the phenomena claimed by theists as a cumulative case for theism, and/or (3) forfeit their credibility as participants in the life of the mind.

33. Burrell, "Religious Belief and Rationality," 107 (see 107–112).

34. Ibid., 108.

35. Collingwood, "Faith and Reason," 137–138.

36. R. G. Collingwood, "Faith Is Reason Cultivating Itself," in *Faith and Reason: Essays in the Philosophy of Religion by R. G. Collingwood*, ed. Lionel Rubinoff (Chicago: Quadrangle Books, 1968), 114.

37. Collingwood, "Faith and Reason," 140.

38. Ibid., 142.

39. Burrell, "Religious Belief and Rationality," 98.

40. Collingwood, "Faith and Reason," 142.
41. Collingwood, "Faith Is Reason Cultivating Itself," 118–119.
42. R. G. Collingwood, *Religion and Philosophy* (London: Macmillan, 1916), 67.
43. Collingwood, "Faith and Reason," 143.
44. Werner Schaaffs, *Theology, Physics, and Miracles*, trans. Richard Renfield (Washington, D.C.: Canon Press, 1974), 43.
45. John Smith, "Faith, Belief, and the Problem of Rationality," in *Rationality and Religious Belief*, ed. C. F. Delaney (Notre Dame, Ind.: University of Notre Dame Press, 1979), 59.
46. Literature on this topic includes John Polkinghorne's *Belief in God in An Age of Science* (New Haven, CT: Yale University Press, 1998) and his *Science and Technology: An Introduction* (Minneapolis, MN: SPCK/Fortress, 1998).
47. Max Jammer, *Einstein and Religion* (Princeton, N.J.: Princeton University Press, 1999), 211–212.
48. Ibid., 214. See also Davies, *God and the New Physics*, 147–148.
49. From Einstein's "Autobiographical Notes" quoted in Jammer, *Einstein and Religion*, 225.
50. Jammer, *Einstein and Religion*, 226.
51. Ibid., 203–213.
52. John Polkinghorne, *Belief in God in an Age of Science* (New Haven, Conn.: Yale University Press, 1998) (see chapter 3).
53. Frank D. Schubert, "Thomas F. Torrence: The Case for a Theological Science," *Encounter* 45 (1984): 133, quoted in Jammer, *Einstein and Religion*, 206.

CHAPTER FOUR

Belief in God's Goodness

The story is familiar. Job is a righteous man with a great deal of wealth. On a single tragic day, however, messengers arrive one after the other bearing news of a series of disasters that leave Job destitute and alone. His servants, oxen, and asses are destroyed by the Sabeans; other servants and sheep are struck by lightning and die; the Chaldeans steal his camels and kill his servants; and a great desert wind destroys the house in which Job's sons and daughters are dining, and all are killed. As if that is not enough, Job himself is afflicted with debilitating boils and reduced to sitting among ashes. Even though Job is devastated by the news that he has lost all, even though he descends into the abyss of grief and despair, even though he feels bitter and betrayed, still he worships God (Job 1:13–2:8).

A second telling of this story is also familiar, but less so. Job is a righteous man with a great deal of wealth. Satan comes before the Lord and claims that Job is not as righteous as he seems; indeed, Job is righteous, he insists, only because the Lord takes special care to bless and protect Job and his family and possessions. Satan further insists that if this were not the case, if Job lost this special blessing and protection, then he would curse the Lord to his face. In response, the Lord agrees to bargain. Satan can have his way with Job short of taking his life. So, at the hands of Satan, Job suffers the horrendous losses already described, including his own health and the support of his justly skeptical spouse. And what is Job's response? "Naked I came from my mother's womb, and naked shall I return; the Lord gave, and the Lord has taken away; blessed be the name of the Lord" (Job 1:6–2:22).

The difference between these two versions of Job's story is clear and critical. The second is a complete and accurate version, far superior to the first in its characters, plot, and dramatic suspense. It is perhaps surprising, then, that the first fragmented, prosaic version of this story is the one preferred by some philosophers of religion, at least if their approaches to the problem of a God and evil are any indication. Regardless of how one chooses to categorize the many modern approaches to resolving the dilemma,[1] many of them collected together, no matter how varied and distinctive they may be individually, hold in common one thing—they presuppose the first rather than the second telling of the story of Job. And therein lies a corruption of consciousness, the tendency toward the fallacy of rationalism, by disowning and writing out of the plot the role of Satan and the satanic. One does not have to look far to discover the source of this denial; many contemporary philosophers feel compelled to disown Satan and satanic power in the world. David Hume, who set the modern agenda to which most contemporary philosophers of religion feel obligated, established that philosophical questions having to do with religious matters must be approached, as with other matters, on a rational, empirical basis quite independent of faith or the beliefs and practices of faith; and many philosophers of religion have followed Hume's lead. This enlightened approach seems somewhat paradoxical: that to solve the philosophical problems raised by religious belief one must bracket the very resources (religious beliefs and experiences) in the context of which the problems arise in the first place. And yet such an "atheological" approach, as Marilyn McCord Adams calls it, requires that the "deployment of the argument from evil" and attempts to defend it are conducted within "the parameters of a religion-neutral value theory. . . ." Although Hume attempts to anchor his own philosophy of religion on just such a religiously neutral, objective basis, today many philosophers would agree that such a value-free, religiously neutral basis is illusory and a self-deception. I agree with Adams that the wide variety of atheological approaches to the problem of evil, including Hume's, fail partly because they aspire to be atheological. What is needed is "to approach the problem *aporetically*," as Adams puts it, by "formulating . . . beliefs about how God is solving the problem of evil using the valuables within a Christian value theory to defeat evils."[2] In this chapter I intend to trace an *aporetic* approach to the problem of evil, an approach that draws on theological beliefs and practices, in this case the Christian ones, whereby not only God but Satan and other particularly Christian beliefs (e.g., incarnation) are summoned in solving the problem of evil. As indicated, other philosophers (Alvin Plantinga, Marilyn Adams) mobilize the local beliefs of the Christian tradition in addressing this issue. I affirm these efforts and hope that by locating them in the context of my methodology (symmetry, asymmetry, and supersymmetry) I might expand on and enhance them.

Of the several ways to categorize atheological approaches to solving the problem of evil, the one that most suits my purposes here is to distinguish between subjective and objective approaches. Some approaches tend toward a subjective solution and others tend more toward an objective one. Both kinds of approaches aspire to be religiously neutral as far as possible and both presuppose that the world is a rational, orderly place constituted by a simple symmetry that can be discovered and explained. That supposed symmetry is perhaps nowhere more greatly challenged than by the reality of evil and suffering, by the world's sometimes horrendous moral asymmetry. Theistic approaches that tend to emphasize a subjective, volitional solution to the problem of evil originate at least as early as St. Augustine and are perpetuated today in the work of philosophers such as Richard Swinburne. They defend theism by appealing to free will, by claiming that all moral evil derives from creatures who are distinguished by freedom of the will. The matter of natural evil (e.g., disease, earthquakes) is addressed variously. To his credit, Plantinga includes the activity of the devil and his cohorts; while Swinburne argues, as Pojman fairly summarizes, "that natural evil is part and parcel of the nature of things, resulting from the combination of deterministic physical laws that are necessary for consistent action and the responsibility given to humans to exercise their freedom."[3] Although advocates of the subjective approach may be Christian philosophers, in the spirit of Hume they tend to minimize any appeal to concrete theological beliefs and tend to maximize religious neutrality.

Approaches that accent objective, rational solutions originate at least as early as Irenaeus and are preserved in the thought of philosophers such as Gottfried Leibniz and John Hick. Although objective approaches generally include free will as a significant feature, their defenses of theism are distinctive in arguing that evil in the world is allowed by God for the purpose of bringing about a good that is greater than it would be in a world without evil. Their appeal is to a larger cosmic context in which God works to realize his purposes. Leibniz argues, for example, that God permits evil in the world in order to achieve the best of all possible worlds; by confronting evil in the world humans propel themselves toward a moral and spiritual destiny far greater than would be the case if there were no evil in the world. Similarly, Hick envisions life as an occasion, established by God, for soul-making. Humans, individually, and the human race, collectively, begin as infants who are fallen and who by God's grace and by properly using their freedom can capitalize on opportunities (i.e., evil, suffering) for soul-making and progress toward the ideal of divine love that characterizes the kingdom of God. Objective approaches such as these, like many subjective approaches, tend toward the atheological, religiously neutral Humean ideal, attempting to minimize appeal to specific and distinctively Christian interpretations of beliefs.

Both subjective and objective approaches possess much that is of value for treating the problem of evil. Both kinds of approaches reflect in common the human quest and desire for symmetry. Both presuppose that the world is symmetrical and rational and that the challenge of evil can be met by reason and by its capacity to situate evil and suffering somehow within that symmetry, whether subjectively as a function of volition or objectively as necessary for achieving God's purposes in the universe. I am in agreement with a great deal in these two approaches and draw on both in developing my own perspective. With subjective approaches, I argue that free will and agency is central, and yet I include in the mix the incommensurability of the satanic, the free will and agency of Satan and satanic legions. With objective approaches, I argue that although evil and suffering may be occasions for soul-making and for realizing God's sovereign purposes, the aim of evil and suffering in the world is not for the sake of soul-making or for fulfilling some divinely appointed end, some best of all possible worlds. I argue instead that evil and suffering are not intended nor permitted by God and that their presence in the world is an asymmetrical moral and spiritual insult and outrage, incommensurable with God's design for the universe. By themselves many subjective and objective approaches tend to fall short of an adequate solution, partly because theologically they are too timid, failing to draw on the considerable, local religious resources provided by the tradition they are defending and partly because philosophically they are too brash, failing to acknowledge that, just as in the physical universe, there likewise belongs to the moral/spiritual universe an asymmetrical being (Satan) without which horrendous evil in the moral universe is not adequately understood and without which the problem of evil cannot be adequately addressed. Many of both kinds of approaches, in other words, tend toward the prosaic version of Job's story. They tend to minimize that most deviant and devious character in the story without which the problem of evil defies its fullest possible treatment.

The approach I take to the problem of evil I refer to as "intersubjective," for various reasons. First, it presupposes that only by and through the mutuality of shared emotional experiences, between God and God's children, only through loving compassion (emotional intersubjectivity) can and will the problem of evil, both theoretically and practically, be satisfactorily addressed. I am in sympathy with the advice of Adams, as already noted, that Christian philosophers must "give up our focus on defense, and its attempt to operate within religion-neutral value-theory, in favor of an aporetic approach to the problem. It is time to devote ourselves to understanding and articulating our own beliefs about the relationship between God and evil."[4] In treating the problem of evil, accordingly, I do not feel compelled to assume an atheological stance, just as the skeptic in arguing against God's existence does not assume a metaphysically neutral, atheological stance. I do feel compelled and obligated, of course, to give good and sufficient reason for my thesis and to justify it retrospectively in terms of a Christian world-version. My belief is that by applying analogically the notion of asymmetry (incommensurability and unpredictability), by retrieving Satan as a significant character in the story of Job, and by reenfranchising God's loving compassion as the supersymmetrical force opposing horrendous, gratuitous evil in the world, the problem of evil can be satisfactorily addressed.

My procedure is first to examine the reality of Satan and the satanic and its relevance for treating the problem of evil and suffering. Second, I show how Satan and horrendous evil introduce into the moral universe an asymmetrical, quantum factor parallel to the quantum reality of the subatomic world of physics. Third, I discuss the relation of God's sovereignty to the reality of Satan, horrendous evil, and suffering, arguing that in the moral universe God necessarily relates to free agents (Satan and humans) persuasively and not coercively. And finally, I show how the power God employs to defeat Satan, evil, and suffering is existential compassion, the persuasive redemptive power of God's loving care.

Asymmetry: Belief in Satan

Any solution to the problem of evil, I am persuaded, must begin by telling the whole story of Job, including Satan and the bargain Satan makes with God. Satan is indispensable to the drama, direction, and design of the story, even though Job seems unaware of this bargain. No doubt the story can be told without Satan, as some philosophers of religion are inclined to do, but we can be sure from the start that it will not be a compelling story.

"The death of Satan," insists Wallace Stevens, "was a tragedy for the imagination"[5] and, I would add, a tragedy for the theological, philosophical, and historical imagination. Writing in 1944, Stevens could not yet have known fully the extent of the grim and ghastly horror that was the Holocaust. He could not have known fully at the time how perniciously and pervasively Satan had penetrated the sinew of European civilization and paralyzed its moral muscle. But we know now, and yet secular and Christian thinkers alike feel themselves far too sensible, reasonable, and progressive to patronize childhood fantasies of angels, spirits, demons, and devils. Nevertheless, what Reinhold Niebuhr observes of original sin, we can fairly and assuredly observe of gratuitous and horrendous evil, namely, that there is no doctrine for which more empirical evidence can be collected than the reality of Satan and the satanic. Not surprisingly, then, all of the major religions of the world, all pagan religions, and many philosophies (e.g., Manichaeanism) incorporate, in some important sense, the reality of the satanic,[6] the reality of an asymmetrical being whose activity is accounted for not by its conformity to any standard model of moral reason but by its deviation from that standard model, by its incommensurability and unpredictability. So, what if we presuppose the reality of Satan and satanic forces in the world, as I think we should? What significance does "the satanic" have for treating the problem of evil? To answer these questions I first explain what I mean by "horrendous" and "gratuitous" evil and then what I mean by "Satan" and "the satanic."

By "horrendous" and "gratuitous" evil I simply mean, for my purposes, a magnitude of evil for which natural and human causal conditions are inadequate explanations and for which "transhuman" or "satanic" explanations are warranted and alone sufficient. In this sense, I use "horrendous" and "gratuitous" to refer to the asymmetrical nature of some evil. Evil is horrendous and gratuitous when, on the one hand, it is situated incommensurably with the standard model in which moral reason is able to discover an entirely satisfying material or human explanation for evil, and when, on the other hand, faith apprehends as a causal condition the activity of the satanic. The Holocaust is an obvious recent example of "horrendous" evil, for which any adequate explanation must include the satanic. There are, of course, many material and human conditions (psychological, racial, political, military, and cultural) that explain the occurrence of the Holocaust. But these, I think it is fair to say, do not sufficiently account for the magnitude of that horrendous evil. What, then, do I mean by "Satan" and the "satanic"?

Few theologians bemoaned the death of Satan like they bemoaned the death of God, even though Satan in our culture preceded God in death. The reason why includes, I think, the fact that the idea of Satan and the satanic is far too scandalous for sophisticated, rational, scientifically sensitive theologians to take seriously. When thinking of Satan and the satanic most people are left with residual childhood images: a sniveling little reddish devil and magnificent medieval stories of goblins, ghosts, and ghouls. Although I think these are wonderfully compelling images of the satanic, they are, of course, insufficient when trying to treat the problem of evil. My aim here is not to provide an inexhaustible exegesis of Satan in the biblical tradition, although I think the view set forth here is consistent with it. Instead, I intend to provide an idea of Satan and the satanic that is relevant to the question of evil, to determining how one can believe in a good and all-powerful God and account for the reality of horrendous evil and suffering in the world. In doing so, I find Arthur C. McGill's essay "Structures of Inhumanity" and Walter Wink's magisterial trilogy on "The Powers" helpful.[7]

Whether one prefers to think of "Satan" and "demons" as actual, fallen angelic creatures or as personifications of demonic forces in the world is beside the point I want to make here. The biblical tradition does sometimes portray Satan as a fallen angelic being who is an adversary of God, but always without status and power equal to God's.[8] C. S. Lewis accents this latter point, arguing that although Satan is an evil force in the world he should not be seen as an equal opposite of God. "Satan, the leader or dictator of the devils, is [in the biblical tradition] the opposite, not of God, but of Michael."[9] My treatment of the problem of evil, in other words, does not collapse into the Manichaeanism that for a time so attracted the young Augustine. My argument does, however, contend for the reality of an asymmetrical satanic being in the moral universe. Since many philosophers are either ignorant of, disinterested in, or scandalized by the notion of Satan and satanic powers, it would be helpful to reinterpret, with the help of McGill and Wink, biblical images of the satanic.

Suppose, then, that Satan and satanic forces, along with human agency/natural phenomena, are a primary source of evil and suffering and as such constitute the asymmetrical dimension of the universe. What picture of the moral/spiritual world results? The term "satanic" refers to "what is encountered as a transhuman powerfulness," as McGill puts it. Its essence is its "power over the human situation, power to change and control, to have disposal over the existence of people." Such transhuman powerfulness, of course, manifests itself either as a morally good (God, good angels) or morally evil (Satan, bad angels) force; but in either case, it is a power that cannot be accounted for merely in terms of natural phenomena or individual or collective human agency. More particularly, the satanic refers "not just to any kind of powerfulness" but to a "powerfulness that seems to come from beyond all human agency." McGill clarifies:

> So far as power seems to emanate from a recognizably human agent, we are not involved with what I am calling the [satanic]. [Satanic] powerfulness is experienced as surpassing the whole horizon of human activity. It releases a destruction or it opens up a magnitude, or it cuts through to a depth, or it involves a finality that no individual or corporate human agency could possibly attain.[10]

Put another way, transhuman powerfulness refers to what the Bible calls "principalities and powers" (e.g., Ephesians 6:12). Wink argues that "what people in the world of the Bible experienced and called 'Principalities and Powers' was in fact real. They were discerning the actual spirituality at the center of the political, economic, and cultural institutions of their day." Typically people then, and indeed many now, personified these powers as good (angels) or bad (demons). Wink's preference is not to personify them but to think of them as "impersonal entities"[11] or forces, forces that are transhuman, whose power is beyond the capacity of human agents to entirely control and manage. These powers should be viewed "not as separate heavenly or ethereal entities but as *the inner aspect of material or tangible manifestations of power*.... These 'Powers' do not, then ... have a separate spiritual existence. *We encounter them primarily in reference to the material or 'earthly' reality of which they are the innermost essence.*"[12] But whether one prefers to personify them or not, McGill and Wink both insist that transhuman, satanic forces manifest themselves in two ways, socially through human institutions and systems (social, political, economic) on the one hand, and physically through material and natural forces (earthquakes, diseases) on the other. Both society and nature, in other words, can "have an actual spiritual ethos, and we neglect this aspect of . . . life," cautions Wink, "to our peril."[13]

In the story of Job we find Satan exploiting both human institutions and nature's forces in his efforts to expose Job's fragility. Indeed, the author links quite closely Satan's bargain with God and subsequent horrendous disasters, both human and natural, which are intended by Satan to undermine Job's righteousness. Satan capitalizes on conventional military institutions, inciting marauding warriors (Sabeans, Chaldeans) to destroy Job's livestock and servants; and he exploits forces of nature to destroy Job's servants and sheep (lightning) and his sons and daughters (desert wind). And what of Satan's bargain with God? What does it presuppose about Satan and his character and role in the moral world? If we look closely at the details of Satan's bargain with God, I think we will see emerging a specific profile of satanic power in the world.

First, the occasion for Satan's bargain with God, the occasion for him exploiting human institutions and natural forces, is not to punish Job for wrongdoing, as Job's friends and believers in general propound; nor is it to provide an occasion for soul-building or a best possible universe. Instead it is to corroborate Satan's doubts about Job's righteousness, to selfishly test Job's convictions and verify whether Satan's suspicions about Job are true. In a sense, then, satanic evil in the world, whether institutional or natural, is asymmetrical; that is, it is incommensurable when measured by the standard model of moral reason in which evil is warranted and correlated to some natural cause or human agency. But in Job's case the evil is horrendous or asymmetrical. It is incommensurable with moral reason and just fairness and is not predicated on any agency for which he is responsible. Its occasion is Satan's arrogance, the self-satisfaction and indulgence he receives in testing and seducing Job and proving his point in opposition to God. The evil Job suffers is not deserved and thereby deviates from the demands of moral reason. Although human actions do have natural consequences that we either enjoy or suffer, the biblical tradition portrays satanic evil as indiscriminate and unpredictable, in that there is not, according to the standard model of just fairness, a rational moral basis for its occurrence, apart from satanic self-indulgence and appeasement. This is why so much evil and suffering seems gratuitous and horrendous. Satanic evil often is without rhyme or reason, an inexplicable and unpredictable reality that undermines the moral symmetry of just fairness. Satan's "reason" for assaulting Job (that Job is only a fair-weather friend of righteousness) is purely selfish, fortuitous, and self-glorifying and an affront both to the Lord and to Job's righteousness and sense of righteousness. In short, gratuitous evil and suffering, such as Job experiences, signifies a moral incommensurability and unpredictability in the universe perpetrated by the agency of an asymmetrical being.

Second, it is clear from the story of Job that although Satan's power is transhuman it is not transcendent; it is not unlimited. His power is limited to and manifest within the constraints of social institutions and natural forces. Satan and Satan's power are not God's equal. Although his power is transhuman, he is not creator or the creator of power. Satan must operate through human agents and institutions (e.g., the military power of the Sabeans and Chaldeans) or through natural forces (lightning) in his effort to seduce Job and win his point. Accordingly and finally, Satan's transhuman power over humans must be persuasive and not coercive. The Lord protects the integrity of human creation as free and in the image of God. Satan, in his transhuman powerfulness, can only try to influence and seduce (in this case unsuccessfully) Job's will, he cannot coerce and determine it. That God forbids Satan to take Job's life indicates the limitations of Satan's transhuman powerfulness. In short, Satan's power in the world, although considerable, is nevertheless constrained, proscribed by the structures of human institutions and patterns of nature.

How, then, are we to understand Satan's transhuman powerfulness as it manifests itself subjectively through social institutions and objectively through natural forces? First, institutional "principalities and powers," says Wink, are the subjective "inner or spiritual essence, or gestalt, of an institution or state or system; [that] the 'demons' are the psychic or spiritual power emanated by organizations or individuals or subaspects of individuals whose energies are bent on overpowering others." Furthermore, Satan is "the actual power that congeals around collective idolatry, injustice, or inhumanity, a power that increases or decreases according to the degree of collective refusal to choose higher values."[14] In the first century, for example, Jews and Christians both perceived in the institutions and policies of the Roman Empire "a demonic spirituality that they called Sammael or Satan." They encountered this demonic power in specific institutions such as "legions, governors, crucifixions, payment of tribute, Roman sacred emblems and standards, and so forth." That within the context of their ancient prescientific view of the world people should personify these evil powers as demonic beings should not surprise nor obscure the fact that "the real spiritual force that we are experiencing is emanating from an actual institution." It should not obscure the fact that "the demons projected onto the screen of the cosmos [by ancient mythologies] really are demonic, and play havoc with humanity; only they are not *up there* but *over there*, in the socio-spiritual entities that make up the one-and-only real world." Indeed, Wink argues that even the "New Testament insists that demons can have no effect unless they are able to embody themselves in people (Mark 1:21–28; Matthew 12:43–45/Luke 11:24–26), pigs (Mark 5:1–20 par.), or political systems (Revelation 12–13)."[15] Wink is willing, as am I, to speak of "demons" as actual, incommensurable, destructive forces in institutional structures and systems, of "the Domination System" as "an entire network of Powers . . . integrated around idolatrous values," and of " 'Satan' as the world-encompassing spirit of the Domination System."[16]

For early Christians, the ethos and immensity of the Roman Empire, its political, economic, and military systems, palpated with dark and destructive demonic powers that the author of Revelation depicts as a dragon (chapter 12) and a beast (chapter 13) that make war on the children of God. Throughout history, similar domination systems can be identified as possessed by transhuman, demonic forces whose evil and destruction are situated asymmetrically in relation to reason and moral order. The United States' "invisible institution," Hitler's Nazi Germany, Stalin's Soviet Union, and Pol Pot in Cambodia are but a few examples of institutions and systems that were "full of foreboding and menace" and "an intensity of evil" that rendered them for a time diabolical.[17]

As already noted, Job and his family experience the social manifestation of the transhuman powerfulness, under the auspices of the institution of war. His servants, oxen, and asses are destroyed by the violence of marauding Sabeans; and the Chaldeans steal his camels and kill his servants. That such guerrilla warfare is a way of life in the region does not diminish the horror of the evil and suffering it generates. Warfare and collective violence in general involves transhuman, demonic forces, it seems to me, because individuals alone would not deign to carry out such violence. But in and through individuals cobbled together, a kind of corrupting conspiratorial force grips the collective consciousness, a transhuman force that by all accounts is greater than the sum of its individual parts. Job feels the helplessness and hopelessness of one whose life has been decimated by unpredictable, asymmetrical forces that not only are beyond his power to control and influence but also are beyond his power to comprehend and justify.

Second, transhuman powerfulness, in the biblical tradition, also manifests itself objectively and naturally in and through material forces, or, as Wink puts it, through "the patterning of physical things—rocks, trees, plants, the whole God-glorifying dancing, visible universe."[18] Such transhuman powerfulness may manifest itself through nature as morally good (of God) or evil (of Satan). One way of referring to this natural kind of transhuman powerfulness, according to Wink, is the biblical concept of "element" or "elemental." Wink explains that "elemental" refers to "that which is the primary and irreducible component of a thing, the most basic constituent of any substance or entity." So, in Colossians 2:8 "'elements' is used . . . to denote the first or fundamental principles of the physical universe." And "in II Peter 3:10 and 12 . . . we find 'elements' meaning not so much the basic principles as the basic stuff, matter: on the day of judgment, heaven and earth will be burned up, and 'the elements will be dissolved with fire.'"[19] What these elements have in common, Wink goes on to show, is not only that they are "the irreducible and basic principles or entities of a particular class of phenomena" but also that "they are powerful, indispensable, and ubiquitous." Indeed, these elemental forces, like gravity, are "boundaries that cannot be transgressed with impunity. They are the very conditions of existence. We cooperate with them or we are 'judged' by them."[20] In other words, "elements" of nature are "not then merely constructs of human thought (though they are, of course, also that). They are given within nature, patterned into organisms and objectified in science, symbols, images, art, rules, and religions." Indeed, these elemental forces operate in nature and society "the way electrostatic bonds function in molecules: they operate to hold the shape or maintain the stability of physical, biological, and cultural systems."[21] Whatever the details of how we interpret these elemental, invariant forces of nature, what is clear is that the magnitude of their transhuman powerfulness, in both benign and beastly manifestations, is tangible and legendary. As Wink puts it,

> We must have food, clothing, and shelter in order to survive. Hurricanes, tornadoes, and typhoons devastate whole cities. Floods and drought destroy crops, and thousands starve. Earthquakes, volcanoes, and dustbowls spur mass migrations of refugees. These are the more dramatic instances of our interaction with the elements, when we are most keenly aware of the fragility of our lives before such awesome powers.[22]

Because our human interaction with nature's elements is ordinarily benign and salutary we are mostly unaware of them until disaster strikes. Then we are painfully and often tragically aware of not only their powerfulness but their apparent incommensurable hostility as well. What of this destructive manifestation of nature's elemental force? What is its nature and how are we to situate it in relation to human and satanic agency?

We must first recognize, as does Wink, that human agency often abuses and misuses the elements of nature with consequences that are destructive of human well-being and of human life.

It is not, in such cases, so much that nature is hostile to humans, but that humans (and satanic forces) are sometimes hostile to nature. God has created the world to benefit humankind, not obliterate it. The abuse and misuse of nature's elemental powers can be interpreted in at least two ways; those instances in which human agency is responsible for upsetting the "balance" of nature and thereby inviting natural disaster, and those instances in which nature's hostility belongs entirely to its own transhuman powerfulness. The view that some natural disasters can be attributed to human agency presupposes that humans are not simply distant and detached observers of nature's elemental forces, but participants in them. We come to understand them and in so doing attempt to control and manipulate them for our own advantage but sometimes with disastrous consequences.[23] Examples are easily and readily identifiable: ill health that results from smog or polluted waters, destruction of ecosystems, construction of villages in flood plains, nuclear weapons, and so on. These are instances in which nature's apparent hostility is a result of human agency, of human ignorance, indifference, or pride. No wonder ancient Hebrew communities were instructed to cultivate and care for the earth and not manipulate and exploit it. It was partly for their own good and safety.

And yet many natural disasters in which thousands of humans and animals tragically lose their lives cannot be accounted for in this way, as the result of faulty human agency. And it is these manifestations of natural evil and suffering that confront and challenge any belief in God's goodness and power. Can we understand these natural manifestations of horrendous evil and suffering as the result of satanic transhuman powerfulness?

Belief in angels is deeply rooted in the Christian tradition, but despite recent interest in angelology, few contemporaries believe that actual spiritual beings are flitting invisibly about the universe seeking to exploit the forces of nature for good and ill. On the other hand, Christianity, or indeed any religious tradition, cannot and should not simply reduce itself to scientific materialism and subscribe to a universe devoid of transhuman powerfulness. Christians believe that God not only created but continues to sustain the universe with a holy presence; so too Christians believe that forces of evil are present in the world, abusing and exploiting the forces of nature to lure people into doubt and skepticism. These satanic forces are not, as already noted, the equal opposite of God. That is why mostly nature functions to the benefit and enjoyment of humankind. But they are transhuman, evil forces nonetheless and use their angelic powers to destroy and defeat forces of good in nature. Wink suggests that we can understand "angel," both good and fallen, as "the code name for the numinous interiority of created things."[24] This "numinous interiority" of nature is the transhuman powerfulness of nature personified in biblical tradition as good or fallen angels whose business it is to work through the forces of nature for the advantage or disadvantage of humankind. The powerfulness of good angels may manifest itself graciously, as the wonder of flourishing crops, the beauty of a sunset, or the birth of an infant or as awe and reverence before the vast expanse of space—and all this to the glory of God. The powerfulness of fallen angles may manifest itself maliciously, in the fury of a hurricane or volcano, in the destructive power of an earthquake or flood, or in the incremental encroachment of cancer; and all this, not as punishment, but to the self-satisfying glory of Satan. As McGill suggests, satanic abuse of nature manifests itself variously. "Sometimes it crushes and violates with overwhelming force," as with "disease or insanity, famine or flood." And sometimes the satanic secures "its mastery over human beings not by crude force, but by subtle insinuation, by playing on the weaknesses and perverse wishes of the human mind and thus seducing people to give themselves over into its power . . . manipulating and enslaving the human ego by means of enticing forms" of addiction and obsession. Alcoholism, drugs, and pornography, as many who suffer these addictions know, are powerful demonic forces that seem and indeed by their nature are beyond the control of human agency. In either manifestation, McGill concludes, the satanic "signifies a powerfulness beyond the human arena that ruthlessly dominates the lives of people"[25] by abusing the natural patterning of elemental forces.

The aim of manipulating the numinous interiority of nature by transhuman agents is not to punish or retaliate, soul-build, or satisfy some abstract, modal criterion for the best possible world. Instead the aim is shameless, satanic self-indulgence and aggrandizement, to seduce humankind, like Job's spouse, away from God, into the dregs of doubt and despair, into the clutches of skepticism and anguish, into the dark pit of hell. As noted already, Job experiences the "numinous interiority" of nature's fallen transhuman powerfulness. Satan exploits nature by making lightning strike sheep and shepherds, killing them all (Job 1:16); and he made a great desert wind destroy the house in which Job's sons and daughters dined and all were killed (Job 1:18–19). Throughout Hebrew and Christian scriptures good and evil transhuman forces are depicted as nature's "numinous interiority," employing the forces of nature in the service of good or evil. Narratives of the flood, the Exodus, crossing the Jordan, drought and famine, blindness, plagues, diseases, healings, and storms at sea portray the numinous interiority of nature as being at the mercy of good and evil forces. True, whether the transhuman powerfulness of nature's numinous interiority is interpreted as good or evil partly depends on how one is situated in relation to the God of Israel. The plagues of Egypt, for example, and especially the angel of death, from the Egyptian perspective, are surely forces of evil while for the enslaved Hebrews they are angels of light and liberation. Nevertheless, transhuman agents, whether good or evil, manifest their powers in and through the numinous interiority of nature.

How does this understanding of Satan and the satanic help us interpret evil and suffering in the world? How does Satan's transhuman powerfulness, manifested socially through principalities and powers on the one hand and materially through elemental forces of nature on the other, begin to address the problem of evil? What use can we make of Satan and satanic asymmetry for addressing the problem of evil in the world?

The case I want to make here is perhaps best advanced by way of analogy: Satan and the satanic are to the moral/spiritual world of evil as incommensurability and unpredictability of antimatter are in particle physics.[26] Satan and the satanic are quantum factors in the moral and spiritual sphere as random particles and chance events are incommensurable quantum factors in physics. How then does the quantum factor of the microworld help us understand the macro-, moral world of good and evil and how does it help us treat the problem of evil?

No doubt most cosmologists agree with Paul Davies when he argues that the new physics not only put to rest Newton's vision of the universe as a giant clock, "unwinding along a rigid, predetermined pathway toward an unalterable final state," but introduced "back into the melting pot" in a new way "the whole issue of freedom of choice and determinism."[27] No longer can scientists and philosophers believe as once they did that on the basis of Newtonian mechanics one can from a single event at a designated moment predict precisely all other possible future events. The new physics brought, or should bring, such a way of thinking to an abrupt halt. The quantum factor's vision of a process in nature that is intrinsically incommensurable, uncertain, and unpredictable permits in principle the possibility of events that are free, self-caused, even uncaused, chaotic, and irrational, events that are asymmetrical and incommensurable in relation to the standard model of uniformity in the universe. Just as the physical universe's quantum factor suggests "nature's rebelliousness," so too the moral universe's quantum factor, human free will and satanic transhuman powerfulness, suggests a "spiritual rebelliousness" that accounts for the horrendous evil and suffering that otherwise remains opaque.

What results from this analogy? What results from acknowledging asymmetries in the moral universe? The answer is in terms of Satan and faith's apprehension of the satanic. Reenfranchising Satan and the satanic provides a transhuman way of explaining and understanding the causes of gratuitous and horrendous evil, while at the same time not justifying them morally. Horrendous evil is a deviation from the symmetry of moral reason both in its trans- or nonhuman, non-natural satanic causal explanation and in the unpredictability of its occurrence. Reason comprehends and explains it as an event that is incommensurable in relation to the standard model of morality; faith apprehends its cause as transhuman and satanic. The horrendous evil we call the Holocaust is a case in point. Although historians and social scientists continue to identify the natural, human causal conditions that brought about the Holocaust, these conditions do not and cannot entirely comprehend and explain it. Reason, on the one hand, comprehends the Holocaust as an instance of horrendous evil that is incommensurable in relation to the standard of moral reason. Faith, on the other hand, apprehends the reality of the satanic in the Holocaust as a transhuman causal force working maliciously and malignantly within social, political, and cultural institutions and phenomena. Neither reason nor faith can or should ascribe to such horrendous, satanic evil as somehow justifiable as "God's will" or "soul-building," or treat horrendous evil as if it somehow conforms to a divine plan. Indeed, horrendous evil is an insult to God; its cause is satanic; it situates itself asymmetrically in relation to the goodness of God and manifestly deviates from God's will and moral design.

God's Sovereignty and Satanic Asymmetry

The treatment for the problem of evil and suffering that I am advocating should by now be clear. I have argued that the reality of the satanic, as a quantum factor in the moral universe, is indispensable to treating the problem of evil. Satanic forces along with human volition and God's goodness and powerfulness form an equilateral triangle in the center of which converges an antidote for the problem of theodicy. God's essential goodness accounts for the presence of moral symmetry and goodness in the world; human and transhuman satanic agency account for the reality of both social and natural evil, including gratuitous evil. The question arises, accordingly, What is the relation of the power of free agency, both human and transhuman, to God's sovereignty? How is human and transhuman freedom situated in relation to divine sovereignty? If God is sovereign and almighty, why does God "permit," as some would put it, humans and Satan to inflict evil and suffering so freely and frivolously, let alone at all? Assuming God's goodness and omnipotence, why does horrendous, gratuitous evil and suffering exist? Why is there evil and suffering at all? Any adequate answer to these questions requires that we make a distinction between two kinds of divine sovereignty or transhuman powerfulness, coercive and persuasive. The biblical tradition, it seems to me, underwrites the view that God manifests both kinds of sovereignty, and in the following way: in relation to nonvolitional creation God employs coercive power, and in relation to volitional creatures, human and satanic agency, God employs persuasive power. How and why so?

I agree in part with Tyron Inbody when he argues that "the problem of theodicy in the late modern West focuses primarily on the question of the nature of God's power." Especially today the traditional notion of divine omnipotence is "problematic for many postmoderns for a variety of reasons, including not only philosophical and religious but political and moral ones as well." Accordingly, theodicy must confront "the problem of the meaning and implications of the theistic notion of omnipotence in a postmodern world."[28] The one qualification I would add is that the problem of theodicy, as I reconceive it, must include an examination of the nature and implications of satanic power and its relation to God's power.

Traditional theism, from at least St. Augustine onwards, has conceived of God's sovereignty and omnipotence largely in terms of coercive power. By coercive power I mean the unhindered capacity to compel, restrain, or dominate by such force as to be able to bring about or cause certain intended effects. In relation to humans

God's coercive power is the capacity to compel an act or choice by force. And that force is omnipotent and divine in that it always can and does accomplish what it wills. In traditional Western theism God's omnipotence is conceived of as just such a coercive force. God coercively causes to happen in the realm of nature and in the realm of human history whatever God wills and intends. As Inbody notes, there are two distinguishable but inseparable features of omnipotence in Western theism. "(1) God is the only or primary cause of every event in the world, and (2) nothing happens in the world that God does not cause within God's all-powerful rule."[29] Inbody goes on to point out that theologians typically attempt to modify and moderate this view somewhat by introducing the notion of God's "permissive will" that allows humans, and by implication Satan, the free will to make choices contrary to God's will. Such an emendation, Inbody insists, is but a "verbal qualification with no real significance." Calvin himself notes, in his *Institutes*, that "[There can be] no distinction between God's will and God's permission.... But why shall we say 'permission' unless it is because God so wills?" and in his commentary on Genesis that "Adam did not fall without the ordination and will of God. It offends the ears of some when it is said that God *willed* this fall; but what else, I pray is the permission of Him, who has the power of preventing, and in whose hand the whole matter is placed, but his will?"[30] This traditional conception of omnipotence and its emendation (permitting human freedom) have proven themselves woefully inadequate, I think, to solving the problem of evil.

There are, of course, biblical narratives in which God in sovereignty acts coercively. The Genesis creation narratives, for example, depict God creating coercively, as it were, to bring into being a certain order of things. The created order is thus situated in relation to God as the result of God's coercive power. It is determined coercively by God's will and is sustained or not (i.e., miracles) at God's discretion. But God includes in that created order, ironically, a quantum factor, free will, a capacity for freedom, a capacity for undermining order, the possibility of human and transhuman asymmetrical agency. This surely is a great risk God takes. For the very nature of that quantum factor, of creatures exercising free will, is not only that the potential for chaotic asymmetry is introduced into the universe but that, to preserve the integrity of human creation, God must now relate to creatures of freedom, whether human or transhuman, persuasively and not coercively. If God relates otherwise (i.e., coercively) toward humans, then God's supreme and climactic creativity, namely, humans created in God's image, is forfeited and falsified.

By persuasive power I mean the capacity to move or attract, induce or influence a subject to believe, act, or live a certain way by means of argument, entreaty, inducement, by love and care and compassion, and not by coercion. Conceiving God's sovereign power in this way reaps several rewards. First, by persuasive power God preserves, protects, and promotes the spiritual integrity of human creation and its divine image, its capacity to freely exercise its will. "As a symbol of divine power," says Wendy Farley, "love . . . represents a fundamentally different *kind* of power than the power of coercion. . . . If the power of God is conceived through the grid of love rather than [coercion], there is 'room' in creation for that which utterly resists and thwarts the will of God."[31] Sovereignty conceived of as love's persuasive power preserves the integrity of human freedom (*imago Dei*) and precludes perversions that interpret evil as punishment or testing or as essential for wholeness and harmony. "The risk or foolishness of divine love is that it creates a world in which real and terrible resistance to God is possible."[32] Second, interpreting God's power as persuasive rather than coercive allows for an explanation of horrendous evil and suffering in the world even though there is no way to morally justify it. "Imagining divine power through the symbol of love," insists Farley, "makes it possible to account for evil without having to justify it."[33] Evil and suffering, as argued above, are indeed incommensurable and unpredictable and are an affront to God's moral sovereignty and persuasive love.

Third, this fact sheds light on the dialectic relationship between God's sovereignty and evil. Unlike coercive power, what love's persuasive power wills is by its very nature not guaranteed a priori and necessarily. God wills that Adam and Eve obey, for example, but alas they do not. Such latitude is not a failure of divine sovereignty. Rather it preserves the integrity of God's creation of humans *imago Dei*, preserves, ironically, the very volitional power that challenges the persuasive power of God's care. So, for example, if a parent has taught and modeled hospitality to his son and asks the son to show hospitality to others, and the son does not, the son's rebelliousness is not caused by or the fault of the parent; the failure does not belong to the will of the parent but to the rebellious will of the son, even if the parent could have coerced the son to do so or by threats of punishment. However, if the parent fails to teach and model hospitality, then the parent can be held responsible, at least in part, for the son's failure. One cannot read very far in the biblical narratives without being struck by the fact that the relationship between God's will and human will is a matter of persuasive and not coercive power. In the opening chapters of Genesis we find God persuading Adam and Eve that it would be to their benefit if they would freely comply with the command not to eat of the fruit of the tree of the knowledge of good and evil. And when they do not, Adam and Eve attempt to persuade God that their failure to comply is really excusable, the fault of another and not themselves. Inbody and others refer to this notion of divine power as "relational": "Power no longer means the capacity coercively to impose one's will on a totally powerless object; it means the power to affect another free center of power through persuasion."[34] In this sense, God's sovereignty and omnipotence might perhaps be retained as an "optimum persuasive power," as John Cobb puts it, but not as "the capacity unilaterally to impose one's will on another."³⁵ The biblical narratives are replete with stories of God relating to humans by means of persuasion and not coercion, in regard to both moral and salvific choices. From Abraham to Moses, from David to Jonah, from the parable of the Good Samaritan to the parable of the rich young ruler, from Peter to Paul, the biblical paradigm depicting the relationship between God's power and human free agency is one of persuasion and not coercion. Human and transhuman free will constitute the possibility of asymmetry; and sin, evil, and suffering constitute the reality of asymmetry in an otherwise symmetrical moral universe. If we conceive of God's sovereignty primarily in terms of comprehensive coercive power, then one is compelled to attempt the impossible, somehow justifying morally the reality of horrendous evil and gratuitous suffering in God's good world. One is compelled to intone the prosaic version of Job's story, laboring to defend God in terms of "permissive will" or "soul-building" or best possible moral world and so on. But the biblical version of Job's story favors drama and poetry, favors the Lord, and Satan also. And in so doing it compels us to interpret God's sovereignty as the persuasive passion of a love so powerful and secure that it is not threatened by human and transhuman freedom. Indeed, it is so secure in that love that not only is the integrity of human and transhuman freedom preserved but the exercise of it is promoted.

Compassion as Supersymmetry

Must we settle for a moral universe constituted by irreconcilable tensions between moral reason and horrendous evil, God and Satan? Is the most we can hope for a kind of benign stalemate between our desire for simple moral symmetry and the reality of asymmetries? My answer to these questions is No. If philosophers reenfranchise faith, if they are willing to speak in the idiosyncratic dialect of their own tradition (e.g., Christianity, Buddhism, humanism), then hope for treating the problem of theodicy is neither an illusion nor mere abstraction. For the Christian a solution emerges from the concrete historical ground of God's ontological compassion and manifests itself existentially in the compassion of redemption and reconciliation.

We know from our discussion in chapter 2 that the world of particle physics includes a holistic, supersymmetrical dimension in which the lines between conventional dualisms (subject/object, mind/body) are blurred and reality in part is constructed by the experimenter (the physicist determines by "peeking" which way the particle will scatter after striking an object). Here again I extend the analogy between the world of subatomic particles and the macroworld of moral practice. Just as in the microworld the electron keeps open the direction it will scatter until the experimenter peeks,³⁶ so analogously the moral world of evil and suffering keeps open the direction it will scatter until those who suffer or empathize with the suffering respond. Although the fact of involuntary suffering (originating in evil) is unpredictable and uncontrollable, the impact on its victims, whether it will be an occasion for responding destructively or constructively, partly depends on those who are victimized and the community to which they belong. This is to say that all evil, including gratuitous evil and suffering, presents itself as an occasion for wholeness and health or an occasion for bitterness and anger, an occasion for hope and compassion or an occasion for despair and hatred. Most of us know of people whose response to debilitating physical accidents and gratuitous suffering is one of anger and bitterness, a profound sense of betrayal by God and God's alleged goodness. The transhuman evil they suffer is found to be too much for them to bear and it becomes, understandably, an occasion for an unrelenting and cynical assault on life and love and God. For others who have similarly experienced debilitating physical accidents, suffering becomes an occasion for courage, growth, and inspiration. Very often the difference in a person's response to such gratuitous suffering is a function of the community in which he participates. If it is a community of love and compassion it is likely that reality for that suffering person will be constructed creatively and beneficially. If it is a community glorifying self-interestedness and self-sufficiency, no doubt the reality occasioned by horrendous evil and suffering will include feelings of bitterness and betrayal. Whether the moral/spiritual universe collapses into a tragic, existential asymmetry of despair or whether it culminates in the redemptive, existential supersymmetry of compassion is itself a function of divine and human agency.

Consider again the story of Job. From the text we know that the horrendous and gratuitous evil Job suffers is involuntary, caused by both human agency (by the Sabeans and Chaldeans) and transhuman agency (a desert storm and disease). The horrendous evil and suffering that victimizes Job and his family manifests the incommensurability and unpredictability that is not uncommon in a fallen world. The material causes of horrendous evil and suffering are known and are not at issue for Job, although the role of Satan in his plight is apparently opaque to him. At issue for Job are two questions. First, are there reasons that justify the evil he suffers, or does he suffer unjustly? Second, how should he respond to the indiscriminate and horrendous evil and pain he suffers? The bulk of the story is a series of conversations addressing these questions. The second question arises early on in the story when Job's wife suggests that his response to gratuitous suffering should be to "curse God, and die" (Job 2:9). If that is Job's response, as it is his wife's, then the opportunity for supersymmetry is forfeited and his life collapses into an abyss of despair. However, even though Job is defiant throughout his conversations, even though he feels betrayal and bitterness, he does not succumb to despair and hatred. Always Job is willing to keep the conversation with God alive, to ask critical, candid questions. He rejects the simple and self-righteous answers of his friends, who argue that the tragic evil Job suffers is not gratuitous and that there are sufficient reasons to justify his suffering. The reasons his friends give assume that Job is somehow responsible for the evil and pain he suffers. These friends are driven by the same insatiable desire of some philosophers and theologians, namely, the desire for simple, moral symmetry, the desire for finding good and sufficient reason for evil and suffering. Their vision does not include the asymmetry of horrendous evil, or the possibility of Satan and incommensurability of satanic agency as a causal condition for indiscriminate evil and suffering. They intone several ready-made, easy answers, one of which is that his suffering is punishment for sins or some failing and that Job should duly repent and restore his relationship with the Lord. Job is adamant about his innocence, however, and refuses to believe that he is responsible for his suffering.

The culmination of Job's story and his dispute with the Lord is on the surface ambiguous and perhaps even baffling. For not only is no specific reason given for his suffering, neither is there any apparent resolution forthcoming. Indeed, there is no justifying reason that can be offered. Sheer, unadulterated, self-indulgent satanic whim to test Job's righteousness is not a justifiable reason, only an incommensurable cause. Satan's bargain is ultimately unsuccessful, although Job's righteousness is certainly at times precarious. We do know that Job eventually relinquishes his defiant stance, but only after the Lord asks, "Will you condemn me that you may be justified" (Job 40:8)? Why is it that Job finally renounces his defiance and relinquishes his quest for self-vindication when no explicit reason for his suffering is forthcoming, even from the Lord? Job says simply, "Now my eye sees Thee" (42:5). Could it be that in his communion with the Lord Job comes to understand the asymmetrical character of the moral universe? that because of satanic forces present in the universe, incommensurable and unpredictable evil is sometimes a reality that even a righteous man such as Job may suffer? that for the gratuitous evil and suffering that victimizes humans there is no justification? Might we suppose that what Job comes to see is that satanic transhuman powerfulness is a reality that causes the righteous to suffer unfairly? That just as quantum events in the subatomic microworld constitute nature's chaos and rebelliousness, evil and suffering constitute chaos and rebelliousness in the moral realm, caused by satanic forces without rhyme or reason to justify them? It is my contention that this is what Job comes to see, so that although he is not vindicated in his search for justice he is somehow assured by the Lord's answer. Ultimately, I would like to believe, Job comes to see that the tragic evil that destroys his family, health, and possessions and the suffering that wastes him is the result of incommensurable and unpredictable satanic forces. After his conversation and communion with the Lord, who out of a whirlwind speaks to Job of the very mysteries of the universe, Job sees what he and his wife and his friends had failed to see or admit, namely, that there exists in the very moral structures of the universe a deviant, satanic rebelliousness and moral incommensurability that faith apprehends but for which there is no moral justification. Apprehending by faith that the satanic is a prime character in the story not only complicates the plot but completes it by casting along its contours a dark shadow that accounts for the horrendous evil suffered by humanity.

But that is not quite the end of the story. Upon admitting the incommensurable reality to himself, Job is confronted by yet another choice. How will he respond to his plight? How will he now reconstruct his world? Will he feel bitter and betrayed, and capitulate, as did his wife, to existential despair? Will there well up within him feelings of pious self-righteousness, as in his friends? Or will he accept the gratuitous reality of his suffering and sorrow and in gracious humility receive the hope that God in compassion offers? All of these options, all of these ghostly unrealities, present themselves as possibilities for Job and his future. Job feels betrayal and bitterness; he feels confused and rightly defiant toward God. And yet the question remains as to how Job will respond to his experience of horrendous evil and suffering. Will he collapse in despair or live in hope? And how he responds depends a great deal on him, on how he has prepared himself, along with his community of faith. Which option, which response, which ghostly unreality he transforms into reality depends on Job. He has the opportunity to contribute to his reality by transforming one of these ghostly unrealities into concrete reality. Which option becomes reality remains open until Job chooses for himself. And which does he choose? When God finally responds to Job "out of the whirlwind" (38:1) it is with a withering series of rhetorical questions that probe the very mysteries of the universe that lie beyond human comprehension. Accordingly, Job's reply to God is no surprise. "I have uttered what I did not understand, things too wonderful for me, which I did not know" (42:3). Nevertheless, says Job, "I had heard of thee by the hearing of the ear, but now my eyes see thee" (42:5). What is it Job now has come to see? What Job by faith apprehends, I imagine, is not only the symmetry of God's universe and not only satanic asymmetry as cause of his horrendous suffering but the healing compassion with which God loves him and all humans. What is disclosed to Job, what he apprehends by faith and feel, is the heart of God. What Job feels finally is God's loving compassion for him and for humanity. Job collapses in a heap of dust and ashes. He humbles himself before the Lord and repents. He accepts God's loving and unmerited compassion; he does not continue to harbor feelings of bitter betrayal. By story's end we imagine Job happy: "And Job died an old man, and full of days" (Job 42:17).

How, then, does existential compassion redeem and reconcile the discrepancy between the goodness of the world's symmetry and its evil incommensurability?

What power does it possess that enables it to embrace and supercede the world in its symmetry and its asymmetry? Even to ask such questions is an anomaly in contemporary Christian theodicies; "divine love," argues Farley, "tends not to play a very central role in Christian theodicies," partly because traditional theodicies conceive of God's power as coercively sovereign and partly because many are reticent to attribute a desire and emotion like love directly to God.[37] My premise is that without reenfranchising divine love into the equation, the puzzle of theodicy will remain fragmented and inscrutable.

Divine love or "existential compassion" refers not to any particular feeling or emotion but to a capacity for intersubjectivity, to the divine and human capacity for sharing emotions, experiences, and feelings. It is this capacity perhaps more than any other (reason, freedom of will) that establishes and elucidates the image of God in humans. This fundamental and fundamentally unique divine/human capacity for intersubjectivity reconciles, redeems, and supercedes the otherwise unrelenting tension between the world's symmetry and asymmetry. Compassion is, for better or worse, God's way of overcoming the asymmetrical evil and suffering that infects the world, and by examining the logic of existential compassion we can see how this is so. A logic of compassion includes at least two dimensions or movements, the first of which I refer to as empathetic identity and the second as redemptive alterity. Through empathetic identity, we shall see, God assumes responsibility for evil and suffering in the world, and through redemptive alterity God fulfills that responsibility of defeating evil and suffering by transforming and healing humanity. This twofold logic of existential compassion in both of its dimensions is referred to by the writer of Hebrews who, in speaking of Jesus, argues that "he had to be made like his brethren in every respect [empathetic identity], so that he might become a merciful and faithful high priest in the service of God [redemptive alterity], to make expiation for the sins of the people. For because he himself has suffered and been tempted, he is able to help those who are tempted" (2:17–18). As empathetic identity, compassion inspires in a person the faith to enter into the tragic asymmetry of the world's evil and suffering, to share in its incalculable pain and alienation. As redemptive alterity, compassion enables one to transform and restore the one suffering, even in the midst of evil and suffering, even in spite of horrendous evil and gratuitous suffering. For Christians, incarnation and atonement, the birth, life, suffering, and death of Jesus are the supreme acts of transhuman compassion in and through which both of these roles of compassion are fulfilled. Paul, in his majestic Christological discourse (Philippians 2), argues that it is loving compassion that inspires God to become human, to experience the same emptiness, the same temptations of evil and pain of suffering and death experienced by humans. And it is loving compassion that inspires God to raise and glorify Christ and thereby resist evil and redeem and restore a broken creation.

Consider more particularly the first movement of compassion as one of empathetic identity, in particular God's empathetic identity. By "empathetic identity" I refer to an intersubjective movement in which the compassionate one approaches and enters into the reality of another, in an act of what Nel Noddings refers to as "engrossment."[38] By engrossing oneself empathetically in the identity of another, the self brackets its own reality and apprehends the reality of another by sharing as far as possible in the experiences and feelings of that other. Jews typically refer to empathetic identity when they speak of the Holy One present in the life of Israel and in historical events (e.g., the Exodus). Christians refer to God's empathetic identity in terms like "God's incarnation." As the writer of John puts it, "And the Word became flesh and dwelt among us, full of grace and truth" (John 1:14). We shall see that this motion of empathetic identity, of incarnation, is God's way of assuming responsibility for the reality of evil and suffering in the world. How so?

We cannot read very far in the Genesis accounts of creation without a keen sense of the symmetry and beauty with which God created the world. Whether in the refrain "And there was evening, and there was morning" or "And God saw that it was good," clearly, it seems, God's original creation is portrayed as an exquisite work of art. But this is not the view of some, like Wendy Farley, who insists that asymmetry or what she calls "tragedy" is a necessary feature of God's original created order. She argues that "suffering . . . is necessary at the very core of the human situation in the world,"[39] that human "finitude itself seems to be tragically structured. . . . This tragic structure is not evil, but it makes suffering both possible and inevitable prior to any human action."[40] Finally, "The conditions of finite existence are tragically structured."[41] Although Farley's view, that God crafted into the very structure of creation a tragic element, sometimes seems more akin to Greek fatalism than to Hebrew-Christian freedom, there is a proper sense, I think, in which the biblical tradition presupposes an original, perfectly symmetrical creation that nevertheless includes an asymmetrical quantum factor. If by the "tragic structure of finitude" Farley means something like the volitional capacity of humans created in the image of God, then what I argue here is something similar. By definition freedom is asymmetrical insofar as the exercise of it is self-caused and its productions uncertain and unpredictable. Freedom is an event for which no cause can be identified other than the event (the exercise of free will) itself. Determinists would object that this free exercise of will is an illusion, and that if we presuppose the law of cause and effect and perfect knowledge then we could predict unerringly what choices a person would make. I have two responses to this: if one presupposes determinism, the problem of horrendous evil emerges with special acuteness. Moreover, as we shall see in the next chapter, laws of nature, like that of causality, are not prescriptive and deterministic but descriptive and susceptible to counteraction. So the capacity and exercise of free will constitute a quantum factor in the moral and spiritual world analogous to quantum events in the microworld of subatomic particles. Freedom as asymmetry, however, does not of itself constitute incommensurable evil and suffering in the world but only the condition and possibility for them. The Fall represents that seminal, cosmic, moral event wherein human freedom succumbed to seductions of transhuman power and forged an alliance that tragically subjected not only humans but the entire world[42] to the evil and suffering that are the fruit of freedom's fall. Thus tragically was the original symmetry of God's creation corrupted by asymmetrical beings and events, which continue to curse and crowd the world today. Freedom as an asymmetrical feature is nevertheless not a flaw of God's original creation. What is a flaw is the rebellious use made of that freedom by human and transhuman powers; and it is this abuse of freedom that subjects the world to the curse of horrendous evil and gratuitous suffering in the world.

Why then is there existential compassion? What is its relation to the symmetry and asymmetry of the created order? In brief, since the asymmetry of evil and suffering is the fruit of the free exercise of the will, so too, then, must the redemption of that will and the restoration of the created order properly be a function of the free exercise of the will. Compassion's movement of empathetic identity is just such a free exercise of transhuman (divine) and human will. Through compassion God chooses to situate Herself (or Himself) empathetically in relation to evil and suffering with such vulnerability that the power of evil and suffering is disarmed, undermined, and transformed into an occasion for restoration and reconciliation. In other words, existential compassion is that power of transhuman and human will that is ultimately able to secure in the midst of evil's chaos and pain a kind of supersymmetrical healing and wholeness. By so empathizing with fallen human existence God not only enters into and shares the tragic asymmetry of evil and suffering but, as Farley notes, "God [also thereby] share[s] responsibility for [evil and] suffering,"[43] shares through empathetic identity a responsibility for the tragic reality of evil.

Consider the second, inevitable movement of any act of existential compassion, namely, redemptive alterity or atonement. In and through this movement God fulfills responsibility for evil and suffering by transforming and healing humans, thereby overcoming evil and suffering. Jews participate ritually in redemptive alterity in and through Passover and the Day of Atonement. Christians participate ritually in redemptive alterity especially at Holy Week and Easter. The incarnate one, the one who in compassion identifies empathetically with those who suffer, at the same time in the very midst of that identity remains as another, so situated eternally by love to be able to redeem and reconcile, transform and heal. At first, redemption as human transformation may seem a pale and pitiful compensation for the horrendous and gratuitous asymmetry of evil and suffering. But on closer examination the power and passion of atonement will, I think, persuade otherwise.

Alterity is essential for addressing evil and suffering, otherwise the empathetic one is just as powerless to redeem and transform evil as are those who are burdened by evil and suffering. Paul recognizes this movement and need for alterity. Not only does Christ suffer and die but, as he goes on to say, he is "highly exalted," endowed with a transhuman power that is able to redeem and transform. John also recognizes the necessity for alterity when after affirming Jesus' empathetic identity he goes on to declare that "we have beheld his glory, glory as the only Son of the Father. . . . And from his fullness have we all received grace upon grace" (John 1:14–16). The one who loves compassionately must be one who stands as the other. In empathetic identity God shares responsibility for evil and suffering; in alterity, in otherness, God assumes responsibility for redeeming humans and creation by the persuasive power of compassionate love. Because God is other, because God is eternal, and because Christians in Christ situate themselves absolutely in relation to eternity, they are enabled through and in Christ's loving compassion to transform the tragic tension between the world's symmetry and asymmetry by supersymmetrical acts of merciful compassion. Any answer to how this supersymmetrical transformation is possible must include the distinctive nature of Christianity's existential compassion, namely, that it is a passion for mercy and not merely for justice.[44] Justice as fairness presupposes a world of simple moral symmetry, a world-version unable to account for the gratuitous asymmetry of much evil and suffering. In such a world, justice as equal fairness is a principle of insufficient moral depth to compensate for the asymmetry of horrendous evil in the world. What is required, in contrast, is the asymmetrical power of mercy. Justice as fairness can sustain civil order, but it lacks the power possessed by compassion and mercy to redeem and restore those who suffer horrendous evil. What is required to counteract horrendous evil is the compassion of mercy, an extraordinary kindness that Richard Stith refers to as generosity.

Stith identifies two ways in which merciful generosity is extraordinary. First, as a moral judgment generosity involves a duty without a right; second, as a moral project it involves benefiting wrongdoers. Consider then these two dimensions of merciful generosity. First, ordinarily we think of "duty" and "right" as correlative: "that for every right there exists a correlative duty, and that for every duty there exists a correlative right."[45] But there are some moral duties one may be required to undertake in full knowledge that the one receiving the benefits of the duty has no right to or claim on the duty. Stith insists that generosity involves just such a moral judgment, that it entails "a duty without a right," and that there are moral occasions when "'duties with rights' can and ought to be rejected in favor of . . . 'duties of generosity.'"[46] Feelings of generosity involve the judgment that I have a duty to act kindly and mercifully toward a wrongdoer even though the wrongdoer is not entitled to any rights that correlate with that duty. A victim of rape who, as Christian, dutifully forgives her assailant, who has no right to that generosity, exemplifies merciful duty without a right. So, God in Christ in assuming responsibility for evil in the world has a duty to show merciful and unmerited generosity toward humankind even though humanity has no right to that duty and its benefits. Second, not only does merciful generosity involve a duty without a right, it also necessarily benefits wrongdoers. In being generous, argues Stith, one has "a duty to benefit precisely and only those who do wrong."[47] By acting mercifully I am necessarily benefiting a wrongdoer; my unmerited generosity endows the wrongdoer with unmerited benefits. When the rape victim shows mercy toward her assailant she necessarily benefits the one who has wronged her by granting acceptance and forgiveness. So in assuming responsibility for evil and suffering in the world, God in Christ shows mercy toward humankind and in so doing benefits wrongdoers whose sinfulness is an affront to God's goodness.

Not only God but also those who claim to follow God's ways are to assume responsibility for asymmetrical evil and suffering in the world. Jesus appeals to his disciples to practice extraordinary and merciful generosity. "If anyone would sue you and take your coat, let him have your cloak as well, and if anyone forces you to go one mile, go with him two miles." Can this injunction be translated into a correlative rights claim? Apparently not, for it seems to presuppose a judgment that certain duties (like, "Let him have your cloak as well" and "Go the second mile") will not correlate with any rights to which the one who compels the cloak and the second mile is entitled. By Roman law, a person did not have "to give as collateral an outer garment—more than what the law could require, which was merely an inner garment."[48] If one has a right only to X, then we cannot say that one also has a right to Y, without speaking at odds with ourselves. The one who has a right only to X cannot also claim a right to Y without violating the rights of another, namely, the other's right to Y. However, there is no contradiction nor confusion in Jesus' injunction. He means that his disciples are to give as he gives, not only what is due another but also what is not due. Even to those who treat them unjustly, their generosity is to be of this extraordinary sort. Jesus' presumption is that even if one had a right (which one does not) to X (the outer coat, the initial strike, the first mile), one does not have a right to Y (the inner clock, the second strike, the second mile). The generosity of the inner cloak or the second mile is a Christian duty that should be delivered even though the wrongdoer has no right to it or to its benefits. What is extraordinary and incommensurable about Christian generosity, then, is its unmerited, merciful graciousness; no rights correlate to its duties and when this is the case such duties will benefit a wrongdoer. What then does all unmerited, merciful generosity have to do with solving the problem of evil?

The premise for which I am arguing is, I hope, becoming clear, namely, that asymmetrical generosity (unmerited, merciful grace) is the concrete way God assumes responsibility for and counteracts asymmetrical, unmerited evil and suffering in the world. Unmerited, gratuitous mercy alone is sufficiently powerful to redeem and restore those who suffer unmerited, gratuitous evil. God's unmerited, merciful compassion toward humanity makes recompense for the unmerited evil and suffering in the world. God's merciful compassion is a countervailing force juxtaposed to the force of horrendous evil and the gratuitous suffering of the innocent, for example. Horrendous evil and gratuitous suffering, on the one hand, are asymmetrical events in the moral world which moral reason cannot justify. Compassionate acts of merciful generosity, on the other hand, are events in the moral world for which there is no justification or explanation; they are duties without correlative rights, duties that necessarily benefit wrongdoers. In so acting with gracious, compassionate mercy (incarnation/ontological compassion and atonement/existential compassion) God not only assumes, through empathetic identity, responsibility for horrendous evil and gratuitous suffering in the world, but fulfills his responsibility by acting in equally countervailing asymmetrical ways, thereby making recompense for such unmerited evil and suffering. God's and God's people's commitment to practice merciful and unmerited compassion constitutes the supersymmetrical healing, wholeness, and harmony by which alone recompense for horrendous evil and gratuitous suffering is satisfactorily made and without which the problem of evil cannot be adequately resolved. We know from the text of Job that in the end God in merciful and unmerited compassion makes recompense for Job's unjust suffering by granting him healing, wholeness, and harmony. For "the Lord restored the fortunes of Job . . . gave Job twice as much as he had before" (Job 42:10). And so "Job died, an old man, and full of days" (42:17).

For the Christian, God in Christ and God's spirit in the community of faithful wield the sword of righteousness into battle against the forces of darkness. Horrendous evil and gratuitous suffering are realities in our world, but they are not final and ultimate realities. As Farley insists, "The church can be a community that mediates both a vision and a power of redemption . . . in its life and in the broader world."[49] Jesus calls his disciples to be in the world as salt and light (Matthew 5:13–16)—salt to heal wounds and light to illuminate a way of life. Thus, "If the cross represents the incarnation of divine compassion in the midst of rupture, the resurrection suggests that evil is not absolute: signs of the kingdom, memories of justice and mercy break into the very midst of history."[50]

In this chapter I have tried to address the problem of theodicy not by minimizing but by maximizing the reality of the satanic, the reality of horrendous evil and gratuitous suffering, in all its ferocity. At the same time I have tried to show how God's equally ferocious life of merciful compassion constitutes a supersymmetrical way of binding Job's and humanity's wounds and bearing wholeness into an otherwise heartless and heartbroken world. But in what sense, if any, is the problem of theodicy in this way solved? For the nagging question remains still: Why are there evil and suffering at all, especially horrendous evil? In a sense, it is never solved. The conditions under which the question of theodicy arises are not by this or any theodicy eliminated. Perhaps it would be better to say that the puzzle of theodicy is completed rather than its problem solved, much as a jigsaw puzzle, when all the pieces are found and properly in place, is said to be completed and yet still a puzzle. Likewise, when all the pieces of the puzzle of theodicy are found and in place, still it is a puzzle, a mystery in which humans finally can only wonder and worship. Or perhaps evil is better seen as a disease, an addiction. Although there is for it no absolute cure, still there is healing and wholeness in the daily discipline and diligence of practicing unmerited mercy.

Notes

1. There are indeed a wide variety of ways philosophers have categorized approaches to the question of evil and a good God. John Hick's distinction between Augustinian theodicy and Irenaeaian theodicy, in *Evil and a Good God*, is one of the more familiar, but there are others. See, for example, Tyron Inbody's *The Transforming God* (Louisville, Ky.: Westminster John Knox Press, 1997), chapters 2 and 3, or Pamela Sue Anderson's *A Feminist Philosophy of Religion* (Oxford: Blackwell, 1998), 40–41.

2. Marilyn McCord Adams, "Problems of Evil: More Advice to Christian Philosophers," *Faith and Philosophy* 5, 2 (April 1988): 121.

3. Louis P. Pojman, *Philosophy of Religion: An Anthology* (Belmont, Calif.: Wadsworth, 1987), 152.

4. Adams, "Problems of Evil," 135.

5. Quoted in Alan Olson's "The Mythic Language of the Demonic: An Introduction," in *Disguises of the Demonic: Contemporary Perspectives on the Power of Evil*, ed. Alan Olson (New York: Association Press, 1975), 9.

6. See, for example, the classic *History of the Devil and the Idea of Evil: From the Earliest Times to the Present Day* by Paul Carus (La Salle, Ill.: Open Court, 1974) and *The Devil: Perceptions of Evil from Antiquity to Primitive Christianity* by Jeffrey Burton Russell (Ithaca, N.Y.: Cornell University Press, 1977). Both of these works treat the idea of the devil and evil in eastern and western traditions.

7. Arthur C. McGill, "Structures of Inhumanity," in *Disguises of the Demonic: Contemporary Perspectives on the Power of Evil*, ed. Alan M. Olson (New York: Association Press, 1975), 116–133. Walter Wink's three books are titled *Naming the Powers*, *Unmasking the Powers*, and *Engaging the Powers*, all from Philadelphia, Pa.: Fortress Press.

8. See chapter 2 of G. B. Caird's *Principalities and Powers: A Study in Pauline Theology* (London: Oxford University Press, 1956), for a brief survey of "Satan" in the Bible.

9. C. S. Lewis, *The Screwtape Letters* (New York: Simon and Schuster, 1996), 6.

10. McGill, "Structures of Inhumanity," 116. The Christian might want to say that the presence of the Holy Spirit in the world is the inverse of the presence of the satanic in the world, a transhuman power of holiness albeit of much greater force.

11. Walter Wink, *Engaging the Powers: Discernment and Resistance in a World of Domination* (Philadelphia, Pa.: Fortress Press, 1992), 8.

12. Walter Wink, *Naming the Powers: The Language of Power in the New Testament* (Philadelphia, Pa.: Fortress Press, 1984), 104–105.

13. Wink, *Engaging the Powers*, 6.

14. Wink, *Naming the Powers*, 104–105.

15. Ibid., 7–8.

16. Ibid., 8–9.

17. Ibid., 8.

18. Ibid., 104.

19. Walter Wink, *Unmasking the Powers: The Invisible Forces That Determine Human Existence* (Philadelphia, Pa.: Fortress Press, 1986), 130.

20. Ibid., 131.

21. Ibid., 132. Wink refers at this point to the work of Ralph Wendall Burhoe, who argues that, in the history of human consciousness, the discovery of these elemental forces of nature, or invariances, was concomitant with the rise of belief in gods. He quotes Burhoe to the effect that "in the history of human thought, among the earliest and most comprehensive systems of abstractions of invariance were those of the primitive myths and theologies, which gave the name of gods to the sources of the invariant and powerful forces or laws which man had to obey if he was to successfully adapt to life."

22. Ibid., 133.

23. See Wink's compelling discussion of this matter in *Unmasking the Powers*, 139–143.

24. Wink, *Unmasking the Powers*, 69.

25. Wink, *Naming the Powers*, 117.

26. For a more complete explanation of these matters, see the section "Faith and Asymmetry" in chapter 2.

27. Wink, *Naming the Powers*, 135. Polkinghorne agrees with this analysis by Davies, for example, in *Belief in God in an Age of Science*, 14, 42.

28. Tyron Inbody, *The Transforming God: An Interpretation of Suffering and Evil* (Louisville, Ky.: Westminster John Knox Press, 1997), 42.

29. Ibid., 45.

30. The quotes from Calvin are included in Inbody, *The Transforming God*, 45.

31. Wendy Farley, *Tragic Vision and Divine Compassion: A Contemporary Theodicy* (Louisville, Ky.: Westminster John Knox Press, 1990), 97.
32. Ibid., 97.
33. Ibid.
34. Inbody, *The Transforming God*, 148.
35. Ibid.
36. For a more complete explanation of this phenomenon, see the section "Compassion and Supersymmetry" in chapter 2.
37. Farley, *Tragic Vision and Divine Compassion*, 97.
38. See Nel Noddings, *Caring: A Feminine Approach to Ethics and Moral Education* (Berkeley: University of California Press, 1984), 19.
39. Ibid., 23.
40. Ibid., 31–32.
41. Ibid., 33.
42. The Apostle Paul writes, in Romans 8:20–23, that even "the creation was subjected to futility" but that "the creation itself will be set free from its bondage of decay and obtain the glorious liberty of the children of God"; indeed, "the whole creation has been groaning in travail together until now."
43. Noddings, *Caring*, 107.
44. Elsewhere I distinguish between a distinctively Christian understanding of justice as "equal mercy" and a conventional secular (Rawls) and religious (Beckley) understanding of justice as "equal fairness." See my *Fidelity of Heart: An Ethic of Christian Virtue* (New York: Oxford University Press, 2001), 118–121.
45. Richard Stith, "Generosity: A Duty without a Right," *Journal of Value Inquiry* 25, 3 (1991): 203.
46. Ibid.
47. Ibid., 208.
48. Craig L. Blomberg, *Matthew*, in *The New American Commentary* series (Nashville, Tenn.: Broadman Press), vol. 22 (1992).
49. Farley, *Tragic Vision and Divine Compassion*, 130.
50. Ibid., 132.

CHAPTER FIVE

Belief in God's Miracles

Toward dawn, Mary Magdalene along with other women go to the sepulchre where Jesus is buried with every intention of anointing the body. On their way they wonder how they might roll back the stone from the sepulchre and are startled, when they arrive, to find that the stone is already rolled away. They enter the tomb and encounter a young man dressed in a white robe who speaks to them. "Do not be amazed; you seek Jesus of Nazareth, who was crucified. He has risen, he is not here; see the place where they laid him" (Mark 16:1–6). And so goes the story of the miracle that is central to the Christian faith. And yet, for people then (e.g., Thomas) as for people today, the possibility of resurrection in particular and of miracles in general is at minimum problematic and at maximum scandalous. Scientists perhaps more than any other community are skeptical of both the possibility and the historicity of miracles. This is not surprising if we recall that what scientists know and do presuppose a world constituted by a simple rational, symmetry. Or at least that was the case until the early decades of the twentieth century, when the implications of certain discoveries (e.g., theory of relativity, quantum mechanics) were drawn and a picture began to emerge of a universe riddled with asymmetrical beings and events.

Although many scientists today are comfortable with some conception of deity, "miracles," claims Paul Davies, "are [still] something that most scientists would rather do without."[1] That this is still true today is largely due, I think, to David Hume, the chief, but far from only, thinker to mold modern discourse on miracles. Ever since the eighteenth century, Hume and his collaborating offspring (both those who jettison and those who justify the possibility of miracles) have routinely committed the fallacy of rationalism and as a result have made several false assumptions on the basis of which the idea of "miracle" has been misconceived and the possibility of miracles distorted. Throughout this chapter I refer to Hume, his offspring, and the rich and varied debate arising among them as the Humean tradition.

This tradition (both the defenders and detractors of miracles) has generally assumed something like Hume's definition of a miracle: "a transgression of a law of nature by a particular volition of the Deity."[2] Even though this definition of miracles is anachronistic, given the collapse of Newtonian physics[3] and the discoveries of the new physics, many philosophers of religion continue to cling to it. James Keller, in rejecting miracles, for example, says that miracles are "temporary suspensions of one or more laws of nature accomplished by divine power";[4] and David McKenzie, in defending miracles against Keller, assumes the same definition.[5] Based on this Humean definition, Nicholas Everitt argues that "a miracle is by definition something which violates a law of nature. To say that an occurrence violates a law of nature means that the claim that there has been such an occurrence is incompatible with a statement of laws of nature. Since these statements are by definition true, necessarily every such claim is false. Necessarily, therefore, there are no miracles."[6] Whether this argument is compelling or not I do not intend to determine here, although I think it is. Neither do I intend to determine whether miracles have actually occurred, nor do I engage the problem with which Hume was preoccupied: that on the basis of testimonial evidences belief in miracles could never be justified. Instead, I attempt to account for the logical and physical possibility of miracles as asymmetrical quantum events that must be apprehended by faith. In doing so, I take issue with the idea of miracle with which the Humean tradition furnishes us and attempt to reconceive it in a way that accounts for miracles, enfranchises the necessity of faith, and renders irrelevant conventional defenses and critiques. My argument presupposes the findings of the new physics, that the world manifests an asymmetrical as well as a symmetrical dimension. My procedure is first to reconceive the laws of nature and second to reconceive the idea of miracle. Third, I apply these reconceptions to a number of miracle stories and then proceed to compare and contrast this new idea of miracles with the traditional Humean one. Finally, I show how a spiritual conception of compassion, at least in the Christian tradition, establishes a supersymmetrical way of reconciling the asymmetry of miracles with the symmetry of nature's laws. By now the reader is familiar with my underlying assumption that the incommensurable and unpredictable randomness of miracles is analogous in the macroworld to the quantum randomness of events in the subatomic world of particle physics.

Laws of Nature and the Idea of Miracles

Those collaborating with the Humean tradition, in arguing for or against the possibility of miracles, uniformly make three assumptions, all of which are false. They assume, first, that laws of nature (symmetry) are necessary in the sense that they are inevitable and irresistible; they assume, second, that miracles (asymmetry) violate or suspend laws of nature; and they assume, third, that belief in God is not properly basic and therefore can be (or cannot be) prospectively justified in various ways (e.g., proofs of the existence of God and the testimonial evidence of miracle events). These are assumptions on the basis of which, and only on the basis of which, conventional Humean arguments about miracles make sense and are at all persuasive. But what of these assumptions? To what extent are they, and the world-version they presuppose, contemporary and compelling? By showing them to be false, as I do in this section, a place is cleared in which we might begin to reconstitute our idea of the laws of nature and to account for the possibility of miracles in ways that conform to the findings of the new physics and confirm the importance of faith.

First, although Newtonian cosmology has long been discredited, vestiges of it survive today in the Humean tradition, insofar as some in that tradition continue, on the one hand, to conceive of laws of nature as fundamentally prescriptive, as inevitable and irresistible and, on the other hand, conceive of miracles as violations of those laws. In theory, if not in fact, it assumes that the simple, natural symmetry of the universe, its forces and processes, are enslaved to deterministic and inviolable laws which admit of no exceptions, so that asymmetrical, miraculous events, as exceptions to those laws, are a fortiori ruled out. Besides begging the question, this simplistic Humean conception of the world's symmetry and its laws of nature is really as incredulous and anachronistic as the Newtonian cosmology from which it is derived. The emerging scientific picture today, especially the one drawn by proponents of the new physics,[7] replaces the old Newtonian model with a model in which symmetrical and asymmetrical events interact in a universe that is open and fluid, one perforated with quantum unpredictability, novelty, and randomness. Paul Davies refers, for instance, to the fact that physicists are well aware of the fact that some natural processes, like radioactivity, include activity that is random and unpredictable and that certain scientific theories, like quantum physics, embrace the notion of a factor within nature that is uncertain and unpredictable. He argues that few would deny that every event has a cause. And yet "the quantum factor ... apparently breaks the chain by allowing effects to occur that have no cause."[8] Because randomness and unpredictability are characteristics of natural processes, the way we interpret the status of the laws of nature must distance itself from Newtonian cosmology. Laws of nature should not be viewed as necessary, inevitable, and irresistible forces clamped on nature like a vice grip. Rather, they should be seen as what Robert Larmer refers to as "explanatory principles" whose function is to account for the "dispositional properties" belonging to natural processes.[9]

Laws of nature are explanatory in that they are theoretical interpretations of the behavior of natural processes studied by scientists. As Larmer suggests, laws of nature are theoretical principles that "serve to explain the experimental laws discovered by scientists. What this means is that, while the term 'laws of nature' refers to a universal condition that may, in principle, be either confirmed or disconfirmed by empirical evidence, the condition will contain terms that refer not directly to observed regularities but to unobservable entities and properties, e.g., electrons, which serve to explain observed regularities."[10] Laws of nature, consequently, are not verified by direct observation but indirectly by virtue of their predictive power. Moreover, as explanatory, laws of nature account for the dispositional properties of natural processes in the sense suggested by E. J. Lowe, who argues for what he calls a "normative conception of natural law." According to this conception "a statement of natural law . . . characteristically implies that 'normal' or 'typical' individuals or exemplars of some recognizable natural kind possess a certain dispositional property. That is, they are disposed to behave or appear in a certain way (usually in certain specifiable conditions)."[11] Hence, laws of nature anticipate what the disposition of natural processes will be under normal conditions, but they do not logically exclude alternative processes that do not conform to this normative disposition. Similarly W. L. Craig and S. S. Bilynskyj insist that laws of nature are statements about the "dispositional properties" of natural processes, where "things of a kind A have a disposition to manifest quality F in conditions C, in virtue of being of nature N." Yet, it is possible to take laws of nature as accounting for universal dispositions of natural processes (e.g., a body upon which no external force is exerted continues in its state of rest or uniform motion in a straight line) without being compelled to claim that they are violated "when behaviour disposed toward them does not occur"[12] or when behavior possessing a different dispositional property does occur.

More than a century ago J. S. Mill, anticipating a kind of dispositional view of natural processes, argued against necessitarianism; causal relationships (whether involving physical or human agency), although uniform and normative, are nevertheless not determinate and irresistible. Rather they are, he insists, alterable and controllable; for although a given cause is disposed to being followed by given effect, that causal disposition is always subject to possibilities of counteraction by other causes. The effects of drinking poison, for example, can be counteracted by an antidote such that, although the causal relationship between poison and death is never violated, death is not the inviolable consequence of drinking poison. Causal relationships "are never uncontrollable, and any given effect is only necessary provided that the causes tending to produce it are not controlled [or counteracted]."[13] Mill, of course, does not and could not at the time argue for the reality of asymmetrical, uncaused random physical events; but the view he does propound lends itself to and accommodates such discoveries of the new physics.

If we assume, in contrast to the Humean tradition and in collaboration with the new physics, that the universe is asymmetrical and susceptible to novelty, creativity, randomness, and unpredictability, and if we assume that laws of nature account for dispositional properties of natural processes under normal conditions, and that these laws can be, and even under normal conditions are, counteracted, then what conception of miracles can reasonably be formulated and sustained? The answer to this question emerges from the soil of a second assumption falsely held by advocates of the Humean tradition. Indeed, the fallaciousness of its first assumption, that laws of nature are determinate and irreversible, tends to commit the Humean tradition to a second false assumption, namely, that miracles are events that violate the laws of nature.

Although it is logically impossible, as Everitt rightly argues, that laws of nature can be violated,[14] his inference that miracles are therefore impossible is hasty and uncritical. He has so thoroughly internalized the fallacy of rationalism and the Newtonian/Humean tradition that he cannot even begin to entertain the possibility that it is the idea of miracles that we must amend and not their impossibility that we are compelled to defend. Paul Davies himself backs into Hume's clutches by distorting Aquinas' definition of a miracle ("something done by divine power apart from the order generally followed in things") to mean "a violation of the laws of nature" and God "breaking the rules."[15] In contrast, given the findings of the new physics, and given that laws of nature account for the dispositional properties of natural processes, it is possible to argue that miracles, as asymmetrical quanta, can be reconceived as events that either conform to or counteract, but never violate, laws of nature. I do not mean to suggest, of course, that advocates of the new physics or J. S. Mill subscribe to any such belief in miracles or that they understand their views as conducive to the idea or possibility of miracles. Novelty and creativity, randomness and unpredictability, according to advocates of the new physics, arise entirely from within the universe. And Mill assumed, in his system of logic, that physical events could be counteracted only by other physical forces or by human agency, and never by an external spiritual force or divine agent. The presuppositions of a physicalist philosophy to which many subscribe, including Mill, exclude the idea of miracles. Nevertheless, although physics' new vision of the laws of nature admittedly does not compel one to believe in the possibility of miracles, neither does it forbid it. Indeed, for the theist, even the scientific theist, the new physics' version of the laws of nature seems to lend itself to admitting such a belief, especially insofar as the scientific version of the world includes not only symmetry (laws of nature) but asymmetry (random, unpredictable, quantum events). How so?

For the Christian theist, all miracle events either conform to laws of nature or are counteractive to them, but in either case they are analogous to asymmetry in the physical universe in two ways. First, they are incommensurable in relation to scientific reason's standard model of nature's uniformity, in that no material or human condition can be identified as their proximate cause. Second, miracles are asymmetrical in that faith apprehends their cause as transhuman and divine. As counteractive to the laws of nature miracles conform to the following pattern: A causes B, unless D (divine agent) counteracts the force of A to bring about M (a miracle). For example, gravity (A) causes a human body to sink in water (B) unless the force of A is somehow counteracted by D, thus producing M. Clearly, what is miraculous in this case is not that the force of gravity is counteracted and a human body made buoyant in water; humans are themselves capable of this. What renders the event miraculous and incommensurable with scientific reason is that the counteractive cause of buoyancy is the direct, immediate act of divine agency, which act must be apprehended therefore by faith and not scientific reason. So, what reconception of the idea of miracles follows from this?

Although both Lowe and Craig argue for its logical possibility, neither goes very far toward developing a clear and compelling reconception of the idea of miracle itself. Lowe concludes his analysis, for example, by claiming that a miracle is "not merely that which violates . . . this or that particular (true) natural law, but that which (supposedly) violates the entire system of (true) natural laws. . . ."[16] Still partially entrenched in the Humean tradition, Lowe seems reluctant to jettison Humean categories and redefine miracles in terms compatible with the new physics and the asymmetrical behavior of certain subatomic particles. Craig goes further than Lowe in that he insists that we must reconceive miracles in terms of "a personal God" who serves as "a transcendent cause to produce events in the universe which are incapable of being produced by causes within the universe. . . ."[17] And yet Craig also falls short of providing a complete and concise conception of the miraculous. Reginald Fuller, a theologian, comes closer to the truth when he says that miracles are "extraordinary interventions" by God but "are not necessarily breaches of the laws of nature or even what cannot be known of nature. . . . They are occurrences which faith recognizes as acts of God."[18]

If we take into account the findings of the new physics we can and must reconceive the idea of miracles primarily in terms of the activity of God and without direct reference to the laws of nature. Properly conceived, then, a miracle (M) is an asymmetrical occurrence whose proximate, sufficient, and necessary causal agent is the intentional action of a divine power (D). First, by "proximate cause" I refer to that condition D, which is most immediately responsible for the occurrence of an event M, such that there is no intervening causal chain of events that links D to M. The causal relationship between D and M, in short, is immediate and direct. Second, by "sufficient cause" I refer to the notion that D is a "causally sufficient condition" for M to occur. Whenever D proximately acts, M may occur such that the immediate agency of D is itself capable of bringing about M. Finally, D is the necessary causal condition of M in the sense that M cannot occur without D. Without the agency of D, M cannot occur. Moreover, all three of these conditions must be obtained for an event to qualify as a miracle. In the story of the parting of the Red Sea, for example, the proximate cause is the presence of Yahweh whose power is both sufficient and necessary for bringing about the miraculous event. Accordingly, miracles by definition are situated asymmetrically in relation to the world's symmetry (laws of nature), because their cause is divine and not natural, and not because they violate laws of nature.

What is especially noteworthy is that by reconceiving miracles in this way, not only are theistic presuppositions seen as indispensable for understanding miracles and their possibility, but the defining postulate (that miracles violate laws of nature) is contravened on the basis of which those who subscribe to the Humean tradition are persuaded of their incoherence and impossibility. That is, the force of this new conception of miracles lies not merely in the fact that it is tradition-constituted, based on faith in a particular set of absolute presuppositions. The followers of Hume themselves hold by faith to certain absolute presuppositions which together constitute a tradition that for centuries determined the rules by which alone, it was assumed, the discussion of miracles could be advanced. Rather its force lies in the fact that this new conception of miracles is constituted in terms of a tradition that makes explicit from the start the theistic presuppositions without which the idea of miracles is inconceivable. Moreover, it is a reconception of miracles that coheres with the advances of the new physics and places miracles within the context of an asymmetrical dimension (the behavior of particles that deviate from the standard model in physics, for which no material cause is identified) that physicists now accept as belonging to the natural universe.

By reconceiving miracles in this way, I do not subscribe to the view, held by some, that God is active in all or even some quantum events. I am in agreement with Peacocke that such a view implicitly supports "total direct divine determination of all events. This is a form of the theological view called 'occasionalism' and entails notorious problems concerning evil and freewill, among many others."[19] Rather, with Peacocke I am arguing that "particular events could occur in the world and be what they are because God intends them to be so, without any contravention of the laws of physics, biology, psychology or whatever is the pertinent science for the level in question. . . ."[20] Accordingly, reason comprehends miracles as deviations from the standard model of material cause and effect; since their cause is transhuman and not material, they are apprehended by faith and not by the sight of reason.

This new conception of miracles entails a difference that makes all the difference and renders false a third Humean assumption, namely, that miracles are events that by definition should be ascertainable by any person, including those whose set of presuppositions excludes belief in a deity. The Humean tradition, as is well known, falls within the parameters of foundationalism. It presupposes that belief in God is not properly basic and that somehow it can be prospectively justified or discredited by determining the success of certain prospective, coercive arguments, such as the arguments for God's existence or the coherence of the idea of miracles or the nature of evidence for supposing that a miracle actually occurred. Foundationalist assumptions in general and arguments for God's existence taken as prospective proofs are, as noted in chapter 3, less than compelling. What I try to show in the following sections is that only from within a world-version presupposing from the start the actuality of God's existence (and thus the proper basicality of belief in God) is the idea of miracles logically possible and is good evidence for supposing a miracle's actual occurrence conceivable.[21]

Asymmetry and Miracle Stories

What results when we apply this recharacterization of the laws of nature and the asymmetry of miracles to specific miracle stories? How can we apply to specific accounts the two ways miracles are asymmetrical? How are miracles incommensurable with the standard model (law of cause and effect) comprehended by scientific reason? And what transhuman being is apprehended by faith as the causal condition of the asymmetrical event?

For Jews and Christians, "in the beginning God created . . ." is the touchstone of all thought and life. It functions as a kind of paradigmatic miracle event, apprehended by faith and depicting quite precisely the three causal relationships set forth above: God as uncaused creator is situated asymmetrically in relation to creation as its proximate, necessary, and sufficient cause. From the Genesis account it is clear that the world is created by divine fiat, that the power of God is the immediate causal condition by which all things are created. That God is the sufficient and necessary causal condition for creating the world is, for Christians, concisely expressed in the prologue to John's Gospel: "In the beginning was the Word, and the Word was with God, and the Word was God. He was in the beginning with God; all things were made through him, and without him was not anything made that was made" (Genesis 1:1–2). From this passage note first that D of itself is capable of bringing about M ("all things were made through him") and, second, that M cannot occur without D ("without him was not anything made that was made"). Note further that creating "the heavens and the earth" is an act that neither violates, suspends, nor counteracts but conforms to the laws of nature. Theists presume, in fact, that by such an act those laws were originally established.[22] It might be objected, however, that an act whereby energy and matter are created ex nihilo violates the first law of thermodynamics, the principle of the conservation of energy. Larmer, I think, has dealt successfully with this objection by distinguishing two senses of "law," a strong and a weak sense. The strong sense, in which "law" is advanced as a metaphysical principle, asserts that "energy can be neither created nor destroyed although its form may change." The weak sense, in which "law" is advanced as a scientific law, states that "in an isolated system the total amount of energy remains constant although its form may change." The strong formulation of "law," which functions as a metaphysical presupposition delineating a physicalist version of the universe, precludes any theistic belief in the divine creation of energy. Nevertheless, the theist, as Larmer points out, can affirm the weaker, scientific formulation of the law that "in an isolated system the total amount of energy remains constant," since such a statement implies nothing concerning the possibility of creation ex nihilo, just as it implies nothing concerning whether, in fact, the physical universe is an isolated system, i.e., open to the causal influence of God. . . . [The theist] is, in short, in a position to accept the Principle of the Conservation of Energy when it is formulated as a scientific law and not as a defining postulate of physicalism.[23] In either case, whether physicalist or theist, the origin of the universe involves an asymmetrical, metaphysical presupposition. Either the universe originates in an uncaused cause (energy) or in an uncreated creator (God). Both are incommensurable with the standard model of material cause and effect discovered by scientific reason and both require an act whereby faith apprehends that asymmetrical transhuman, causal origin of the universe. By faith, Christians believe that the originating cause is the proximate, sufficient, and necessary activity of God; by retrospective reason, Christians cultivate a cumulative case for the world-version implied by this belief.

The idea of a virgin birth has always seemed to Humeans like an oxymoron of sorts, a curious but quite inconceivable idea, a violation of laws of nature, a contradiction, an impossibility. But if we begin to think carefully and clearly about it, if we begin to think of it in terms of asymmetry and of miracles as incommensurable events, we shall find that "virgin birth" is an idea that is logically coherent and an event that is physiologically possible. This is perhaps more clearly evident today than at any time in the past. Current practices of in vitro fertilization, in vivo fertilization, and artificial insemination compel us at minimum to admit both that the idea of a virgin conceiving and giving birth to a child is logically coherent and that the act of doing so conforms to laws of nature and is therefore physiologically possible. As Larmer argues "The miracle of the virgin birth can be seen as an event in which an act of creation by God, i.e., the creation of a spermatozoan in the body of Mary, combined with existent natural processes, i.e., the normal growth and development of a fetus during pregnancy, to produce the miraculous event we call the virgin birth."[24] But how is a virgin birth analogous to quantum events? First, analogous to the asymmetries of particle physics and their deviation from the standard model, a virgin birth, insofar as it is an event with no material cause, deviates from the standard model of cause and effect anticipated and predicted by scientific reason. Second, virgin birth is an asymmetrical event, as I have defined such metaphysical events, in that its cause is transhuman and divine and not material.

The virgin birth as caused by God is situated asymmetrically in relation to the principle of cause and effect. But no law of nature is violated, suspended, or even counteracted in order for a virgin to be inseminated, conceive, and bear a child. For what is necessary for conception, of course, is not sexual intercourse but fertilization of an egg by sperm. So the medical insertion of sperm into a virgin, although rare, is entirely in concert with laws of nature and escapes conventional charges of incoherence or impossibility. Accordingly, as J. S. Mill argues: "We cannot admit a proposition as a law of nature and yet believe a fact in real contradiction to it. We must believe the alleged fact, or believe that we are mistaken in admitting the supposed law."[25] In this case we are mistaken by insisting on the supposed law that a virgin birth violates laws of nature and by insisting, as Everitt does on that erroneous basis, on the incoherence of the idea of miracles.

Instead, the understanding of miracles with which our new definition furnishes us establishes an idea of the miraculous that conforms entirely to the laws of nature and yet, insofar as no material cause is present, is incommensurable in relation to the principle of cause and effect. The causal agent of the virgin birth is a divine power which is its proximate, sufficient, and necessary condition: proximate, because conceived by the Holy Spirit; sufficient, because divine power is itself capable of fertilizing an egg; and necessary, because the birth of a divine human person cannot occur independently of divine agency. In short, that a virgin birth might be accomplished naturally, medically by human agency not only does not logically preclude but rather suggests that such a birth might be accomplished miraculously by divine agency. Again, the miracle (as caused by divine and not natural agency) is situated asymmetrically (divinely caused) in relation to what science predicts, namely, a material cause; and yet it does not violate the law of cause and effect, for it has a cause, albeit not a material one, but a transhuman, divine one. So, although we can account for the miracle, it is incommensurable and unpredictable in relation to the standard model established by scientific reason. Thus, miracles, like the virgin birth, must be apprehended by faith, for no pattern of reasoning can otherwise lead one to accept the reality of such an asymmetrical event.

Perhaps most important as well as most difficult of all to account for are resurrection stories, in which a corpse is somehow reanimated or resuscitated.[26] The women who arrive at the tomb of Jesus carrying spices are startled, the evangelist says, that the stone is rolled away from the sepulchre, and even more amazed to find the tomb empty. That they would be reticent to tell other disciples what they had seen is understandable; but when eventually they do, the disciples first respond with skepticism, doubt, and curiosity and then with belief and affirmation. Today the Christian community embraces the same range of responses to the notion of Jesus' resurrection. Recalling that belief in resurrection makes sense only within the context of a certain world-version, and recalling a couple of theistic presuppositions, however, surely helps assuage the doubts we quite naturally have regarding the notion of resurrection. First, recall that the causal agent of resurrection is deity, and second, that the agent by which life is recreated-out-of-death is itself the original and uncreated creator of that life. Only within the context of some such theistic version of the world can the asymmetry of resurrection be adequately accounted for. So, how is it that resurrection miracles are analogous to quantum events in particle physics? First, like quantum events, resurrection is incommensurable with the standard model, established by scientific reason, that all creatures are mortal and no material cause is sufficient to resurrect them from the dead. Second, that the cause of resurrection, apprehended by faith, is a transhuman, divine cause does not violate any law of nature, for science determines only that no material or human cause can effect a resurrection. Recall that since laws of nature are not prescriptive, irresistible, and deterministic but rather explanatory principles, it is physically conceivable that a dead human body can be reanimated, but if and only if a divine and not material power (from which the possibility of life is derived and sustained in the first place) counters the force of corruptibility and revitalizes the corpse. In the theistic view, then, the law of mortality is natural and normal but not irresistible and deterministic; its power is efficacious only so long as it is not countered by a greater divine force. Faith in Christ's resurrection, of course, appears to scientific reasoning as a random, quantum event, situated asymmetrically in relation to nature's symmetry. This is because the cause of resurrection is not a natural condition but the proximate, sufficient, and necessary activity of God.

Other recorded miracle events (e.g., feedings, healings, parting waters, stilling storms, walking on water) can be similarly interpreted. They appear quite properly to scientific reason as random, unpredictable events that are inexplicable and unjustifiable. They can be accounted for; but since they are situated asymmetrically in relation to the world's natural order, belief in them cannot be compelled by reason but must be apprehended by faith.

Faith and Miracles

Several observations are implicit in what has been argued above, observations that will help place the position for which I have been arguing in relation to the Humean tradition.

First, I advance an idea of miracles that is conceived entirely in terms of their threefold causal relationship with God. The claim that a divine agent is the proximate, sufficient, and necessary cause of miracles is logically independent of any thesis about how miracle events interact with the laws of nature. Hence, the conventional charge of incoherence—because M violates natural laws—to which miracles have traditionally been subjected by the Humean tradition is simply irrelevant. The physical possibility of miracles, however, raises the question of the way miracles are related to laws of nature. I have argued that the physical occurrence of miracles is not impossible on the basis that miracles, like certain physical events, either counteract laws of nature or simply conform to them, with the difference (which of course makes all the difference) that the causal agent of that counteraction or conformity is divine and not natural or human. The cumulative case developed by Christian philosophers accounts for miracles even though, as I have indicated, they are incommensurable in relation to scientific reason's standard model. Larmer, for example, accounts for them by arguing that miraculous acts of God are analogous to acts of human agents; just as human acts may either conform to or counteract laws of nature, so too, according to the theistic version of the world, may divine acts conform to or counteract laws of nature.[27] Just because miracles are situated asymmetrically (Divinely caused instead of naturally caused) in relation to the science's standard model of what constitutes natural symmetry, does not mean that they violate laws of nature.

Second, the conventional Humean conception presupposes that miracles, as violations of laws of nature, are necessarily accessible to and identifiable by anyone who happens to witness them, whether theist, nontheist, atheist, or agnostic. Skeptics are as perfectly capable of recognizing when or if an event violates a law of nature as are devotees. Thus, one need only be rational, not also theistic, in order to identify an event as miraculous, as a violation of laws of nature. But since for Humeans violations of the laws of nature are logically impossible, as Everitt argues, a nontheist is not very likely to be able to see let alone admit the occurrence of such events. The Humean assumption is that all possible physical events must conform to a single and simple symmetry. It disregards and disowns what today virtually all scientists believe, that the world is cluttered with asymmetrical events. My new conception of miracles as asymmetrical, quantum events, in contrast, presupposes that they will likely be ascertainable and identifiable only through the "eyes of faith," only to those whose set of absolute presuppositions includes belief in God and for whom, therefore, belief in a divine power acting in nature and history can be retrospectively and cumulatively accounted for, although not prospectively justified and explained. If one presupposes with Hume that miracles are logically impossible and if one does not presuppose that miracles conform to or counteract but do not violate laws of nature, then that person is not likely to recognize a miracle in his own living room. Belief in miracles presupposes already a complex structure of beliefs whose *conditio sine qua non* is belief in God. Miracles are woven into the fabric of a theistic world-version and point retrospectively, rather than prospectively, to a divine agent to which one already by faith stands committed. Moreover, miracles, as metaphysical (caused by God), quantum (no natural cause) events situated asymmetrically in relation to the world's symmetry, are simply unrecognizable by scientific reason, just as are random, unpredictable quantum events in the subatomic world. Only by faith apprehending miracles as they are in their fully flourishing asymmetry can the mind retrospectively account for and make sense of them, although never rationally justify them.

Properly understood, then, Everitt's conclusion in "The Impossibility of Miracles" (that it could never be reasonable to believe in the occurrence of a miracle) is based not simply and only on a belief that miracles are events that violate laws of nature and are therefore inconceivable. It is based more fundamentally on a fallacious absolute presupposition, namely, that the natural order is constituted of a simple symmetry that precludes asymmetrical, quantum events—that all possible events will always and without exception conform to inviolable laws of nature as we know them and that they can be counteracted only by a higher-ranking physical law, never by a divine agent. This belief presupposes that certain patterns of thought will and certain others will not count as rationally possible. Accordingly, for Everitt, evidence of two thousand miracles will no more convince him of miraculous activity of a deity than the evidence of one or none. From the start the idea of miracle is inadmissible because his received set of naturalistic presuppositions compels him to mistakenly regard the idea of miracle as logically and materially impossible.

Conversely, reconceiving miracles in terms of God as proximate, sufficient, and necessary causal agent suggests that the miraculous nature of an event can be recognized and counted as conceivable only, or at least primarily, by one whose set of absolute presuppositions already includes belief in a divine power. In other words, only within a community of faith (or at minimum only within the context of theistic belief) is belief in miracles acceptable and evidence for miracles recognizable. The asymmetrical miraculous is ascertainable only to those who already participate in a community of faith or who at least lay claim to some kind of theistic belief, however vague or underdeveloped. Miracles, and the belief that there are miracles, should thus be understood as directed to a specific type of audience, one composed of devotees to a divine being, who by faith are accustomed to apprehending the asymmetries that result from divine activity in the universe.

Hume inadvertently illustrates the point I wish to underscore. In a note[28] making a different point, he writes of the Indians of Sumatra who, having always seen water fluid in their own climate and having therefore never seen water freeze, are not and perhaps never will be in a position to experience and understand the meaning of what to them would be quite an incredible occurrence—ice, frozen water. Yet, even though they have never seen water in Moscow during winter, and even though they cannot conceive of frozen water as something a rational Indian would look for, nevertheless, for those who are placed or who place themselves in relevant circumstances, looking for and conceiving of an asymmetrical event like frozen water is perfectly appropriate. Analogously, a person whose version of the world does not include belief in God is not in a position to experience and understand the meaning of what for them is surely incredible—the occurrence of miracles. Since such persons are not in a position to experience or recognize them they cannot therefore reasonably conceive of or even look for them. Only persons who have positioned themselves within a community of faith, or at least a culture of theistic belief, can even begin to look and account for experiences of the miraculous. They alone will have had the kind of beliefs and experiences that enable them to look for and understand the fact, nature, and meaning of miracles.

To put the same thing differently, that which is situated asymmetrically (miracles) in relation to the world's symmetry (scientific reason) must first be apprehended by faith, as argued in chapter 3, before reason can begin to account for them. Even though miracles properly conceived are not violations of laws of nature and not thereby contradictory, as the Humean tradition insists, nevertheless they are asymmetrical events in a symmetrical world and cannot be grasped by reason alone or employed by reason to substantiate faith. As Reginald Fuller puts it, miracles "are occurrences which faith recognizes as acts of God. . . . Not that faith makes them acts of God. It merely recognizes them for what they are. But faith is always a free decision. It is never coerced by overwhelming proof."[29] Faith as an act of will is the way a person freely commits himself to God and God's ways in the world. Reason's task is not to function prospectively, not to try and coerce the mind to faith. Instead, reason properly functions retrospectively, comprehending what faith apprehends and commits one to. Accordingly, Humeans who attempt to employ reason to coerce or deny faith find themselves begging the question. For they first assume that what is by definition asymmetrical and unjustifiable (miracles, violations of laws of nature) can never be justifiable by reason whose function and capacity, by the way, is restricted to comprehending and justifying that which situates itself symmetrically, instead of asymmetrically, with nature's laws. This again is to commit the fallacy of rationalism, which excludes from the start faith and the local faith community from which alone belief in miracles can be accounted for.

Third, it follows from the previous points that these two contrasting treatments of miracles imply that they play two quite distinct epistemological roles. The Humean conception requires that miracles play a major apologetical role, providing the believer and skeptic alike with a persuasive evidential basis for believing or not believing in the divinity of Jesus or in the historicity of Christ's resurrection and so on. Foundationalism, which the Humean tradition assumes, argues that the evidence for or against miracles establishes one of several bases by which belief in the existence of God or the divinity of Jesus is prospectively and rationally validated or invalidated. This claim falsely assumes that genuine philosophers of religion must be ventriloquists, that their voice must speak as if disembodied, on the basis of a neutral body of ahistorical, rational principles and universal truths, as if independent of any commitment to a specific world-version. Yet, as I have argued in chapter 3, the perspective of the Humean or any tradition regarding the status of laws of nature and miracles is not neutral and ahistorical but very much dependent on a constellation of absolute presuppositions and the version of the world implied by them. In contrast, the epistemological role played by the reconception of the idea of miracles suggested here is somewhat more modest. Miracles cannot and do not function prospectively as evidence by which one might or might not, if truly rational, coerce oneself or another into believing in God's existence or the divinity of Jesus. Recognizing and understanding by faith that they are asymmetrical events in a symmetrical world presupposes already a cumulative case, a certain set of metaphysical beliefs, including belief in God.

So, if miracles cannot be employed as stones in the foundation upon which belief in God is erected, of what use are they? If not apologetical, then what significant role do miracles play in a Christian version of the world? Put succinctly, miracles are a means by which the healing power of God's loving compassion transforms and redeems the asymmetrical evil and suffering afflicting God's creation.

Supersymmetry: Compassion and Miracles

Miracles are situated asymmetrically in relation to creation's symmetry, as I have argued, not because they violate nature's laws but because they are events whose proximate, sufficient, and necessary cause is God. But why, in the midst of creation's symmetry, do such asymmetrical, quantum-like events pop up? Why miracles? For the Christian, what purpose and significance do they have? What role do they play? The key to answering these questions lies in what I refer to as "spiritual compassion." At least in the biblical tradition, the purpose of miracles is to redeem creation and restore it to health and wholeness; that is, its purpose is spiritual compassion. Miracles are glimpses of God's kingdom, of the loving compassion by which God's kingdom heals and redeems. Here again, we shall see, God's loving compassion functions supersymmetrically, not only by mediating the world's asymmetry (miracles) and symmetry (laws of nature), but by transforming the disparity between evil (asymmetry) and good (symmetry), between human disobedience and obedience to God's will, into the harmony of God's peaceable kingdom. My aim here is not to provide a comprehensive exegesis of biblical miracles; nor is it to suggest that compassion/redemption exhaust the raison d'être of miracles. My aim, rather, is to show that the role of miracles is not primarily theoretical, not primarily in order to "prove" divinity. Rather the role of miracles is practical: to provide windows of light through which shines the promise and power of God's kingdom, to provide moments of grace wherein is manifest the healing compassion of God's peaceable kingdom. My analysis revolves around three points: first, the context of miracles; second, the role of miracles; and third, the accomplishment of miracles.

First, what is the context in which miracles occur and what significance does this context have for understanding the occasion for God's miraculous activity? In answering this question we might keep in mind especially the supreme miracles of the Bible (the Exodus and the Resurrection). It is clear, I think, that the relevant context for the occurrence of these and other miracles is the fallenness and brokenness of creation. The fact of human and transhuman rebelliousness introduces into creation a moral and spiritual asymmetry, a moral and spiritual chaos and randomness that undermines, as argued in the previous chapter, the moral symmetry God intends for all of creation. The occasion for the Exodus is the bondage and suffering of God's people and by implication of all peoples; and the occasion for the Resurrection is the whole of humanity oppressed by sin and suffering. God through miracles is indulging neither the doubts of Jesus' contemporaries nor the intellectual curiosity of scholars. Rather, as the practical matter that miracles are, God through them shows compassion for a humanity suffering from self- and satanic-inflicted evil, evil that wounds and alienates humans from God and each other. That is why this particular chapter follows directly a chapter on evil and suffering, because evil and suffering are indeed the occasion for God's compassion, and miracles are one powerful means by which that compassion is practiced. As Fuller argues, "The miracles of Jesus are preliminary rounds in the final conflict with the powers of evil," on the one hand, and on the other, "the preliminary manifestations of the final revelation of the glory of God."[30]

The story that perhaps most clearly links miracles and evil, apart from those of the Exodus and the Resurrection, is that of the healing of the paralytic man at Capernaum, whose friends lower him through an opening in the roof of a house. "And when Jesus saw their faith, he said to the paralytic, 'My son, your sins are forgiven.'" And when accused of blasphemy because only God can forgive sins, Jesus replies, "Which is easier to say to the paralytic, 'Your sins are forgiven,' or to say, 'Rise take up your pallet and walk.'" Jesus goes on to say, "But that you may know that the Son of man has authority on earth to forgive sins—he said to the paralytic—'I say to you rise, take up your pallet and go home,'" which the man did (Mark 2:1–12). Is not "My son, your sins are forgiven" a strange way to address the man who is paralytic, as Jesus does? Why not just heal his body? Barclay insists that in "your sins are forgiven" Jesus is acknowledging a common but mistaken belief of many Jews that ill health and misfortune are the result of sin; such a belief was held by the friends of Job, for example, and a rabbinical tradition which believed that "No sick person is cured from his sickness until all his sins are forgiven him."[31] Perhaps the paralytic believed this, but Jesus did not. And yet for Jesus forgiveness of sins and healing of body are of a single, seamless fabric. Not only are they both miraculous events, but both manifest the loving compassion God has for humanity, for redeeming its sinfulness (forgiveness of sins) and its suffering (healing of paralysis). Fuller puts this interrelationship of sin and suffering this way, "The remission of sins is the total gift of salvation of which physical healing is a part."[32] Sin and suffering, as evidence of the work of Satan in the world, are the context and occasion for God to manifest through the miracles of Jesus the power to heal both body and soul. What Jesus wanted those who accused him of blasphemy to "know" is that his "authority on earth to forgive sins" is of the same divine source of loving power as his authority to heal bodies; both manifest the presence of God's kingdom of love on earth. Without acknowledging this context of sin and suffering, miracles degenerate into magical, self-glorifying tricks by which to impress the crowd and "prove" an abstract point (e.g., the divinity of Jesus).

Second, if the occasion for miracles is evil, what then is the role of miracles in a fallen and morally chaotic world? Already I have argued that miracles primarily do not and cannot function apologetically, a position propounded most persuasively by William Paley's *Evidences of Christianity* (1794) and the position against which David Hume explicitly argues. Already I have argued that asymmetrical events (miracles, Jesus' divinity) cannot be justified by reason (whose capacities are restricted to tracing the world's symmetry) but must be apprehended by faith. As Fuller puts it, "You cannot prove that an occurrence is an act of God: only faith can recognize it as such."[33] There is general consensus among biblical scholars and theologians, however, that whatever else their role may or may not be, the role of miracles, as occasions for spiritual compassion, includes their function as "signs," to which I add the modifier "sacramental." Hence, their function is as "sacramental signs."

As "signs," miracles point to the promise and presence of God's kingdom, to a kingdom whose power of love and compassion is calculated to redeem creation and restore a moral and spiritual supersymmetry. As Fuller puts it, a miracle is "an occurrence pointing beyond itself to some further meaning...."[34] Or as Barclay insists, a miracle is a sign that "tells us... of the nature of God; it is a door opening in the eternal to give us a glimpse of God."[35] As "sacramental" I do not suggest that I consider miracles to be institutionalized, ecclesiastical rites by which the church administers God's grace to the faithful. What I suggest is similar to what Peacocke suggests by the phrase "the world as sacrament,"[36] in this case referring particularly to miracles. As sacramental miracles are events through which the power and grace of God's kingdom is made known to those who have ears to hear. As signs, miracles point to the loving compassion of God's kingdom; as sacramental they convey the actual power of God's loving compassion without which redemption and restoration is impossible. Both Fuller in *Interpreting the Miracles* and Barclay in *And He Had Compassion* argue that miracles are signs that manifest the loving compassion, the forgiveness and mercy, of God's kingdom on earth. This should not surprise us once we acknowledge, as we have above, that the occasions for miracles are sin, evil, and suffering in the world. For it is only the power of God's loving compassion, only God's miraculous acts of mercy and forgiveness that are of sufficient moral and spiritual strength to defeat the evil and heal the suffering polluting creation

One has only to think of the two supreme biblical miracles—the Exodus and the Resurrection—to be persuaded that biblical miracles cannot be properly understood except as practical responses to a practical problem (evil and suffering). The Exodus, of course, is that miraculous event, remembered and reenacted at Passover, through which God in compassion delivers Israel and all humanity from the moral and spiritual chaos of oppression and in truth reveals at Sinai a vision for restoring moral and spiritual order, for living holy lives together. Similarly, Jesus' Resurrection is that miraculous event, remembered and reenacted at Easter, by which God demonstrates the supersymmetrical power of loving compassion to redeem humankind and indeed all creation, and restore them to health and wholeness, restore moral and spiritual symmetry. The Apostle Paul, for instance, writes that the occasion for the miracle of Christ's cross and Resurrection is the fact that humans are alienated from God. Christ is "our peace, who has made us both one, and has broken down the dividing wall of hostility.... [T]hat he might create in himself one new man in place of the two, so making peace, and might reconcile us both to God in one body through the cross, thereby bringing the hostility to an end" (Ephesians 2:14–16). The context for God's miraculous activity is the hostility of sin, evil, and suffering in the world.

Miracles are one primary way God responds compassionately to the world's moral and spiritual asymmetry and redeems and restores its health and wholeness.

Or consider Jesus' healing of the man who was deaf and dumb (Mark 7:31–37). The text says that "looking up into heaven, [Jesus] sighed, and said to him, 'Ephphatha,'" that is, "Be opened." Biblical scholars have interpreted "sighed" or "groaned" in at least a couple of ways. For some, Jesus exhales "a prayer so intense that it sounded like a desperate cry." Others find in that sigh a groan of compassion. "As Jesus looked at this poor man in all his wretchedness, a sigh of sympathy was wrung from him for the man's wretched case." Barclay insists that we should embrace both interpretations. As Jesus was "moved with compassion" he cried out to God for power sufficient to heal the man's suffering. This story "tells how [Jesus'] compassion joined hands with the power of God and how then a miracle happened."[37] In short, miracles are moments of compassion through which God's grace redeems, reconciles, and retrieves into a fallen world the supersymmetrical healing and wholeness of God's peaceable kingdom.

If philosophers of religion disregard evil and suffering as the occasion for miracles and if they ignore their role as sacramental signs of God's kingdom of compassion, then miracles are likely to become, as they are for rationalists, little more than bourgeois amusements to indulge scholarly curiosity. Or they are likely to become, as they are for fideists, a carnival sideshow of magical, conjuring tricks calculated to rejuvenate the otherwise insidious spiritual boredom of those for whom God's reality is a rusted curiosity. Indeed, a portrait of magical, conjuring tricks is one we have of miracles in those apocryphal gospels, like the Gospel of Thomas, written long after the canonical gospels. These gospels, Barclay tells us, "purport to tell the story of the infancy and boyhood of Jesus. They are works of pious fiction, designed to fill in the gaps in the life of Jesus." One Sabbath, while playing with friends, for example, the boy Jesus commands the waters of a stream to pool so that he can take the mud and make clay sparrows that he then causes to fly away. When he is rebuked by a friend for performing this miracle on the Sabbath Jesus withers the boy up like a parched fruit tree. In another story, Jesus, irritated by a child who runs and crashes into him, promptly kills him. In yet another story, Jesus magically lengthens a slab of lumber for his father Joseph, so that a carpentry project can be completed.[38] These miracle stories, says Barclay, "do not ring true because they are only glorified conjuring tricks; they fail to do what every miracle of Jesus did—they tell us nothing of the nature of God,"[39] they tell us nothing of God's kingdom, nothing of how through Jesus God's compassion heals people wounded by evil and suffering. The spiritual boredom reflected in the Gospel of Thomas that requires Jesus to perform conjuring tricks is not so different from the spiritual boredom that today requires evangelists to entertain crowds by performing conjuring tricks. In the authentic stories of Jesus' miracles "the heart of God is displayed." They are events that allow "us to see something of God's attitude of love towards humanity."[40]

Finally, what do miracles accomplish? The answer is implicit in what has already been argued. Through miracles God demonstrates a loving compassion of such power and passion as to be able to heal, redeem, and reconcile; through miracles compassion transforms the tension implicit in creation's dichotomies (symmetry and asymmetry) into a supersymmetrical fellowship of difference. The Jewish notion of *tikkun olim*, healing a wounded world, is perhaps most precisely and perceptively to this point. The power of God's compassion, miraculously conveyed, heals the wounds of the world, overcomes the hostility of creation's fallenness caused by human and transhuman disobedience, transforms, redeems, and retrieves the harmony and wholeness that God intended for creation. What miracles promise is hope and what they provide is vision, both of which are realized in the supersymmetrical harmony biblical writers refer to as the kingdom of God. How is this possible? How can God's loving compassion accomplish such reconciliation and harmony?

You may recall our discussion from the previous chapter on the principle of dialectical moral equilibrium: the asymmetry of horrendous evil in the world requires an equally asymmetrical moral event which moral reason as justice cannot supply. Horrendous evil and gratuitous suffering require a comparable good like mercy and meekness ("turn the other cheek") which stands asymmetrically in relation to the moral reason of just fairness ("an eye for an eye"; reward and punishment according to just desserts). Only morality incommensurable with moral reason, and only compassionate mercy and meekness, as sometimes manifest in and through miracles, are able to heal and restore. The spiritual depth of compassion that Jesus demonstrates through miracles "is not [simply] humanitarian compassion . . . ," as Fuller puts it. Rather, "As indicated by the broader context in which the word is sometimes used, and by Matthew's normal preference for 'mercy' in the context of Jesus' healings, the compassionate mercy of which the evangelists speak is the compassion and mercy of God."[41] In this sense God's merciful compassion manifest in the Exodus and Resurrection is itself miraculous in all the ways indicated above. For such quantum mercy and compassion requires that God be the proximate, sufficient, and necessary cause. The women who stand astonished at the empty tomb soon come to understand the Resurrection not merely as a miraculous event but even more as a manifestation of God's miraculous and unjustifiable mercy, a merciful compassion of such power as to be able to make recompense for the unjustifiable evil and suffering in the world. Just as much evil and suffering in the world is unjustifiable, so also must God's compassion be so much more unjustifiably merciful, loaded with unmerited love more than sufficient to make recompense for that unjustifiable evil and suffering. Through the miracle of the Exodus in the Hebrew tradition and the miracle of Christ's Incarnation/Resurrection in the Christian tradition, God's merciful compassion accomplishes a supersymmetrical harmony between God's will and human practice; they are miracles that reveal the nature of God's will, on the one hand, and they empower humans, on the other hand, to practice that will.

Consider these two supreme miracles, the Exodus and the Resurrection, more specifically. How do they accomplish a supersymmetrical harmony between God's will and human life? Each "foundation" miracle, as Fuller calls them, is anticipated by "preliminary" miracles. "Before the Exodus come the plagues of Egypt and before the death and resurrection of Christ the healings, exorcisms . . . and the so-called nature miracles."[42] These minor miracles are like warnings (plagues, exorcisms) to the forces of darkness (Pharaoh, Satan) that God in his mercy intends to defeat evil and heal his creation. Along with these preliminary miracles are what Fuller refers to as "'accompanying miracles' occurring alongside of and as part of the great miracle itself."[43] The miracles accompanying the Exodus are the dividing of the sea, the pillar of fire and cloud, water from the rock, and manna. Accompanying Christ's Resurrection are the miracles of incarnation, baptism, and transfiguration. All of these accompanying miracles enhance and bolster God's intention to heal and restore through loving compassion the world to its rightful harmony. They bear into reality the extraordinary meaning of God's kingdom and prepare humanity for a righteousness that by all accounts is supersymmetrical, a righteousness in which the power of God's unmerited mercy defeats the power of Satan's unmerited evil, invokes a vision of a new Jerusalem, and grants the grace and power necessary for God's people to practice the promise of that vision.

The rest of the story is that the women who first witness the empty tomb "fled . . . ; for trembling and astonishment had come upon them; and they said nothing to anyone, for they were afraid," even though the angel at the tomb had instructed them to go and tell the disciples what they had seen. When they finally do tell the other disciples, "they would not believe it" (Mark 16: 8–11). Eventually, however, many do believe and by so doing become participants in the continuing miracle of Christ's resurrection. For the community of faithful believers, insofar as it continues to practice in its own life the unmerited mercy and compassion of Christ's resurrection, participates in that miracle for which God alone is the proximate, sufficient, and necessary cause.

In the preceding three chapters I have shown how God's loving compassion manifests itself ontologically, existentially, and spiritually. Collected together these three dimensions provide a profound and provocative supersymmetrical way of solving the problems typically treated by philosophy of religion. But together they accomplish even more. For as we shall see in part III, compassion, as emotional intersubjectivity, functions in civilization as a normative experience, and it does so in two ways. First, it is the normative basis for conversation and cooperation between the world's religions and, second, it is the normative basis for determining the role of religion in society. I address these two matters in the next chapter.

Notes

1. Paul Davies, *God and the New Physics* (New York: Simon and Schuster, 1983), 197.

2. David Hume, *Enquiry Concerning Human Understanding*, X. Others who assume Hume's definition of miracles are Richard Swinburne, *The Existence of God* (Oxford: Oxford University Press, 1982); Davies, *God and the New Physics*; Brian Davies, *Thinking About God* (London: Geoffrey Chapman, 1985); J. L. Mackie, *The Miracle of Theism* (Oxford: Oxford University Press, 1982); and Nicholas Everitt, "The Impossibility of Miracles," *Religious Studies* 23 (1987): 347–349.

3. Peter Harrison argues that Newton and some of his most prominent followers "came to understand miracles in a way quite different from their seventeenth-century predecessors, and that in developing this new conception of the miraculous they managed to avoid those conceptual confusions which are thought to afflict the cognitive worlds of their earlier contemporaries." In other words, Newton himself did not believe that his view of the world required that he view miracles as "violations of the laws of nature" as did some thinkers, like human. See Peter Harrison, "Newtonian Science, Miracles, and the Laws of Nature," *Journal of the History of Ideas* (1995): 531–552.

4. James Keller, "A Moral Argument Against Miracles," *Faith and Philosophy* 12 (1995): 54.

5. David McKenzie, "Miracles Are Not Immoral: A Response to James Keller's Moral Argument Against Miracles," *Religious Studies* 35 (1999): 73–88.

6. Nicholas Everitt, "The Impossibility of Miracles," *Religious Studies* 23 (1987): 349.

7. See, for example, two books by Paul Davies, *The Cosmic Blueprint* (New York: Simon and Schuster, 1988), and *God and the New Physics* (New York: Simon and Schuster, 1983).

8. Davies, *God and the New Physics*, 101–102.

9. Robert Larmer, "Miracles and the Laws of Nature," *Dialogue* 24 (Canada) (1985).

10. Ibid., 227–228.

11. E. J. Lowe, "Miracles and the Laws of Nature," *Religious Studies* 23 (June 1987): 273.

12. W. L. Craig, *The Historical Argument for the Resurrection of Jesus During the Deist Controversy* (Lewiston, N.Y.: Edwin Mellon Press, 1985), 483–484. See also Stephen S. Bilynskyj, *God, Nature, and the Concept of Miracle* (Ph.D. dissertation, University of Notre Dame, 1982), 117–146.

13. J. S. Mill, *A System of Logic* (London: Longmans, Green, 1949), book 6, chapter 25, see 2, 3.

14. Everitt, "The Impossibility of Miracles," 349.

15. Davies, *God and the New Physics*, 190.
16. Lowe, "Miracles and the Laws of Nature," 276.
17. Craig, *The Historical Argument for the Resurrection of Jesus*, 483–484.
18. Reginald H. Fuller, *Interpreting the Miracles* (Philadelphia, Pa.: Westminster Press, 1963), 9.
19. Arthur Peacocke, *Paths from Science Towards God: The End of All Our Exploring* (Oxford: Oneworld Publications), 105.
20. Ibid., 109.
21. Craig argues, I think rightly, that "only the atheist can deny the possibility of miracles, for even an agnostic must grant that if it is possible that . . . God exists, then it is equally possible that He has acted in the universe" (*The Historical Argument for the Resurrection of Jesus*), 490–491.
22. There is, perhaps, some basis for arguing that the act of divine creation counteracts the rule of chaos in the universe (Genesis 1:2). The earth was without form and void, and darkness was upon the face of the deep; and the spirit of God was moving over the face of the waters. Here is depicted the greater power of deity countering the forces of chaos and degeneration to bring about order and goodness in creation.
23. Larmer, "Miracles and the Laws of Nature," 232–233.
24. Ibid., 235.
25. Mill, *A System of Logic*, book 3, chapter 25, 2.
26. Theologians sometimes distinguish "resurrection" from "reanimation" or "resuscitation," with the former referring to the reception of a new, incorruptible body and the latter referring to the temporary rejuvenation of a body's biological life. In my discussion, I have in mind neither of these senses but have in mind "resurrection" in the sense of rejuvenation of biological life and reception of a new, incorruptible body.
27. Larmer, "Miracles and the Laws of Nature," 231.
28. Hume, *Enquiry*, section 10, part 1, n. 20.
29. Fuller, *Interpreting the Miracles*, 9.
30. Ibid., 10.
31. William Barclay, *And He Had Compassion: The Miracles of Jesus* (Valley Forge, Pa.: Judson Press, 1992), 13.
32. Fuller, *Interpreting the Miracles*, 51.
33. Ibid., 12.
34. Ibid., 15.
35. Barclay, *And He Had Compassion*, 5.
36. Peacocke, see chapter 9 of his book *Paths from Science Towards God*.
37. Fuller, *Interpreting the Miracles*, 71.
38. See Barclay, *And He Had Compassion*, 3–5.
39. Ibid., 5.
40. Ibid., 6.
41. Fuller, *Interpreting the Miracles*, 13.
42. Ibid., 10.
43. Ibid.

PART III

FAITH AND CULTURE

> Where do we go from here?
> Asks the voice of the prophet.
> Continents drift.
> Faces of the dead
> and the yet unborn
> drift in my head.
> Love drifts into dream
> too distant to touch.
> Think of a world with
> No prisons, no prisoners.
> I remember one man
> A maker of words
> Who said simply,
> Start from where you are.
> Spread out. Nourish.
> Reach. Be wind.
>
> Margaret Gibson, *Signs: A Progress of the Soul*

CHAPTER SIX

Christian Faith and Other Faiths

Jesus, weary from his journey, rests beside Jacob's well. A woman of Samaria comes to draw water and Jesus asks her for a drink. And so begins a conversation about living water and true worship. The woman draws water, and Jesus tells of water he can give that will so satisfy that she will never thirst again. The woman speaks of differences between her religious tradition and Jesus', and Jesus tells her of true worshippers who worship in spirit and truth. She perceives that Jesus is a prophet and is drawn by his disarming but caring way with her. Jesus perceives that, although she has strayed from her own faith, she cares deeply about her spiritual welfare (John 4). So, what is the significance of this remarkable encounter between Jesus and the Samaritan woman? What can we make of it? Or rather, what can it make of us? How can it interpret and inform our experiences and struggles? One can read and interpret this story in a variety of ways. One way of reading it that perhaps has been somewhat neglected is to read it as a paradigm for interreligious conversation about interreligious cooperation. And this is the reading of John's story to which I wish to draw attention.

"The question of the existence, or extent of shared territory between the different faiths," says Chris Arthur, "remains one of the most difficult (and important) questions...."[1] It is a perennial and precarious dilemma: How is it possible to protect and preserve religious diversity and at the same time promote a common, normative criterion for interreligious conversation and cooperation? How can we affirm the distinctive particularity of each local religious tradition while at the same time affirming a universal criterion for making interreligious judgments? How can we profess devotion to a unique, local narrative tradition and at the same time propound a meta-narrative to which all religions can subscribe? Customarily one can locate conventional solutions to this dilemma between two poles. Objectivism as a form of rationalism seeks to discover what S. Mark Heim refers to as the "common core of religion"; it accents the constitutive, universal substance of religion and all religions.[2] John Hick's "soteriological criterion"[3] and Paul Knitter's more recent "soteriocentrism"[4] tend toward this pole and the fallacy of rationalism. Subjectivism, as a form of fideism, resigns itself to what Heim refers to as the "incommensurability between faiths"; it accents religious pluralism and the difference and distance between religions.[5] Paul Griffiths' *An Apology for Apologetics* and Knitter's earlier *No Other Name* tend toward this pole and the fallacy of fideism.

Today it is fashionable to affirm diversity and abstain from fashioning some normative common ground among religions. Notable exceptions include Paul Knitter, who expresses an increasingly common sentiment when he says, in his *One Earth Many Religions*, that

> The obsession of so many contemporaries with preserving diversity at all costs, with not wanting to impose any kind of common agenda or seek after common criteria by which we decide what is true or false (right or wrong) can easily lead to what David Krieger has called . . . a "relativist agnostics." What he means is simple and frightening; if we have no common agenda, if there are no common criteria to be discovered or fashioned by nonviolent consensus, then ultimately what is "true" will be decided by power—by who has money or the guns.[6]

The normative approach implied by Knitter in *One Earth Many Religions* "marks a change in course," as he puts it, from his earlier approach in *No Other Name*.[7] In *No Other Name* he proposed a "non-normative, theocentric" approach to interreligious dialogue, whereas in his more recent *One Earth Many Religions* he advocates what he refers to as a "multinormed, soterio-centric" approach,[8] or a "correlational globally responsible model"[9] for interreligious dialogue.

Knitter explains how his correlational model is situated relative to a variety of postliberal perspectives. Postliberalism, as a version of fideism, assumes, he argues, that religious traditions "should for the most part stay in their own back yards, or in Lindbeck's phrase, in their own 'cultural-linguistic system.'" This implies that for postliberals "there is no 'commons' which all the households share. Postliberals are therefore wary of venturing beyond their own back yards to find some kind of common ground for mutual understanding."[10] Although at one time subscribing to this view, Knitter is now eager to venture one step further by suggesting that neighbors, without leaving their own backyards, can nevertheless "stand and talk to each other over our backyard fences," or engage in what some call "'ad hoc apologetics'—provisional opportunities to give and receive witness."[11] Knitter's correlational model of globally responsible interreligious dialogue exemplifies this "over the backyard fence" opportunity to "give and receive witness." The normative approach I take here proposes that neighbors should take yet one further step, beyond postliberalism and ad hoc apologetics, beyond Knitter's correlational model, to a place not constrained by the boundaries of backyard fences. This place is in fact a common public space where not only neighborly conversations but neighborly cooperation already takes place, and does so without requiring devotees to forsake their own backyards. Specifically, the common human experience of compassion establishes a public space and normative criterion where neighborly conversation and cooperation among religions takes place. By cooperating compassionately, neighbors are not compelled to foreclose on their personal homes; indeed, flourishing in their own homes and feasting with their own families is vital for engaging publicly in compassionate, neighborly conversation and public cooperation.

In distinction from both objective and subjective approaches, I propose an intersubjective approach that satisfies both the demand for a diversity of religious traditions and the demand for a universal, non-multinormed ground for interreligious cooperation. My view is that the common, universal, intersubjective, supersymmetrical experience of compassion meets both of these demands. Indeed, my thesis is that compassion is an experience that is of sufficient depth to embrace the diversity of religious traditions while establishing a normative space in which they may and should converge. My procedure is, first, to review what is by now commonly accepted, the cognitive status of emotions; second, to set forth a logic of emotional intersubjectivity underlying compassion, an intersubjectivity that embraces both the diversity and unity of religions; third, to show how compassion as supersymmetrical and emotional intersubjective affirms diversity among religions and provides a universal, normative criterion for interreligious conversation and cooperation; fourth, to show how compassion, as normative, functions as a criterion for critique and conversion; and finally, to show how this normative view of compassion situates religions in relation to truth and to each other.

Emotions as Cognitive

The possibility for normative interreligious conversation and cooperation is found neither in the abstract, generic beliefs of modern rationalism nor in the withering diversity of sectarian postmodern pluralism, neither in the objective universality of reason nor in the subjectivity of religious particularity. Rather, I argue that it is to be found in the universal particularity of emotional intersubjectivity, in the mutuality of shared emotions. I must first remind us of what today is widely accepted, namely, the cognitive status of emotions. The time is long since past that emotions can properly be regarded as irrational or even nonrational experiences, which are inherently misguiding or misguided. Evidences from a variety of disciplines (including biology, philosophy, psychology, and theology) supporting the cognitive status of emotions is vast and compelling. Elsewhere I have argued for a cognitivist view of emotions[12] and will only sketch that argument here for purposes specific to this thesis. My premise is that emotions are complex experiences constituted by three essential elements: judgments, projects, and energy.

To begin with, emotions include, as Martha Nussbaum puts it, "judgments about the world in such a way that the removal of the relevant [judgment] will remove not only the reason for the emotion but also the emotion itself."[13] Emotions arise in the first place because a judgment is made about an intentional object. Remove that judgment and the emotion dissipates. Consider the case of the prophet Nathan, King David, and Bathsheba (2 Samuel 11 and 12). Nathan tells David of a wealthy subject of his kingdom who has stolen the lamb of a poor man in order to entertain a sojourner. David makes the obvious and intentional judgment that the wealthy man has treated the poor man unfairly; and that judgment triggers in him anger toward the wealthy man. A short time later, when David realizes that he is the wealthy man about whom Nathan's story is told his emotion changes concomitantly with his judgment. He now judges himself to be the unjust culprit and his feelings turn from anger to feelings of guilt and remorse. In either case, the emotions David feels are initiated and altered by cognitive judgments he makes about the world.

The same holds for emotional projects. There is "an intimate . . . connection," as Roger Scruton puts it, "between . . . knowing what to feel and knowing what to do." Simultaneously with judgments, emotions involve "recognizing patterns of appropriate behavior,"[14] which I refer to as emotional projects. Jonathan Edwards similarly recognizes this dimension of emotions when he states that God made the emotions "the basis of human actions"; they are "like springs that set us moving in all the affairs of life and its pursuits." If they were "taken away, the world would be motionless and dead."[15] In his *Religious Affections* and *The Nature of True Virtue* Edwards speaks of the affections as the actual "exercise," "practice," and "habit" of a benevolent heart. And Paul Lauritzen speaks of emotions as "culturally constructed . . . 'social practices organized by stories that we both enact and tell.'"[16] In short, emotions involve practices or projects that are triggered by emotional judgements, socially constructed, and very often moral in character. The feeling of guilt, for example, is triggered by a judgment about the world I have made for myself, that I have done something wrong. But guilt also involves me in certain appropriate actions, a project—that repentance is required and forgiveness and restoration are available.

Thus, when his "anger was greatly kindled against the man," David knew immediately the nature of the project to be undertaken: the rich man must "restore the lamb fourfold," and he "deserves to die" (2 Samuel 12:5–6). The project that David's emotional judgment triggers is in this case already stipulated by and through the community to which he belongs. David shares a culture, a system of accepted beliefs and practices. Not only has his community educated him as to the appropriate emotional judgment to make regarding the injustice, but it has educated him with respect to the emotional project appropriate to that judgment. The matter becomes more complicated, of course, when Nathan reveals to David that he is the rich man who has committed the injustice. The new self-understanding that David comes to generates not only a different family of emotions, not only a different emotional judgment, but a different project. His feelings of guilt and remorse, appropriate now to a new understanding of himself and his world, concomitantly alter the emotional project he undertakes. David and his family participate in a project of healing appropriate to his community's conception of sin, punishment, and reconciliation.

But emotions, as we all know from our own experiences, consist not simply of judgments and projects but of potent forces, of passionate energy that invigorates our lives and empower us to put into practice those emotional judgments and projects. Emotions, in their dimension as passionate energy, possess a transformative power that is legendary, inciting people to undertake deeds of great heroism as well as deeds of malicious savagery. As in physics, where power is transferred from one form to another, so emotions constitute a system of transference and transformation in which energy expresses itself in various forms, such as anger, love, fear, and joy, transferring its power from form to form as the occasion calls for it. Initially David is angry toward the rich man of Nathan's narrative, but only momentarily. When he recognizes himself as the culprit in the story his emotional energy is transformed into feelings of guilt, remorse, and repentance. The transformative forces of our emotions empower us to put into practice certain moral projects triggered by the emotional judgment we have made.

A Logic of Emotional Intersubjectivity

Not only are emotions potent cognitive experiences, as I have just argued, they are also powerful intersubjective experiences that entail a paradoxical structure. I refer to emotions as intersubjective, first of all, because humans of vastly different cultures, religions, races, and genders can and do in fact share common emotional experiences, constituted by common emotional judgments, projects, and energy. And I refer to their logic as paradoxical because shared emotional experiences possess a power of satisfying at one and the same time the demand for objectively intelligible and universal truth and the demand for distinctively local and particular meaning. It is precisely this paradoxically intersubjective character of emotions that makes it possible for me to argue that compassion constitutes the normative criterion for interreligious conversation and cooperation. How so?

To begin with, emotional intersubjectivity is simply a way of conceptualizing what ordinary people feel daily, the experience of shared emotions, the experience of compassion. It implies that a person's or community's emotional experiences are not privileged but accessible to others. Robert Solomon recognizes the intersubjectivity of emotions when he insists that in emotional relations "we 'open ourselves' to others, allow ourselves to share their experiences and opinions, [even] their worldviews, and ultimately, their other emotions."[17] When we feel for and with friends who have lost jobs, with women who do not receive comparable pay for comparable work, or with parents who have lost a child to cancer, we share emotionally something of their experience, we feel in ourselves something of the feelings that they themselves feel. One does not have to read far in Christian scriptures to recognize that this capacity for emotional intersubjectivity constitutes the true beating heart of Christian faith and the normative criterion of its life. It is the heart of incarnation, of Jesus' ministry and morality, of death, resurrection, and redemption. Of the incarnation the writer of Hebrews says, for example, that Jesus feels in himself all the sorrow, fear, and anxiety of human life but without sinning (Hebrews chapters 2 and 4). Jesus sympathizes with the huge crowd gathered to hear him and feeds them; he pities the woman caught in adultery and forgives her; he feels the sorrow of Lazarus' family and weeps with and for them; in the garden and on the cross he feels in his own soul the dark fear, anguish, and despair felt by humans in their sinfulness, guilt, and alienation. Many of Jesus' parables likewise presuppose the capacity for shared emotions as the criterion whereby his followers should relate to others, especially those with whom they differ most radically. The story of the good Samaritan is the most famous of them because it draws such a compelling picture of the extent to which shared emotions, the extent to which compassion, can traverse differences of race, religion, and culture and establish community. Jesus' encounter with the woman at the well is, as we shall see, another.

But what is it that is shared in emotional intersubjectivity? What do humans share when they feel what others feel, when feeling compassion? I must note, first of all, that the idea of compassion does not refer to any single emotion or feeling; rather, by feeling compassion we experience a wide variety of emotions, such as care, fear, anger, mercy, guilt, joy, and so on. Compassion refers to the intersubjectivity of those emotional experiences, not to the emotions themselves, to the fact that they are shared, that one feels in himself something of the feelings of others. Second, what humans share is not something diffuse, mysterious, magical, and irrational but something specific and concrete. Put simply, when humans share an emotional experience they experience in common the judgment, project, and affectional energy constituting that emotion. Consider a child who has been sexually abused by a father. I, along with certain neighbors, make a common moral judgment that this abuse is tragically evil, and I feel intense loving care for the child and anger at the father for exploiting his child, who intuitively trusts him. Moreover, in feeling caringly toward the child and anger toward the father, I am inspired by those feelings to undertake a common project to heal the child and to discipline and restore the father. The emotional feelings, triggered by this common judgment, also supply sufficient energy and inspiration so that all concerned are empowered to undertake compassionate projects of healing. Such emotional intersubjectivity, of sharing emotions, suggests that emotions are not private, privileged experiences exclusive to the life of a particular individual or individual community. They are universal and universally accessible to peoples of diverse cultural traditions.[18] For the rest of the story is that the neighbors who feel the same loving care as I do for the child and anger toward the father belong to wildly different ethnic, cultural, and religious traditions. Hindus, Buddhists, Marxists, Jews, Christians, Muslims, and humanists together make the common emotional judgment, share those common feelings of concern and anger, and undertake common projects of healing. Of course, my claim that the intersubjectivity of emotional truth-judgments are universal and universally accessible does not intend to meet modernity's abstract criterion of objective universality. But it does acknowledge a truth about human experience, that people of diverse traditions have access to a common experience of compassion, to common emotional judgments, projects, and energy on the basis of which, as I shall show, interreligious conversation and cooperation are possible.

But to say that my feelings of love or fear are intersubjective is not to say that they are exactly the same as yours; for they will differ insofar as our narrative traditions, local communities, and biographies differ. How this is so presupposes that emotions are structured not only intersubjectively but paradoxically as well. By claiming that emotions are structured in a peculiarly paradoxical way I mean this: that although emotional experiences (their judgments, projects, and energy) may be universally shared by people of profoundly different cultural and religious communities, each community will express, justify, and sanction that common, universally accessible feeling in distinctive narrative ways, ways that are loaded with tribal particularity and local meaning.

Enlightenment objectivism presupposed that the rational activity of human mind is such that particular, specific beliefs must always be justified, if justified at all, in terms of increasingly abstract, objective, and universal principles. Emotional intersubjectivity, in contrast, inverts the objectivist strategy by presupposing paradoxically that the more general, universal, and universally accessible is explained, justified, and inspired by the increasingly local, particular, and tribal. Hence, to share more fully and faithfully in the common, universally accessible feelings of compassion, like fear, awe, mercy, just anger, love, and so on, a person must participate more fully and faithfully in the distinctive beliefs and practices of his local, tribal community. For it is in and through a community's nourishing, comforting arms, in and through its cultic practices and local stories that a person is inspired and empowered to venture beyond his or her backyard into the public square, beyond one's tribal community into the global community beyond familial intimacy into projects of public compassion. Indeed, it is in and through practicing its unique idiosyncrasies that a community of faith is inspired to share in emotional judgments and projects with peoples of all faiths or no faith who similarly are inspired by practicing the idiosyncratic practices of their own tribal communities. George Santayana recognized this paradoxical relation between the universal and particular. "Every living and healthy religion has a marked idiosyncrasy," he explains. "Its power consists in its special and surprising message and in the bias which that revelation gives to life." Santayana goes on to argue that it is precisely the power of a religion's marked idiosyncrasy, its special and surprising message, that paradoxically opens for it common, global, and universal possibilities. "The vistas [a religion's idiosyncrasies] open," he goes on to say, "and the mysteries it propounds are another world to live in,"[19] in our case the world of compassionate cooperation with peoples of different faiths. The particular idiosyncrasies of a religious tradition, Santayana seems to be rightly arguing, open access to what is more universal. Or inversely, as I have been arguing, the universal and universally accessible truths constituting emotion's judgments and projects are expressed, justified, and inspired by the local, tribal meanings embedded in the cultic practices of particular communities.

Take, for example, the movement against apartheid in South Africa. The combined effort and weight of a wide diversity of religious and secular communities contributed to its demise. And the intersubjectivity of compassion constituted the common human experience that inspired that effort and bore that weight. The intersubjectivity and universal accessibility of compassion's feelings (of anger toward oppression and loving concern for those suffering) established the possibility for widely different communities to align themselves against apartheid. Hindus, Muslims, Marxists, humanists, Christians, and Buddhists shared feelings of compassion. They shared in common an emotional truth-judgment, that the world as it is (apartheid) is unjust and oppressive; and they shared a common emotional project, to alter the world as it wrongfully is into the world as it ought to be, one of freedom and justice. But for each of these communities the universally shared feeling of compassion is not inspired by and justified in terms of increasingly abstract and universal principles of rationality. Rather for each tradition, public compassion, paradoxically, is inspired by and justified in terms of increasingly particular, tribal practices and local meanings. Marxists are inspired by the meaning of class struggle, Jews by Yahweh's deliverance of a chosen people from bondage, Christians by the liberating power of Jesus' Resurrection, and so on. And yet, at the same time, these local practices and distinctive meanings in no way forfeit but rather foster the practical possibility of universal and universally accessible feelings of compassion. Put similarly, compassion refers to a profoundly ironic experience to which Søren Kierkegaard sometimes refers.[20] On the one hand, says Kierkegaard, compassion does not concern itself with distinctions and yet, on the other hand, it does concern itself with distinctions. How, then, does compassion both not concern itself with distinctions and at the same time concern itself with distinctions? I now turn to answering these two questions.

Because compassion by its very nature involves shared emotional experience it traverses (not transcends) that which distinguishes and distances one person or community from another. By feeling in myself, like the Samaritan in Jesus' parable, what the other feels I overcome the difference that distances me from the other. Compassion possesses a power whereby peoples, who are otherwise profoundly different in their religious cultures, are able to participate in a common emotional experience, making mutual emotional judgments and undertaking mutual emotional projects. It possesses a quality whereby diverse peoples are empowered to become what Martha Nussbaum in *Cultivating Humanity* refers to as "world citizens." "Habits of empathy and conjecture conduce to a certain kind of citizenship and a certain form of community: one that cultivates a sympathetic responsiveness to another's needs, and understand the way circumstances shape those needs, while respecting separateness and privacy."[21] "The world citizen," in other words, "must develop sympathetic understanding of distant cultures and of ethnic, racial, and religious minorities within her own."[22] Compassionately entering into the experience of other communities traverses distance and difference and establishes a common global citizenship. But to disown the universal intersubjectivity of religious experience is to commit the fallacy of fideism and neglect interreligious cooperation as it is actually practiced by devotees of different traditions.

Jesus' encounter with the Samaritan woman at the well is illuminating in this regard. The differences between Jesus and the woman could hardly be more stark and striking. Both are members of communities between which ancient animosities and hostilities are legendary. Differences in race, religion, culture, gender, and social status together create a seemingly intractable abyss between them. The woman is surprised that Jesus, a Jew, asks her, a Samaritan, for a drink of water (John 4:9). And when they return from town Jesus' disciples marvel that he is talking to a woman (John 4:27). Jesus manages these differences of race, gender, class, and religion, not by dissolving or disowning them, not by yielding or surrendering to them, not by transcending or surmounting them, but by traversing them. Not by discovering common, universal beliefs but by compassionate love for the woman Jesus is able to bridge the distance created by their differences. Indeed, Jesus treats her with such tender acceptance and intimate vulnerability that despite the distance she is drawn into the comfort of the love he offers. His loving care establishes with the woman a relation of spiritual intimacy that makes them vulnerable to each other's joys and sorrows. The intimacy of conversation between Jesus and the Samaritan is really quite remarkable. Their openness to one another traverses their differences and draws them progressively into a relation of personal disclosure and emotional fellowship, but without dissolving these differences. When questioned about her relationships with men, the woman feels no need to defend herself. Instead, she is drawn by Jesus' accepting care into a relation of self-discovery and transformation.

In another sense, however, compassion does concern itself with distinctions, as Kierkegaard suggests, by affirming and loving difference between peoples. By conversing with a Samaritan and a woman Jesus breaks traditional law but in so doing accepts and affirms her in her racial and gender difference. But Jesus also affirms the woman in her religious difference, acknowledging and accepting that she worships in a place and way that differs from his own (John 4:20–22). And he does so without condemning or disowning her in her religious difference. Jesus recognizes that what distinguishes him from the woman most particularly, religious faith, is also what makes it possible for both of them to affirm and care for each other most profoundly. As argued already, so it is with Jesus and the Samaritan: that which inspires communities to practice compassion toward one another is precisely that which distinguishes them from the other, their own uniquely local religious beliefs and practices. Those communities that are truly and authentically compassionate toward others different from themselves will fairly acknowledge for those others what they insist on for themselves, namely, that their own distinctive religious beliefs and practices are indispensable for practicing compassion, for participating as world citizens in a global community. Accordingly, compassionate communities, insofar as they are compassionate, will not only affirm but love affirming the differences and distinctiveness of peoples of other faiths. As we shall see in the following section, this does not forfeit but rather fosters a compassionate basis for witness and conversion. But to disown the idiosyncrasies of a local religious tradition, to suppress differences and diversity is to commit the fallacy of rationalism and neglect religion as it is actually practiced by devotees.

Jesus and the Samaritan woman acknowledge and affirm their religious differences, mutually accepting the fact that the woman's community worships at Mount Gerizim and that Jesus' community worships at Jerusalem. Jesus moves this interreligious conversation about interreligious cooperation a step further, however. He places worship at Mount Gerizim and worship at Jerusalem on equal footing when he exclaims that the day is coming when devotees of these two different religious traditions will recognize that true worship of God is a matter of spirit and truth and not merely of sacred place and time (John 4:20–24). There will come a time, says Jesus, when Samaritans will not worship at Gerizim and Jews will not worship at Jerusalem. Yet that does not mean that true worship comes to a halt. For wherever its sacred place and time and however a community ritualizes that place and time, authentic worship is a matter of spirit and truth.

Loving compassion is the most fundamental dimension by which any community worships God in spirit and truth. For not only does it protect, preserve, and promote worship in distinctly local sacred places, it also constitutes an experience whose very spirit and truth is necessarily and universally intersubjective, an experience requiring distinct communities to share, in the midst of difference, an experience of such spiritual depth and profound truth that they are able to traverse those differences while embracing them. Jesus does not mean that devotees should forsake worship at Gerizim or Jerusalem. He himself continues to worship in Jerusalem and in synagogue, and he does not ask the woman to forsake her worship in the temple at Gerizim. But he is insisting that worshipping at Gerizim or Jerusalem does not empower and transform a community of faith, but that worshipping God in spirit and truth empowers and transforms Gerizim and Jerusalem into authentic sacred space and time.

What, then, can we infer from the fact that compassion, as shared emotional experience, both does and does not concern itself with religious difference and diversity? By now the answer to this question should be clear. What it means is that each religious community will intentionally devote itself single-mindedly to its distinct and particular religious tradition, preserving and appreciating its difference from other traditions, and at the same time mutually promoting and participating in projects of loving care. Compassionate religious communities will not try to invent generic beliefs and practices to which all traditions should subscribe, thereby demolishing fences between backyards. Nor will they settle for affirming each other from afar, befriending each other only as neighbors over the backyard fence, as Knitter puts it. Instead, with compassion as normative, each religion will accept that its practice of compassion is by its very nature intersubjective, common and public, not private and privileged. Each will cooperatively practice what each religion worth preserving preaches, namely, compassion. In so doing the religions of the world will find themselves collaborating in public projects that protect, preserve, and promote the dignity of human life and God's creation. Even further, not only is compassion not the private privilege of a single religious tradition, it is not even unique or exclusive to religious experience.

The parable of the good Samaritan, as William Prior notes, is "not exclusively or even primarily a religious story: the representatives of organized religion are not cast in a favorable light, the hero is a member of a nation of religious outcasts, and he does not justify his actions by appeal to religious principles," although the storyteller does. Compassion is an intersubjective moral experience "shared by . . . people of many religious and cultural backgrounds, including those who profess no religious faith at all."[23] From the grassroots of a local neighborhood to national and international policies and programs, from religious to nonreligious, each tradition individually and all collectively have every reason to function as a moral vanguard, leading peoples and nations of the world in projects of compassion, projects that promote human dignity, peace, justice, freedom, and hope.

In this way, then, the paradoxical nature of emotional intersubjectivity (concerning and not concerning itself with distinctions) establishes the basis on which interreligious conversation and cooperation is possible. Communities who faithfully practice their faith in all its fertile and furious particularity can very well leave their yards without leaving them behind, and participate publicly with peoples of other faiths in the perpetual work of compassion.

Compassion as Normative

From the paradoxical logic of emotional intersubjectivity examined above we can infer that compassion is both a universal, normative criterion whereby interreligious conversation and cooperation is possible as well as a criterion whereby we can judge whether our own and other religious traditions are spiritually and morally compelling. What, then, do I mean when I say that compassion is universal, and what do I mean when I say it is normative?

How is compassion universal? In what sense is it universal to all humans of every religious and nonreligious tradition? Compassion is universal in at least two senses, objectively and subjectively. Compassion is objectively universal in that it is a capacity common to all humans, a characteristic of the divine image, as Christian theologians might say, in which humans are created. Just as reasoning is a capacity common to all humans, so also is the capacity for feeling compassion, the human capacity for mutually sharing emotional experiences, of weeping with those who weep and rejoicing with those who rejoice. Along with qualities such as reason and free will, compassion is uniquely human and partly distinguishes humans from other creatures. In the seventeenth and eighteenth centuries, notes Norman Fiering, "the idea of irresistible compassion became a psychological drama, and more than ever a touchstone not only of true civility but of human status itself."[24] Compassion as a "touchstone . . . of human status itself" is what I mean by compassion as an objectively universal capacity. Such thinkers as Malebranche, Hutcheson, Smith, and Hume insisted that compassion is a natural and irrepressible human capacity, a passion in which even reason is rooted and a passion by which public life should be guided. Today we might find doubtful many of the details ascribed to compassion by these philosophers; but their claim for compassion as a universal touchstone of being human is, I think, compelling. It follows that compassion is likewise subjectively universal insofar as the actual experience of compassion is commonly available and accessible to all humans if they so choose. I would dispute, in other words, the assumption of many eighteenth-century thinkers that as a natural passion compassion is an inevitable human reaction to suffering. Rather, the actual experience of compassion is volitional, a subjective, voluntary choice all humans very well can and may make if they choose. In short, compassion is subjectively universal in that the practice of it is freely accessible to all humans. Regrettably, many twentieth-century ethicists, unlike their eighteenth-century predecessors, have largely abandoned the sentiment of compassion; and what has resulted, says William Prior, is a "distorted picture of our moral lives."[25] By retrieving compassion as a choice all communities of faith can and should make, each local faith community is enabled to live morally as global citizens. By so living compassionately toward the universal other, all peoples are thereby invited to partake of the grace of living compassionately.

My claim, however, is not only that compassion is objectively and subjectively universal but that it is somehow normative as well. How so? In what sense does compassion function as a normative criterion for peoples of all traditions? How does it help us decide what faith traditions collectively ought to do? We can answer these questions, I think, by directing remarks to three matters: discerning the occasion for compassion, practicing the "ought" of compassion, and fulfilling the aim of compassion, all three of which must be present for an occasion to warrant compassionate response.

First, on what bases can we properly discern occasions for acting compassionately? At least three conditions are relevant to answering this question—the presence of suffering, the relative centrality of the suffering, and the involuntary nature of the suffering. Lawrence Blum argues that the proper occasion for compassion is restricted to persons "in a negative condition, suffering some harm, difficulty, danger. . . ."[26] This is the most obvious condition properly eliciting compassionate response, that someone is suffering some kind of pain—whether physical, psychological, social, or spiritual. The Samaritan woman that Jesus encounters surely suffers, whether self-consciously or not, the effects of class and gender discrimination and therefore suffers pain. Likewise the Jew in Jesus' parable of the Good Samaritan, assaulted on the road to Jericho and left for dead, suffers. Second, Blum suggests that suffering must be a condition that is "relatively central to a person's life and well-being, describable as pain, misery, hardship, suffering, affliction, and the like."[27] A wealthy person whose investments are greatly diminished by stock market losses or whose coastal cottage is destroyed in a storm perhaps suffers the pain of severe loss. But his loss is not such as to be considered central and crucial to his survival and well-being, and therefore not an occasion for interreligious projects of compassion. The suffering a laborer experiences upon losing his job, however, is central to his well-being, as is the social and existential suffering of the Samaritan woman and the physical harm endured by the man injured on the Jericho road. Finally, the suffering of the other must be involuntary; it must result from conditions for which one is not directly responsible and from which he neither possesses the power nor the means to extract himself. Victims of natural or military disasters, of abuse or gang violence, of political or economic exploitation suffer involuntarily and are properly occasions of interreligious compassion. Both the Samaritan woman and the injured man suffer involuntarily at the hands of forces outside of their control and thus warrant compassionate response. This requirement, that suffering be involuntary, acknowledges that some people or communities, for whatever religious or ideological reasons, willingly place themselves in or invite conditions of suffering. Christians and Christian communities not infrequently invite voluntary, sacrificial suffering in order to redeem and reconcile. In such cases, they are to be respected and admired and even emulated; but their suffering is not properly an occasion for compassionate interreligious action.

No doubt disagreement amongst the world religions may sometimes arise regarding whether an occasion warrants compassion. Female circumcision is perhaps a case in point. Certainly women on whom circumcision is involuntarily practiced are legitimate subjects of compassion. But what of women, families, and communities who voluntarily subscribe to this practice? Then, traditions, for whom it is an occasion for compassionate action, must both acknowledge that fact and attempt, through the hard work of persuasion, to influence (what they consider to be) the offending tradition to alter its practice. Capitalism is another case in point. Religious traditions, internally and externally, are divided as to whether capitalism is a condition causing much suffering throughout the world. And yet, they are often unanimous in believing that the suffering caused by poverty is an occasion for responding compassionately. In addition, each religion can also undertake the difficult task of persuading others of their judgment, that capitalism as a system is itself a causal condition of poverty in the world, and invite others to participate in efforts to alleviate this systemic causal condition.

Second, how is it that the experience of compassion guides us in determining what we ought to do? What is normative about it? At least three criteria are relevant to addressing this question—love your neighbor as yourself, do unto others as you would that they do to you, and alleviate suffering, all of which are rooted in the emotional intersubjectivity of compassion. As an experience of intersubjectivity, compassion establishes between the self and suffering other a profound mutuality of shared feelings and emotions, a relationship which is encapsulated in the second commandment. Although the word "compassion" does not refer to any particular emotion but to the intersubjectivity or mutuality of emotions, the experience of compassion always entails the particularity, concreteness, and affectional energy constituting specific emotions. That compassion inspires us to love others in the same way that we love ourselves is to say that we should first feel for others the same care and concern that we would feel for ourselves or wish others to feel for us were we suffering as they are.[28] The human capacity to imagine in ourselves what it must feel like to suffer what others are experiencing is itself a prerequisite for discerning and practicing the "ought" implicit in love's compassion. Only if I am willing to open myself to the risks and vulnerabilities of the suffering other, as Jesus habitually did, only if I am willing to feel in myself what they must be feeling, will I know what it is that I ought to do for and with them. In his loving compassion for the Samaritan woman, surely Jesus imagined and felt in himself what it would be like to be a social and religious outcaste, feeling in himself the alienation and loneliness, thirst for acceptance and reconciliation, that the woman must have felt. Such experience of shared emotions is not, then, incidental or parenthetical to compassion's normative function. Rather, it is central and vital, for, as argued already, constituting any emotional experience are cognitive judgments and projects on the basis of which normative cooperation amongst religious traditions is possible.

By loving my neighbor as I myself would want to be loved, I am in an important way establishing in each occasion for compassion the norm by which I and others ought to act. What moral norm will emerge from my love of neighbor as myself may differ from the norm that emerges from your love of neighbor as yourself; but those norms will have in common one thing: they will produce compassionate moral projects, will manifest and entail criteria two (centrality) and three (involuntariness). For not only does compassion entail the emotional engagement of intersubjectivity but also specific emotional judgments and projects manifest in the golden rule, *Do unto others as you would that they do unto you*. This rule presupposes already the mutuality of shared emotions entailed by the second commandment. But, in addition, it makes explicit what is often only implicit in moral emotions, namely, the moral judgment that triggers the emotion and the moral project implied by that judgment. The normative moral judgment and project I should undertake emerges from feeling in myself the pain and anguish that the suffering other feels. Genuine feelings of compassion presuppose a judgment that I make, that the other, for example, suffers unjustly and involuntarily.

The emotional project implied by that moral judgment must then address and correlate with my judgment that the other suffers an injustice. What is it that I would wish others to do for me if I were feeling in my suffering such as this other is feeling? Accordingly, I ought to do to and for the other what I would want done to and for me if I were the suffering other. The moral project I ought to undertake is one which addresses directly the feelings of anger and sadness generated by the judgment that the other suffers unjustly. Jesus in his compassion for the Samaritan woman feels in himself her passion for something that will quench forever her profound spiritual thirst; and so he offers her living water. The Good Samaritan, having compassion on the injured man, judging him to be a victim of random violence, feels for him in his physical pain and undertakes a normative moral project of tender care that meets not only the man's immediate but also his future physical and medical needs. Note that the project of compassion the Samaritan takes toward the Jew is one that persons of any other or no religious tradition might justify and justifiably undertake.

But what is it specifically that compassion as normative compels us to do? What is its aim? What is a compassionate community morally obligated to do? What emotional project should it undertake? What is it that I would want others to do for me in my suffering? The answer is, in a phrase, to alleviate suffering. To the greatest extent possible, compassionate communities ought to commit themselves to alleviating as far as possible the pain and hurt of the suffering other. For the Samaritan woman's existential and spiritual pain Jesus offers "living water" with which she will never thirst again. For her social exile his love effects conversion and social reenfranchisement. For the man's physical injuries the Good Samaritan offers ongoing physical and medical assistance. In both cases compassion obligates the compassionate to undertake normative projects whose ultimate purpose is to alleviate the pain and hurt suffered. But discerning exactly when pain and suffering are alleviated is a complicated matter. The immediate pain and hurt one suffers, for example, may very well be alleviated while the conditions producing them remain. Accordingly, any compassionate project will address and alleviate not merely the symptoms but the causal conditions of suffering. Ultimately, not only the marginalized Samaritan woman but the social conditions causing her marginalization, not only the injured man's physical wounds but the social conditions causing assault and theft, must be addressed by genuinely compassionate religious communities.

And exactly how should suffering be alleviated? Surely there is no single and exclusive compassionate way suffering may be addressed. Any number of projects may alleviate suffering; indeed, the conditions and complexities causing suffering may be such that a variety of compassionate projects are required. In any case, faith communities, for whom compassion is a compelling value, can and should cooperate in making compassionate judgments and undertaking compassionate projects which aim at alleviating the symptoms and conditions of suffering. The one stipulation guiding such projects is that in alleviating suffering they should protect, preserve, and promote the dignity of humans, they should enhance rather than diminish, as Martin Luther King Jr. says, the integrity of the person.[29]

All traditions, both religious and secular, worth preserving, then, are those for whom compassion is a normative spiritual and moral value. Indeed, all the world's major religions do in fact treat compassion as normative, central, and vital to moral life. So claims one, the Dalai Lama, who in his study and travels has interacted with each and all of them. "The world's major religious traditions," he concludes, "each give the development of compassion a key role. . . . But even without a religious perspective, love and compassion are clearly of fundamental importance to us all. . . . [W]e need to take others' feelings into consideration, the basis of which is our innate capacity for empathy."[30] Of course, this does not mean that these traditions have always conducted themselves compassionately, and yet they all lay claim to compassion as a supreme and enduring normative value, as one not only to prize but to practice.

Suppose, then, that the world religions practiced compassion as normative for conversation and cooperation. What would result? What conditions between them can we expect to follow? First, no one single, generic justification for compassionate cooperation will be sought among the traditions, but a multiplicity of justifications will be embraced. Each religion, as noted already, will justify its practice of compassion in terms of the particularity of its own local narrative tradition. There will be no need for comparative religionists to try to construct a single, universal generic theology of world religions or for devotees of each religion to subscribe to such a theology. Even though there is an important place and role for comparative religions, it will be important that in practicing compassion cooperatively no such singularity of justification be sought or sanctioned, but that a multiplicity of justifications be encouraged and embraced. For, paradoxically, it is only in accepting and affirming local difference that the distance between religions can be compassionately traversed. Gratefully, then, there will and should be as many justifications for acting compassionately as there are traditions willing to so act, as indeed there were amongst the many world religions that cooperated in bringing to an end apartheid in South Africa. Second, in acting cooperatively, religions will aim not at uniformity but at harmony. To any occasion that warrants it, there may very well be a wide variety of compassionate responses. Indeed, some occasions may be better treated by a diversity of compassionate responses than by any single one. Moreover, certain kinds of compassionate responses may be more conducive to the priorities, principles, and preferences of some traditions and not so to others. For example, there may not be consensus among world religions as to how to address global poverty. But that should not preclude them working harmoniously in diverse ways to address the problem. There need not be a uniformity and consensus on how to act compassionately, only a mutually respectful support of all efforts to do so. This does not mean, however, that on significant and perhaps frequent occasions (e.g., apartheid, famine, war, poverty) the world religions will not find themselves acting largely in concert to treat suffering humanity. Third, the aim of cooperative compassion is not religious colonialism or globalization but voluntary reconciliation. Undeniably, the world's religions have often promoted and participated in the imperialistic endeavors of nations and in so doing forfeited the practice of loving compassion without which ironically they otherwise would not exist. Compassion by its very nature as a voluntary moral judgment precludes such colonialism; it affirms and accepts people in their difference and works to preserve them in their difference while at the same time compassionately traversing the distance created by difference. The aim of cooperative compassion among the world's religions, rather, is reconciliation and renewal, between oppressed and oppressor, between those who suffer and those who cause their suffering. Perhaps the most recent, notable example is the work of the Truth and Reconciliation Commission in South Africa, whose members represented a variety of religious traditions and who nevertheless jointly aimed at healing the deep wounds, scars, and conditions of apartheid.

Compassion as Transformative

But of course Jesus has more to say to the Samaritan woman. He also says to her what to our postmodern ears screeches like fingernails across chalkboard. "You worship what you do not know; we worship what we know, for salvation is from the Jews" (John 4:22). How might we interpret this saying? Or, how might it interpret us? Conscious of speaking to a Samaritan, Jesus is well aware that Samaritan religion includes belief in an expected messiah. Thus, Jesus might be interpreted as simply reminding the woman what she perhaps already believes, namely, that from the Jews would come the Messiah and the hope of salvation. But loaded into Jesus' declaration is something more profoundly problematic. He is presupposing a normative criterion whereby religious traditions might be evaluated and converts solicited. And it is this that our postmodern, marginally religious ears flinch upon hearing. Moreover, when addressing this issue from within the Christian tradition, as I am doing, one encounters a seemingly inexorable obstacle, namely, Constantinian Christianity and the triumphalism implicit in it. Since the fourth and fifth centuries, Christian triumphalism has thoroughly subdued and monopolized the tradition, so much so that it is difficult for devotees to find a foothold independent of triumphalism while remaining within the tradition. It is sometimes difficult to see how to interpret Christian scriptures, for example, in a way that does not simply assume a triumphalist perspective. But that is what I try to do here, to interpret scriptures in a nontriumphalist way that is anchored in the moral supersymmetry of compassion and mercy. Even passages that seem impervious to any but a triumphalist reading, such as John 4:22 or "no one comes to the Father but by me" (John 14: 6), lend themselves to alternative interpretations by presupposing the supersymmetry of grace, compassion, and mercy.

What, then, is the criterion Jesus presupposes in his encounter with the Samaritan woman? Does Jesus' witness emerge from a keen sense of human rights, including the right to proselytize? As a foreigner in Samaria, does Jesus feel the clash of human rights, identified by John Witte Jr. in the preface to the book *Sharing the Book*: namely, "the foreign religion's free exercise right to share and expand its faith versus the indigenous religion's liberty of conscience right to be left alone on its own territory"?[31] Or does Jesus seem to presuppose something of the spirit of S. Mark Heim's approach in which it makes sense, he says, "to speak of salvation in the plural," a multiplicity of salvations, each religion with its own unique aim and with practices suited to fulfil its aim?[32] Or does Jesus' witness both affirm difference while offering a normative criterion for critique and conversion? If we look carefully, John's narrative itself provides a clue and an answer. For devotees of any religion to worship in spirit and in truth, they must (Jesus is both practicing and preaching) live compassionately, thereby transforming enemies into neighbors. Loving compassion constitutes the essence of Jesus' witness and the basis on which he can claim any right to witness on foreign soil. As Jesus acts compassionately toward the Samaritan woman, his enemy, so all who witness must live compassionately toward enemies, toward difference. Indeed, practicing compassion is the *conditio sine qua non* of true witness, of critique and conversion. As God acts with loving compassion toward humans and as prophets of all religious traditions in turn act compassionately toward humans, so transformation in any tradition consists of acting compassionately toward neighbor and enemy. Jesus is only repeating verbally what he has already practiced with the Samaritan woman: that salvation lies in the strength of grace required to love enemies with the same merciful compassion with which God loves humans. It is Jesus' compassion toward her that redeems the Samaritan and sends her enthusiastically to her neighborhood as witness. It is precisely this extraordinary gift of loving compassion, embodied and practiced by Jesus, that constitutes salvation. And it is the saving power of loving compassion that, for Jesus as a Jew, is from the Jews but nevertheless not restricted to the Jews. This practice of loving compassion, in short, is the normative criterion whereby religious traditions might be critically evaluated and whereby a person might convert or be converted from one tradition to another.

Compassion as Critique

Any faith community whose life is authentic and whose love is reliable is one whose voice is not only pastoral but prophetic, not only affirmative but evaluative. So devotees in each religious tradition bear the prophetic burden of critical self-evaluation; and the criterion that seems most compelling for doing so is the practice of loving compassion. Jesus is keenly aware that his first responsibility as prophet and preacher is to his own faith community and to his disciples. He excoriates religious and political leaders of his community for their hypocrisy and for lack of humility and compassion toward the marginalized of society (e.g., poor, prostitutes, and publicans). And he criticizes his own disciples for grasping after power and prestige and for neglecting the disenfranchised, like children and lepers. As Christian, then, I am obligated, first and foremost, to stand prophetically in relation to my own community, employing loving compassion as the measure of all things. Sadly and very often I find my own faith and the faith of my community terribly and tragically wanting in compassion, even toward members of our own community. From petty factions in local churches to the horrors of the Inquisition, from Christian racism in the United States to sectarian violence in Ireland, Christians often fail to live up to their name and claim to be followers of Christ. With loving compassion as guide, Christians must assume responsibility for speaking and living prophetically to and in their own community.

But compassion is normative not only for critical self-evaluation but also for critical evaluation of all faith traditions. It is the only normative, comparative criterion available, it seems to me, whereby to fairly evaluate faith communities other than my own, for a couple of reasons. First, because, as argued above, compassion is the only experience universally accessible to and shared among peoples of all religions; second, because it is the only criterion in terms of which I believe my own tradition can fairly and legitimately be evaluated by those of different faiths. When those of other faiths evaluate my tradition, as they properly should, I would want them to do so in terms of compassion. Indeed, this is the criterion by which Jesus evaluates those of other religious traditions, like the Samaritans. He praises the Samaritan who out of compassion helps the Jewish traveler assaulted on his way to Jericho (Luke 11). For his faith and loving concern for his paralyzed servant, Jesus praises the Roman centurion. Similarly, the Apostle Paul's norm for addressing and evaluating Greek religious tradition is God's love and compassion for all peoples. At Athens he comments on statues dedicated to the many gods of ancient mythology, even a statue to an unknown god (Acts 17). But his primary concern is not that they believe in many gods, although as a Jewish Christian he would certainly take issue with Greek polytheism. Instead, his concern is to preach God's compassion, a criterion universal to human experience. Paul himself not only demonstrates compassion toward the

Greeks by bringing gospel to them, but he does so also by telling them a gospel story in which God's compassion is available to them through the incarnation, death, and resurrection of Jesus (Acts 17). What authentic religious tradition would not claim that its way of transformation is voluntarily available to all and that loving compassion is the heart of that transformation?

With compassion as normative, then, the religions of the world mutually possess a fair criterion for intra- and interreligious evaluation. Jews have every right and even obligation to criticize Christians for their magnificent failures toward Jews throughout history, especially during the Holocaust. The norm for doing so is not whether Christians believe properly, whether their belief in the Trinity or the Incarnation, for example, makes sense. With compassion as norm, Jews have a right and an obligation to criticize the Christian community because its belief in the Trinity and Incarnation failed to inspire in them loving compassion toward Jews. We can imagine an indefinite variety of occasions when between faith communities compassion fairly can and should function as normative for critical evaluation and constructive redemption. Critical questions like, To what extent does my or other religious traditions encourage and practice compassionate world citizenship?, then, provide a common, universal criterion for assessing and evaluating religious traditions and a standard for transforming and reforming traditions. Compassion establishes a normative moral criterion for judging and condemning traditions, like Nazism or Stalinism, for example, or common practices within traditions, like racism in Christianity or classism in Hinduism.

Compassion as Conversion

By now it is clear, I should think, what inferences we can draw regarding religious witness and conversion. A legitimate place and role for witness and conversion is purchased by compassion's intersubjectivity. Compassion functions not only as occasion for cooperation and not only as a criterion for critical evaluation but also as normative ground on which witness and conversion can and should take place. In order to show this, however, it is perhaps helpful to distinguish "conversion" from "proselytizing." To proselytize, as Martin Marty suggests, is a process in which a person, a proselytizer, "induces someone [a proselytizee] to convert" from the place where he is to the place where the proselytizer is.[33] Such change of place can be induced by persuasion or even sometimes by coercion, by threats and intimidation. Since the activity of proselytizing is often identified with a kind of dogmatic imperialism or "religious balkanization,"[34] I prefer to distinguish it from "conversion." In religious balkanization, proselytizing devotees of one religion, on presumption of superiority, try to pressure, persuade, or coerce (socially, religiously, politically, or militarily) devotees of other or no religions to "change places." I find the word "proselytizing" at minimum inadequate and at maximum repulsive. It undermines the legitimate role of witness and conversion among religions. I employ "conversion," in contrast, to refer to a valid and viable, albeit not inevitable, consequence of religious communities that practice toward those of other traditions projects of loving compassion. The witness of loving compassion, in other words, is a fair and compelling basis for a person of any or no tradition to voluntarily "change places" if for that person converting is perceived as beneficial. Jesus' encounter with the Samaritan woman is again a case in point. The witness that Jesus embodies and the offer of salvation that he delivers is distinguishable from repugnant proselytizing and balkanization. First of all, Jesus does not try to induce and recruit the woman to join his Jewish faith community, as would the proselytizer. Nor does he surreptitiously bring with him an economic-political agenda for which his religion is a front and foil. Indeed, Jesus revokes and nullifies both proselytizing and balkanization, in two ways. One, simply by declaring that true worship of God requires neither Mount Gerizim nor Jerusalem but requires a heart situated rightly in relation to God and others. This does not mean that Jesus thinks one can worship God independently of a local community of faithful people but only that worship, whether at Gerizim or Jerusalem, is authentic only when done in spirit and in truth. And it is precisely that spirit and truth, second, which is the basis for Jesus' witness and the woman's conversion. Loving compassion, as already noted, is the crux of Jesus' witness and it is that compassion, embodied in the actions and words of Jesus, which draws her into a spiritual intimacy with him and God that is nothing short of remarkable.

Likewise today, witness and conversion should be in spirit and in truth, in the spirit of love and in the truth of God's compassion for humankind. Accordingly, if the persistent racism of Christianity in America is problematic for young African-American men, for example, and if black Muslims show loving compassion, meeting needs for self-esteem and acceptance, then that surely is a legitimate basis for witness and conversion. Or if a Hindu woman of low caste feels emancipated spiritually, socially, and politically by Buddhism then that is a legitimate basis for witness and conversion. What tyrant has authority to say that I must remain in the suffocating prison of a tradition that no longer satisfies? What tyrant can decree that I should not be helped by those of other traditions whose compassion heals the hurt and hunger in my soul? In short, a religion's compassionate witness is the common interreligious norm for conversion. No religious tradition should compel devotees of other traditions to convert, nor should traditions prohibit one of its own who voluntarily chooses to "change places." Compassion is, then, in a sense, its own justification for witness and conversion; as a supersymmetrical experience, it is an antidote to Christian triumphalism. By its very nature it precludes the imperialism of proselytizing and globalization. By the act of loving the other as one loves oneself, a person witnesses to God's love, which love by its very passion and power invites and draws others to a feast in which all will be satisfied and never thirst again.

Compassion as Practical Truth

What, finally, are the implications of this thesis (of compassion as normative basis for interreligious cooperation) for addressing the question of truth and world religions? What is the relative truth of religious traditions? And how does compassion stand in relation to a tradition's truth or falsity? A religion might be said to be true or false in a number of ways, four of which I discuss here. We might evaluate it regarding its claim to historical/scientific truth, to metaphysical truth, to existential truth, and to practical truth. I treat the first three of these only briefly in order to address the latter more completely. In doing so, we will find that, in the first three cases, a religious tradition's truth is situated in a way more or less symmetrically or equally with truth in other traditions, and yet also in a way asymmetrically. In the case of practical truth the matter is more complex; for the truth of a tradition depends on praxis, on living compassionately.

For a religion to be true or false historically/scientifically it must be shown to be objectively true; its truth-claims must be justified objectively. Customarily there are at least two ways of doing so. A claim might be justified empirically, according to the extent to which it corresponds to our sensory experience of the world. Or a claim might be justified logically, according to whether it coheres with other true ideas and all the rules of correct thinking. Thus, can a tradition's claims to historic and scientific truth be decided in terms of these two objective criteria, correspondence and coherence? Based on objective evidence, for example, a case can be made for the historicity of lives and teachings of persons such as Confucius, Moses, Siddhartha Gautama, Jesus, or Muhammad. And what results from such a comparative analysis, it seems to me, is that world religions are situated more or less equally in relation to claims to historical/scientific truth, each tradition properly claiming for itself certain beliefs that are shown to be historically and scientifically sound. But, of course, the truth of religions cannot fairly be reduced simply to historical/scientific claims. Religious traditions likewise make metaphysical truth-claims (whether the law Moses received is from God, or whether Siddhartha Gautama is the Buddha or Jesus the Son of God) and can be examined accordingly. These truth-claims are not simply historical/scientific; they are properly examined, as I argued in chapter 3, in terms of retrospective reason and the cumulative case that can be made for them, in terms of the coherence of the total world-version to which they give rise. *Credo ut intelligam*, insists St. Augustine; the beliefs of faith imply a world-version in terms of which those beliefs are justified, and it is to the persuasive power of this comprehensive world-view that the claim to metaphysical truth must appeal. Here, too, the world's religions are situated, it seems to me, more or less equally in relation to their cumulative and metaphysical truth-claims. In addition to historical/scientific and metaphysical truth, religions also claim for themselves existential truth. For something to be true existentially it must be shown to be true subjectively and its claims justified subjectively. By subjective truth I do not mean subjectivism or relativism. Indeed, I mean quite the opposite, along the lines of what Kierkegaard (the modern founder of the phrase "subjective truth") means when he claims that subjective truth is absolute, truth to which a person situates herself or himself absolutely, with unswerving commitment and single-minded conviction. Subjective truth, therefore, refers to that truth within which a person lives inwardly with infinite passion and devotion, a truth which endows a person's, a community's, life with ultimate meaning and absolute conviction. Indeed, what religious traditions wish to lay claim to perhaps more adamantly than all else is their capacity for existential truth, for truth that endows human existence with meaning, truth to which devotees commit their lives absolutely. Here again religions are situated equally in relation to existential truth-claims; all traditions claim, and devotees substantiate, that their religion provides them with existential truth and meaning.

If scholars were to compare and contrast religious traditions in terms of their historical, metaphysical, and existential truth claims, what likely would result? Could they thereby decide which religion(s) is(are) true or comparatively more true than others? Could they determine whether there is one true religion, independent of devotees simply and passionately asserting theirs to be so? We must, I think, answer these questions in two ways, one of which suggests a symmetry between religions, and the other of which suggests an asymmetry between them. First, we can conclude that in relation to historical, metaphysical, and existential truth-claims, religions are situated more or less symmetrically. The extent to which these three kinds of truth-claims are justifiable in each tradition is more or less equal and equally compelling. So, it makes sense to say, with S. Mark Heim, that not only is there a multiplicity of salvations, each with its own aim and way, but there is a multiplicity of religious truths presupposed by those ways, each as equally true as the others.[35] Hence religions stand in equal and symmetrical relation to each other. Now, to deny and disown this symmetrical relation among world religions and to assert the superiority of one's own tradition's historical, metaphysical, and existential truth-claims is to commit a form of the fallacy of fideism, a kind of dogmatic imperialism. It is dogmatic in that it uncritically and prejudicially asserts as absolute its own truth-claims and, in opposition to the diverse claims of other traditions, condemns them as false. It is imperialistic because, in privileging its own truth claims as alone absolutely true, it implicitly if not explicitly subjugates all other religious traditions to its claims of absolute truth.

And yet neither do I think we should conclude that there is only and simply equal symmetry among the world's religions, a kind of benign relativism. To conclude this and nothing more is also to distort reality and disown a significant asymmetrical dimension of religious experience. For most devotees believe, from within their respective traditions, that their tradition's claim to truth, in all the ways identified above, is somehow, at least for them, more compelling and satisfying than other traditions. The reason for this may be simple familiarity. Or devotees may be able to give more sophisticated and compelling reasons why they are Baha'i or Taoist and not Christian or Muslim. Devotees do not treat, if only by default, the beliefs and rituals and practices of all religious traditions as if they are equal and equally compelling for them personally. A Baha'i is Baha'i because of that tradition's intentional dedication to unifying all religious traditions, and this belief for him trumps other religious traditions, so much so that he would not be happy and at home in other traditions. And so the typical devotee will stand in an asymmetrical relation to the truth of all other religious traditions. As devotee, she will be persuaded that her tradition, more than any of the others, is better able to satisfy her moral and spiritual hunger. This is not to say that devotees do not acknowledge the truth and wisdom and value of other traditions. Most do. But it is to suggest that the preference implicit in her devotion to her own tradition implies a judgment that, at least for her, her tradition is, if it may be put this way, more true and meaningful. This is generally so for devotees of every religion. Devotees typically find their tradition's truth and meaning more suitable for them and thereby inevitably situate themselves in asymmetrical relation to other faith traditions, even if that relation is in good faith. To deny this asymmetrical relation and to assert no more than a simple and equal symmetry among religions is to disown the experience and reality of most devotees; it is to default to a kind of benign, uncritical relativism.

Is that, then, what we must settle for, either dogmatic imperialism or benign relativism? I think not. What is most vitally significant when evaluating the comparative truth of religious traditions is not simply how far they are true historically, metaphysically, and existentially but how far they are true practically, how far they inspire devotees to actually put into practice what they claim is true. My premise is this: for devotees of religions to fairly and persuasively lay claim to the truth of their tradition in relation to others, that claim must be repeatedly and continuously justified not simply scientifically, metaphysically, or existentially but practically. Their truth-claims are justified, if justified at all, not simply or primarily in theory but in practice. The unique dimension and responsibility of religious/moral communities, and that which distinguishes their claims to truth from other communities (e.g., political, social, academic), is that their claims to truth are justified in practice. And it is precisely this feature, practical justification, whereby the relative tension between religions is superceded and a kind of supersymmetrical harmony among religions made possible. Practical truth, in short, is the ultimate, climactic way of overcoming the stalemate between dogmatic imperialism on the one hand and benign relativism on the other. How so?

A unique characteristic of practical truth that distinguishes it from other truths is that it is self-referential, self-justifying, and self-authenticating. By this I mean that practicing compassion is its own justification, in the way that Martha Nussbaum, for example, argues for the "cataleptic" self-certifying character of emotions,[36] and that Patricia Greenspan argues for "emotional justification" as self-referential.[37] In the Christian tradition, theologians typically treat self-justifying experiences, such as compassion, as a species of *argumentum spiritus sancti*, the inward presence of the Holy Spirit manifesting itself. Proof of the presence of the Holy Spirit lies in the practice of a life of holiness, a life of loving compassion. Kierkegaard puts it provocatively. The law of truth is this: "If the proclamation is true, it must produce what it proclaims."[38] The proof of the truth of a religion, in other words, is its practice. The extent to which it is practiced is the extent to which its teachings can be said to be justifiable and justifiably true. If a religion's teachings are found to be discontinuous with human practice or if they tend not to inspire humans to practice them, then that tradition's truth and reliability is rightfully cast in doubt. This does not mean that a religion's devotees must be perfect but that in their imperfection they acknowledge their distance from their religion's teaching, make restitution for failures, and reconcile with their tradition by practicing it. Thus, Christians demonstrate the truth of their tradition to the extent that the Holy Spirit inspires them to practice loving compassion toward neighbor and enemy. Traditions justify themselves religiously, prove themselves true and false, insofar as they produce the loving compassion they proclaim. If they are not thusly productive, then the truth they claim for themselves cannot be considered compelling, should not be considered true.

That seems to be what Jesus especially practiced and taught. In response to those who questioned the authority with which Jesus taught, Kierkegaard explains that "Christ had only one proof, 'If you do my father's will, he shall know whether the teaching is from God or whether I am speaking on my own authority.'"[39] The will of the Father, of course, is love of God, self, and others. Proof of the truth of religious belief that is of spiritual significance, accordingly, lies not merely in discursive reason, not only in heightened insight into the rationality of one's belief, not in how literally or metaphorically one interprets sacred text and tradition, but in the actual practice of loving compassion. Proof of religious faith, in other words, is not primarily a function of theory or of correct belief, for "even the demons believe and shudder" (James 2:19). It is rather a function of how one lives.[40] It is not by intoning "Lord, Lord," that faith is authenticated, says Jesus, but by practicing compassion, by feeding the hungry and liberating the oppressed (Matthew 7:21–23; 25:31–46). The conversion of the Samaritan woman and her neighbors seems to have been inspired by Jesus' compassion toward her, by his disregard of conventional barriers (such as racism, sexism, classism, and religious fanaticism), by entering compassionately into her world, so that she might make a choice as to whether she wanted to enter the intimacy of love's spirit and truth. The spirit and truth of Jesus' religious convictions are authentic and authenticated for the woman, in other words, by his loving compassion toward her. What is that spirit but the practice of compassion itself? What is that truth but the healing, transforming power of compassion? Not this dogma or that, not Mount Gerizim or Jerusalem, not this ritual or another, but the compassion God and God's people practice in the world.

Gotthold Lessing, in his play *Nathan the Wise*, adapts an old parable in which he answers the question, How do we know which religions are true? Nathan tells of a wise man who inherited a marvelous ring. The ring possesses secret powers to make the owner especially loving and loved of God and humans. This fortunate fellow has three obedient sons whom he loves dearly and equally; and because of his love he promises each son individually that he will inherit the wondrous ring. When the time comes to fulfill his promise, the father secretly commissions a skilled artist to craft two exact replicas of the original ring. The two rings so perfectly replicate the original that even the father cannot tell them apart, the original from the other two. Upon the father's death the sons begin to quarrel, each claiming that his inherited ring is the one and only authentic ring. But alas the rings are so exactly alike that one is indistinguishable from the others. The dispute between the sons becomes so acrimonious that they appeal to a judge to adjudicate the case for them. The judge learns that the genuine ring will be the one that empowers the wearer to love God and others freely and selflessly. The judge addresses the brothers: It seems to me that each of you love yourself the best, and not God and others. All three of you are deceived deceivers; none of you possesses the genuine ring. But if any of you are interested in proving that your ring is the truly authentic one and not merely interested in claiming that it is, then it would behoove you to devote yourself to loving God and others in such an extraordinary way that your compassion and benevolence, your gentleness and loving kindness indubitably prove your ring's authenticity.

Compassion is the way devotees can properly insist and justify their claim that a religious tradition's truth-claims are absolute. By practicing loving compassion, devotees and devoted communities situate themselves in absolute relation to God and to their tradition. For in those moments and projects of compassion, that at which a religion aims is absolutely and fully realized. In compassion a community situates itself intentionally and absolutely in relation to truth and God so that the truth it claims is justified not in relation to increasingly abstract, universal principles of reason external to it but in relation to the practice of compassion itself. Its persuasiveness belongs simply and uniquely to practicing compassion, which for Jesus constitutes true worship, worship in spirit and truth. Jesus taught as much to his disciples—that as I love you, you should love one another—for it is by doing so that all people will know you are my disciples, that they will know that the truth you claim is authentic (John 13:34–35; see also Luke 6:43–49). The one who truly confesses to God, says the writer of I John, is the one in whom God's love abides and who abides in God's love. Loving compassion, in short, is not only the true and enduring basis for witness and conversion (John 4:13–21); it is the true and enduring basis for justifying the truth of one's religious tradition in general and one's claim to truth in particular.

Practicing loving compassion, accordingly, not only is its own justification but is the primary way, it seems to me, in which interreligious asymmetry is superceded. Devotees of any tradition can justifiably lay claim to absolute truth only insofar as their tradition inspires and empowers them to practice toward others, and especially toward their enemy, works of loving compassion. In projects of compassion are realized most fully and absolutely that for which religions exist, love of God, self, neighbor, and enemy. In projects of compassion is realized a kind of moral and spiritual supersymmetry between religions. By practicing compassion a religious community does not elevate itself to a status of truth superior to that of the other who is cared for. Rather in loving compassion it raises with and in itself the other, the one cared for, situating the others in relation to itself and its truth in such a way that all people experience in common the harmony of compassion's supersymmetrical truth. In loving God and neighbor as one's self, God, self, and other converge absolutely in the mutuality of compassion and thereby supercede the conceit of dogmatic imperialism and the critical detachment of benign relativism, ascribing to each other the absolute and intrinsic worth of all God's creatures. Both dogmatic imperialism and benign relativity are, we might say, bourgeois solutions to the problem of comparative truth; for the persuasiveness of neither of them is contingent on a community practicing what it proclaims. No way of life must be practiced for truth to be claimed. In contrast, the supersymmetrical harmony resulting from love's compassion is a proletarian solution; it results from a wage earned and battle won. Its truth requires the grace of actual work and practice. Its truth requires a faith community to risk in practice what it claims in theory. If it does not, its claim to truth is fraudulent and forfeited. So, what is unique about religious truth-claims, and the justification of those claims, is that they are true in any meaningful and absolute sense only if they produce what they claim. And what all religions claim in common is the power to produce in devotees the practice of loving compassion. By God's grace and the joyful sweat of compassion's hard labor, religious communities can practice mutually among themselves in public life that which alone justifies their truth-claims and supersedes the dogmatic imperialism and benign relativism into whose lairs they may otherwise be lured. Jesus and the Samaritan woman are not lured into these lairs; Jesus speaks simply to her of worshipping in spirit and in truth. By loving her compassionately he embodies that spirit and truth, thereby proving that the ring he wears is authentic.

Compassion as Supersymmetry

For Christianity, at least, one additional problem arises that must be addressed. Christianity is sometimes seen to stand in relation to the truth in a way that perhaps differs from other religions. The originating founders and teachers of all the world's religions, Confucius, Lao Tzu, Siddhartha Gautama, Moses, Muhammad, generally claim for themselves the role of prophetic witness to the truth, but none claim the status of divinity itself. Christians, on the other hand, believe that Jesus is not merely a prophetic witness to the truth but is truth itself, indeed, claiming that Jesus is the only way and truth (John 14:6). This claim is not, of course, an issue for devotees of other traditions, since they simply deny it. Nor is it an issue for many Christians who prefer to see Jesus as simply a great and gifted prophet. Yet, many Christians do believe that "Jesus is Divine" and that claim is problematic for them and others. For implicit in that claim is a triumphalism that scrapes the nerves of modern and postmodern humans. In light of what I have argued above, is there any sense that can be made of this claim? How does it fit, if at all, in the framework already established? Two responses may at least clarify if not entirely resolve this question. One response has to do with contextualization and the other with interpretation.

First, the passage in which Jesus claims that "I am the way, and the truth, and the life; no one comes to the Father, but by me" (John 14:6) must be purged of Constantinian triumphalism. Jesus should be interpreted as standing historically in a "crease" between religious traditions, and not finally possessed of and by any. On the one hand, Jesus is not Christian; on the other hand, he is not Jewish. The Jesus who makes the claim to truth originates, of course, the Christian tradition historically but he does not stand within that tradition personally. The particularity of Western civilization that bears the name "Christian" and distinguishes itself from and in competition with other religious cultures is not a tradition within which Jesus stands, although he is the source of its origination. Jesus can and must be seen as standing apart from the particularity of Western Christianity; it is simply one particular historical and for some persuasive version of who and what Jesus is. The most compelling evidence for this is simply that Jesus was a devoted Jew, identified himself and was identified by others as such, and remained so to the end of his life. And yet, in a significant sense, neither is Jesus a Jew. He is rejected by the authorities and institutions of his religious community of origin. He is not accepted as one who faithfully embodies and manifests the heart of the Jewish tradition. Indeed, Jewish tradition rejects from the beginning Jesus' claim that he is the fulfillment of the messianic promise and the Son of God.[41] Jesus does attract a few Galilean followers and other (often marginalized) Jews, but they are uniformly without religious power or portfolio and have no authority to speak for, even while speaking from, their Jewish tradition. Jesus finds himself spiritually homeless; he is rejected by his originating religious community, and in the lifetime of his ministry, no distinguishable Christian tradition emerges, although eventually one does. Yet, during his lifetime Jesus and his followers continue to identify themselves as Jews, even though they are not accepted by the Jewish community. In short, Jesus is dispossessed and not yet possessed. He stands independently and alone historically, culturally, religiously. There is no Christian or Jewish tradition to stand with or speak for him. He has nowhere to lay his head.

Second, what interpretation should Christians then make of Jesus' claim to be the only way and truth and life? What is the religiously homeless Jesus claiming for himself? Well, he certainly cannot be claiming that only through the Christian tradition is transformation delivered to the world, for that tradition does not yet exist. Nor can he be claiming that only through me as an embodiment of Judaism is transformation possible, for he was well aware of being dispossessed by Judaism. Is there, then, a nonimperialistic, nonprejudicial, and nonprivileged, transreligious, supersymmetrical way of interpreting Jesus' claim to be the only way and truth? Consider Jesus saying, "I am the incarnation of God's loving compassion. Loving compassion is the only way, truth, and life whereby all peoples come to God. All people come to God, if they come at all, only through the transformative grace of God's loving compassion that I am, that I incarnate." Jesus, who stands without religious portfolio in the crease and at the crossroads between religious traditions, declares to peoples of all traditions that "I am God's loving compassion incarnate, and it is precisely this love that is the only way, truth, and life by which all peoples come to God." Throughout history prophets of all traditions witness in their own way, if they are witnesses at all, to God's loving compassion: in Judaism, Moses; in Buddhism, Siddhartha Gautama; in Christianity, the Apostle Paul; in Islam, Muhammad, and so on. All are witnesses to God's loving compassion which Jesus incarnates as the way, truth, and life. This line of argument, of course, is seen as quite irrelevant and perhaps even repulsive to devotees of traditions other than the Christian one. They view Jesus at most as another great prophetic witness, and understandably insist that their own prophets and prophetic witnesses to God's loving compassion are at least equal if not superior to Jesus, and certainly sufficient for them, and sufficient to inspire them to practice it. And yet the status of Jesus and his claim to be the only way, truth, and life, are the concern of many Christians. Many Christians want to know that, as Heim insists, the common Christian belief in the "finality of Christ" is not "mutually exclusive" with affirming the "independent validity of other ways."[42]

The Apostle Paul has often been seen as an advocate of Christian triumphalism and has been frequently exploited as such by the Constantinian tradition. But what if we assume the supersymmetry of compassion as a starting point for interpreting Paul? A familiar passage will suffice to show how Paul's perspective is consistent with Jesus' interaction with the Samaritan woman. Paul argues that in Christ "there is neither Jew nor Greek" (Galatians 3:28). Neither Paul nor any other Jew or Greek had a conception of "Jew" or "Greek" to which religion was not essential and intrinsic. For him, the covenantal relationship with Yahweh could not be separated from being a Jew; and participation in pagan ceremonies or belief in many gods (see Acts 17) could not be separated from being Greek. Paul's case is similar to Jesus', in insisting that the crux of being in Christ is not the Jewish religion or the Greek religion, not the temples at Mount Gerizim or Jerusalem but living by faith in God's grace. Indeed, Paul introduces his comments (Galatians 3:23–28) by saying that people are "no longer under a custodian" or "confined under the law" or "kept under restraint" by a religious tradition. Rather by faith in Christ all are "sons of God," "neither Jew nor Greek," "slave nor free," "male nor female." For Paul being "in Christ" by faith is living in God's grace, mercy, and compassion; it is not and could not mean being religiously "Christian," since Jesus embodied no such tradition. Nor could it mean being Jewish and keeping Jewish law, since Paul himself, in a dispute with Peter, insisted that being in the grace of Christ did not necessarily include keeping the Jewish tradition (Acts 15). That does not mean that Paul is advocating grace without a religious tradition, but like Jesus he is arguing that true religion is worshipping in spirit and in truth. So, whether Jew or Greek, a person should live in grace and with the compassion and mercy practiced perfectly by Jesus in his life and death and resurrection.

What are the implications of this view for interreligious conversation and cooperation? Typically, the metaphor that is compelling for Christians and devotees of all religions is an image of many roads, all of which lead to a common end: God, Nirvana, the Ultimate, the Real. Each road requires of its travelers beliefs and practices distinct to that road, but ultimately all travelers arrive at the same destination. This metaphor, however, is too weak to bear the weight of what I am trying to argue in this chapter. I prefer instead a metaphor suggested by Kierkegaard in his analysis of the parable of the Good Samaritan.[43] Represented in this parable are devotees of at least two religions who are traveling only one road. The road these devotees walk is one and the same road, not different roads. The parable tells of a single road, between Jerusalem and Jericho, and of five travelers (the injured man, the thieves, the priest, the Levite, and the Samaritan), all who are walking the same road physically but who spiritually are walking that one road differently. The injured man, a Jew we presume, walks the road peacefully; the thieves walk the same road violently; the priest walks the road indifferently; the Levite walks it selfishly; and the Samaritan, the other, the enemy, the heretic, walks it compassionately. Of the Samaritan Kierkegaard says, "He found the poor unfortunate man on the road of mercy. He showed by example how to walk the road of mercy; he demonstrated that the road, spiritually speaking, is precisely this; how one walks. This is why the Gospel says, 'Go and do likewise.'" The road each walks is the same road, but for Jesus what makes all the difference is how they walk that one road. All walk the same road; all religions embrace devotees who walk that road differently—some violently, some indifferently and callously, some selfishly and self-righteously, and some mercifully and compassionately. The traveler that is acceptable to Jesus, the one who walks the road truly, is not a devotee of Jesus' own religion but is of a hostile religion. So, for Jesus the critical issue and criterion is not which religious tradition the devotee happens to claim; it is not what one claims that demonstrates how one walks the road; its is not that the road is walked in the garb of this religion or that, but how devotees of any tradition walk the road. Do they walk the road in self-righteousness and violence? Or does their religious tradition inspire in them the grace and power with which to walk the road mercifully and compassionately? This seems to be Jesus' criterion; this seems to be the crease Jesus occupies between religious traditions that nevertheless invites devotees from all religious traditions. "Worldly sagacity," says Kierkegaard, "teaches that the road goes over Gerizim, or over Moriah, or that it goes through some science or other, or that the road is certain doctrines, or certain behaviors," or all of these magnanimously embraced together. But not according to the life and teaching of Jesus, who repeatedly rails against such worldly wisdom even when its origin happens to be priests and professors of religion. "But all this is a deception," insists Kierkegaard, "because the road is how it is walked." As Scripture says, "Two people can be sleeping in the same bed [religious tradition]—the one is saved the other is lost. Two people can go up to the same house of worship—the one goes home saved and the other is lost. Two people can recite the same creed—the one can be saved, the other is lost."[44] How can this be? How can this happen? How can two devotees of the same religious tradition not both be acceptable to God? How can devotees of different traditions be acceptable to God? The deception of worldly wisdom is twofold; to believe dogmatically that the key to transformation is for all to walk the road you walk, or to believe benignly and naively that any road you walk suffices. Jesus rejects both of these deceptions, as do all the great prophets. Knowing that all humans of all religious traditions walk the same road, Jesus preaches what he lives, namely, that it is not what road you walk that matters but how by God's grace you walk the road, whether by loving compassion or selfish ambition. This "how," this grace of mercy and compassion, embraces both the particularity of a local tradition and the universality of interreligious fellowship; it possesses supersymmetrical powers of such strength as to treasure differences between self and other and at the same time traverse differences and enter into a universal fellowship of spirit and truth. This "how" fills the crease between and in and through all religions, and it is the grace of this "how" that for Christians Jesus incarnates as the way, the truth, and the life.

Notes

1. Chris Arthur, "A Revolution in Religious Consciousness," in *Bulletin* 29, 1 (February 2000): 14.

2. S. Mark Heim, *Salvations: Truth and Difference in Religion* (Maryknoll, N.Y.: Orbis Books, 1997), 132.

3. John Hick, *An Interpretation of Religion* (New Haven, Conn.: Yale University Press, 1989), 299.

4. Paul Knitter, *One Earth Many Religions: Multifaith Dialogue and Global Responsibility* (Maryknoll, N.Y.: Orbis Books, 1996), 56.

5. Heim, *Salvations*, 132.

6. Knitter, *One Earth Many Religions*, 56.

7. Ibid., 17.

8. Ibid.

9. Ibid., 54.

10. Ibid., 52.

11. Ibid., 52–53. For Knitter this neighborly conversation over the backyard fence, or ad hoc apologetics, takes the form of a conversation about global responsibility.

12. See chapter 2 in my book *Fidelity of Heart: An Ethic of Christian Virtue* (New York: Oxford University Press, 2000).

13. Martha Nussbaum, *Love's Knowledge: Essays on Philosophy and Literature* (New York: Oxford University Press, 1990), 291.

14. Roger Scruton, "Emotion, Practical Knowledge and Common Culture," in *Explaining Emotions*, ed. Amelie Rorty (Berkeley: University of California Press, 1985), 529.

15. Jonathan Edwards, *Religious Affections* (Portland, Ore.: Multnomah Press, 1984), 5.

16. Paul Lauritzen, "Emotions and Religious Ethics," *Journal of Religious Ethics* 16, 2 (1988): 315.

17. Robert Solomon, *The Passions* (Notre Dame, Ind.: University of Notre Dame Press, 1976), 272.

18. Exactly how emotional intersubjectivity or compassion is universal is a question I address in the subsequent section of this chapter, "Compassion as Normative."

19. George Santayana, *Reason in Religion*, quoted by Martin E. Marty, "Proselytizers and Proselytizees on the Sharp Arete of Modernity," in *Sharing the Book: Religious Perspectives on the Rights and Wrongs of Proselytism*, eds. John Witte Jr. and Ralph C. Martin (Maryknoll, N.Y.: Orbis Books, 1999), 9–10.

20. Søren Kierkegaard, *Works of Love: Some Christian Reflections in the Form of Discourses*, trans. Howard Hong and Edna Hong (New York: Harper & Row, 1962), see page 252.

21. Martha Nussbaum, *Cultivating Humanity: A Classical Defense of Reform in Liberal Education* (Cambridge, Mass.: Harvard University Press, 1997), 90.

22. Ibid., 69.

23. William J. Prior, "Compassion: A Critique of Moral Rationalism," *Philosophy and Theology* 2 (Winter 1987): 173.

24. Norman Fiering, "Irresistible Compassion: An Aspect of Eighteenth-Century Sympathy and Humanitarianism," *Journal of the History of Ideas* 37, 2 (1976): 198.

25. William J. Prior, "Compassion," 173.

26. Lawrence Blum, "Compassion," in *Explaining Emotions*, ed. Amelie O. Rorty (Berkeley: University of California Press, 1980), 508. Blum points out that experiences of human happiness and pleasure are also positive occasions for mutually shared emotions of joy and exhilaration, but not of compassion.

27. Ibid.

28. For a discussion of what it means to "feel with" and "feel for" suffering others, see my discussion in *Fidelity of Heart: An Ethic of Christian Virtue* (New York: Oxford University Press, 2001), 143–146.

29. See King's "Letter from a Birmingham Jail." April 16, 1963.

30. Dalai Lama, *Ethics for a New Millennium* (New York: Riverhead Books, 1999), 76–77.

31. John Witte Jr., "Preface," in *Sharing the Book: Religious Perspectives on the Rights and Wrongs of Proselytism*, ed. John Witte Jr. and Richard Martin (Maryknoll, N.Y.: Orbis Books, 1999), xiii.

32. Heim, *Salvations*, 6; see also the development of Heim's argument in chapters 5–8.

33. Martin Marty, "Proselytizers and Proselytizees on the Sharp Arete of Modernity," in *Sharing the Book: Religious Perspectives on the Rights and Wrongs of Proselytism*, ed. John Witte Jr. and Richard Martin (Maryknoll, N.Y.: Orbis Books, 1999), 1.

34. This is a phrase that John Witte, in a slightly different way, uses in his Preface to *Sharing the Book*, xii.

35. See Heim, *Salvations*.

36. Nussbaum, *Love's Knowledge*, 265–266.

37. Patricia Greenspan, *Emotions and Reason: An Inquiry into Emotional Justification* (New York: Routledge, 1988), 3–5. Throughout this book Greenspan argues for the notion of emotional justification and it self-referential character. It is an argument with which I largely agree and recommend to the reader who would like to pursue this notion

only introduced here. Robert C. Roberts similarly makes a case for the self-referentiality and justification of emotions in "Emotions as Access to Religious Truths," *Faith and Philosophy* 9, 1 (January 1992): 83–94, especially 90–92. See also my discussion of practical justification in chapter 2 of my book *Fidelity of Heart*.

38. Søren Kierkegaard, *Søren Kierkegaard's Journals and Papers*, ed. and trans. Howard V. Hong and Edna H. Hong (Indianapolis, Ind.: Indiana University Press, 1975), vol. 3, 609.

39. Ibid., vol. 2, 335–336. Kierkegaard is quoting from John's gospel, chapter 7:16–17.

40. Ibid., 25.

41. See Jocelyn Hellig, "Antisemitism and Proselytism," in *Sharing the Book: Religious Perspectives and the Rights and Wrongs of Proselytism*, ed. John Witte Jr. and Richard Martin (Maryknoll, N.Y.: Orbis Books, 1999), 63.

42. Heim, *Salvations*, 3.

43. Søren Kierkegaard, *Upbuilding Discourse in Various Spirits*, ed. and trans. Howard V. Hong and Edna H. Hong (Princeton, N.J.: Princeton University Press, 1993), 289–291.

44. Ibid., 291.

CHAPTER SEVEN

~

Christian Faith and Society

The young woman, so captivated by the drama of recent events, can contain herself no longer. Her heart soars with the purpose and passion of a Hebrew prophet who has received a word from the Lord. And such a word it is—of indignation as well as exaltation: indignation toward the proud and powerful and rich who are scattered and dethroned and sent away empty; exaltation for the humble and hungry and lowly who fear God. No wonder Mary "magnifies the Lord" and her "soul rejoices in God [her] Savior," for she and her descendents will be blessed, and the hungry will be fed and satisfied, and the lowly will be exalted (Luke 1:46–55). But how can this be? How can promises such as these be anything more than flights of fancy, as even today they seem to be? How is it possible that the rich and powerful will ever be dethroned and scattered? How is it possible that the lowly and disenfranchised and poor can be exalted and finally satisfied?

In answering these questions, we may be tempted to say with the text that it is the Lord who will do these things, who is well equipped to do so. And yet, we know that the Lord, in infinite and inscrutable wisdom, chooses to bring these great things about through the labor and lives of God's people. It is they who are endowed with divine purpose and power sufficient to dethrone the powerful and exalt the lowly. Indeed, it is the community of God's people who are called to carry out and fulfill Mary's vision. It is the purpose of this chapter to say how that is possible and how a community of faith fails or succeeds in doing so. How that is possible is by now a familiar refrain—faithful communities practicing the same loving compassion that they have received from God. I show how the practice of compassion by Christian (or Muslim or Hindu) communities makes possible the fulfillment of Mary's vision. I argue that compassion, in its supersymmetrical role, inspires religious communities in general and Christianity in particular to play in any society two indispensable roles, a prophetic and a pastoral role. By practicing a prophetic role the proud are scattered, and by practicing a pastoral role the lowly are exalted. Properly, then, Christianity and indeed all religions should situate themselves in relation to any society prophetically and pastorally. It is urgent that they do so if societies are to thrive as stewards of civility instead of savagery. My aim is to show not only how this is possible but also why it is urgent.

It is as curious as it is unfortunate that some philosophers of religion today, groping in the shadow of the Enlightenment, have largely abandoned this particular problem—the role of religion in society. This was not always the case. The great classical philosophers of religion in the Christian tradition, Tertullian and Origen, Augustine and Aquinas, even Hobbes and Kant, regarded it as one of the most central and urgent, whose solution requires not only the moral vision of theology but the critical scrutiny of philosophy. Neither religion nor society can afford to have philosophers abandon and disown them in this way; both are always with us and both have proven themselves unable on their own, without the critical tools with which philosophy is equipped, to relate civilly to each other. Indeed, on their own society and religion in the modern world have tended to collapse into one of our two fallacies, the fallacy of rationalism or the fallacy of fideism. Partly my aim in this chapter is to show from modern European history how religion and society have committed in turn each of these fallacies and how in so doing they jointly sparked the most brutal, barbaric conflagration from whose ashes some semblance of civilization is still struggling to arise. And partly my aim is to show how, by employing the critical tools of philosophy, religion and society should and can situate themselves civilly and compassionately in relation to each other.

My procedure is both logical and historical. I first show how the Enlightenment commits the fallacy of rationalism (simple symmetry) and what impact this has had on religion and society in the modern European world. Second, I show how committing this fallacy clears a historical space in which the fallacy of fideism (irrational asymmetry) emerges and how in the form of neo-paganism (e.g., fascism, Nazism) it flourishes and crushes civilization. Finally, I argue that if religion and society are to situate themselves civilly in relation to each other, fidelity of mind is essential. The mind's fidelity to both faith and reason inevitably inspires a community to practice compassion in a way that supersymmetrically transforms and civilizes forces that otherwise savage society. To do this, religion must properly assume its prophetic and pastoral responsibilities, roles without which society degenerates in a dystopia. Throughout, my analysis is historical as well as logical. I apply the logic of my argument to specific historical conditions that permitted and produced European fascism, Nazism, and the Holocaust. Although my constant reference is to these specific events, the structure of analysis set forth here nevertheless establishes a universal paradigm by which similar historical events might be examined and evaluated.

A caveat is in order, however. My analysis of the role and significance of religion in society, especially in modern European society, is intended to be neither comprehensive nor reductive. Many other forces are of equal if not greater power in shaping and driving societies and civilizations. One has only to consider the power of certain forces (e.g., material, economic, political, military, psychological, racial, or cultural) to know that the collective forces that drive and shape societies are multiple, complex, and perhaps finally inscrutable. My intention, rather, is to trace the role and contribution of religion, in general, in shaping society and the role of Christianity and neo-paganism, in particular, in shaping modern European society. I do not want to overemphasize its role, but neither do I want to minimize it. As Western civilization should by now have learned, it ignores the role and power of religion at its own peril, as I shall show.

I again draw heavily on the thought of R. G. Collingwood, who lived during the Nazi rise to power.[1] He did not endear himself to his British colleagues when he accused them of creating with their philosophies an intellectual climate in which fascism could emerge and flourish,[2] and partly because of this he was isolated philosophically, professionally, and personally. I blend several ingredients from Collingwood's later writings that help carry out and demonstrate this thesis. Specifically, I blend his metaphysics, social and political thought, and philosophies of history and religion. I by no means agree with all he has to say on this matter, especially, for example, his insistence that the survival of Western democracy depends on the survival of Christianity. And yet Collingwood's analysis is profound and persuasive and points us in a direction and down a path that provides, I think, an answer to our query as to the role of religion in society, even though he himself does not pursue that path to its very end.

Reason and Symmetry: The Enlightenment

The Enlightenment was very much interested in the question of the relation of religion and society; virtually all of the primogenitors of the Enlightenment treated it in one way or another. Some, like d'Holbach, wanted to banish religion from society entirely; some, like Hume, wanted it restricted to the private lives of the faithful; some, like Locke, wanted its doctrines transposed into universal rational principles; and some, like Kant, wanted it confined within the limits of reason. What these philosophers in particular and Enlightenment thinkers in general insisted in common was that if society is to be genuinely civilized, then scientific reason must be the touchstone of all thought and practice. Religion, accordingly, must in one way or another be purged of its irrational, emotional, and superstitious elements, or at minimum society must be protected from the deleterious effects of such elements. To believe this, as did these prophets of the Enlightenment, is to suffer a corruption of consciousness that commits the fallacy of rationalism. This fallacy revolves around several foci. First, it presupposes that the world is fundamentally and entirely constituted of a simple symmetry. Second, it presupposes that scientific reason is fully and adequately equipped to discover this symmetry and to civilize society accordingly. Third, it presupposes that the asymmetrical forces and artifacts typical of unenlightened human experience—the irrationality of emotions and the superstitious rituals and practices of religion—should be either thoroughly rationalized or exterminated entirely from society. In short, the Enlightenment preaches civilization by reason alone and so inaugurates a process of secularization that combines two simultaneous motions: a motion of demythologizing in which the beliefs of Christianity are transposed into rational principles underlying modern science and liberal politics, and a motion of disenfranchisement in which the alleged irrational, emotional, and ritualistic superstitions of Christianity are disowned and suppressed. It is these two motions of secularization that my analysis of the Enlightenment's fallacy of rationalism tracks.

Rudolf Otto is perhaps better known than Collingwood for his view, set forth in *Das Heilige*, that religion consists fundamentally of two elements, rational and nonrational. Collingwood advances a similar view, but he uses the terms "rational" and "irrational."[3] These two elements are the basis for him explaining the role of religion in civilization. He held that any attempt to understand the source and nature, success and failure, of civilizations must examine the interaction of these two elements. Collingwood's guiding proposition is that religion's rational element endows a civilization with those presuppositions from which it derives its principles of thought and life (its values and ideals), while its irrational element,[4] the emotional energy invoked by ritual and worship, endows a civilization with the inspiration and passion necessary to put these principles into practice and sustain them over time. What, then, of the two motions, demythologizing and disenfranchising, by which the Enlightenment accomplishes its process of secularization? How does it commit the fallacy of rationalism?

First, how did the Enlightenment implement its project of demythologization? The answer, in brief, is by reinterpreting as scientific principles those beliefs of Christianity that are rational, that reflect the world's symmetry and lend themselves to the scrutiny of critical reason. By Christianity's rationality Collingwood refers to those propositions of faith "capable of logical formulation as a system of first principles." Whatever beliefs are in the nature of thought (God, creation), whatever can be conceptualized and codified intellectually, forms the rational component of any religion.[5] Collingwood went so far as to argue that the collective intellect of a society, insofar as we can speak of a society's ideals, values, and beliefs, is at bottom a function of the beliefs of religion. "All scientific and philosophical ideas, before they have been worked out in explicit intellectual terms, are present to men's minds in the form of religious beliefs."[6] This claim is not unique, of course. F. M. Cornford, to name only one other claimant, similarly argues that the principles of Greek philosophy and science are rational refinements of Greek religion, a conversion of thought from its mythological manifestation in religion to its explicitly rational manifestation in philosophy and science.[7] Collingwood's premise is that a similar process of transposition links the beliefs of Christianity to the intellectual principles of the modern European tradition. This premise has its detractors, of course. Marxist materialism, for instance, claims that the intellectual structures of society, including religion, are themselves products of economic forces. Nevertheless, Collingwood believes that through a positive process of demythologization Enlightenment philosophers "succeeded at a kind of distillation by which the rational contents of the Christian faith [were] separated out from the mass of superstitious ideas and magical rituals in which they were embedded."[8] In sweeping away the accumulation of Christianity's irrational, emotional dimension the Enlightenment did not sweep away all. Instead, it extracted from that tradition whatever was "capable of logical formulation as a system of first principles . . . as the axioms upon which our sciences of nature and history, our practice of liberal economics and free or democratic politics—in short, all of the things which make up our civilization, are built."[9] The process of Enlightenment secularization transposed the foundation of modern science and liberal politics from their superstitious formulation in Christianity to a new formulation that was wholly rational and naturalistic.

In *An Essay on Metaphysics* Collingwood develops this particular view in terms of his theory of absolute presuppositions, introduced in chapter 3. If we trace back the line along which the intellect of any civilization evolves, our inquiry, he argues, will encounter a *terminus a quo*, a point beyond which that civilization's unique set of first principles does not recede. This *terminus a quo* consists of a "constellation" of absolute presuppositions, and, for Collingwood, it is a matter of historical fact and logical demonstration that in any civilization this constellation is initially formulated in terms of religious beliefs. In part III of *An Essay on Metaphysics*, for example, Collingwood identifies four beliefs (that there is one God, that the activity of God assumes many modes [e.g., incarnation], that God created the world, and that this creative activity is the source of motion in the world) that comprise the set of absolute presuppositions from which the principles of our modern way of life and thought are derived.[10] Throughout his later writings,

Collingwood claims that persons committed to modern science and liberalism are bound a fortiori to certain presuppositions about the world initially set forth in the creeds of Christianity.[11] Indeed, one could scarcely put the case for their interconnectedness more strongly than Collingwood does: "Take away Christian theology, and the scientist has no longer any motive for doing what inductive thought gives him permission to do. If he goes on doing it at all, that is only because he is blindly following conventions of the professional society to which he belongs." Indeed, he goes so far as to say that modern civilization, including modern science, is "based on Christianity and could not for a moment survive its destruction."[12] And he makes the same case in terms of Christianity and liberal politics.[13]

Clearly Collingwood overestimates Christianity's role and importance. It simply is not true that engagement in modern science or liberal politics logically or even tacitly entails commitment to the Christian creed. Although Christianity did play a vital, if sometimes ambiguous, historical role in the rise of modern science and liberal politics,[14] practicing science and liberalism in no way logically necessitates the creeds of Christianity. Collingwood could persuade himself otherwise because he confused historical causation with logical necessity. Those with historicist tendencies, like Collingwood and Marx, often confer on history determinate laws and internal logical relations where there are only causal relations. Karl Popper, in his *Poverty of Historicism*, faults such philosophers for neglecting to distinguish laws from historical tendencies and patterns of behavior. Collingwood made this mistake, I think, in ascribing to Christianity exclusive logical as well as historical rights to modern science and liberal politics. Nevertheless the general thesis, that historically and culturally modern science and liberal politics are rooted in the soil of Christian belief, is persuasive and widely held. Indeed, most Enlightenment thinkers did not, like d'Holbach, seek to eliminate Christianity or religion entirely from civilization but recognized in some of its beliefs certain rational principles that, when demythologized and purged of their explicitly religious character, retain intellectual value as absolute presuppositions of scientific inquiry and liberal politics. John Locke is an example of one who carries out this kind of argument. In *The Reasonableness of Christianity* he demythologizes certain Christian beliefs and shows how interpreted as rational principles they provide a basis for understanding the world scientifically; and in his *Two Treatises on Government* he grounds his case for liberal, democratic politics and private property on the rationality of certain Christian beliefs. Similarly, in *The Social Contract* (IV, 8) Rousseau grounded his version of democratic ideals in what he called "the dogmas of civil religion," dogmas that at least marginally reflect Christian faith.[15] Collingwood has some basis, then, for arguing that the original historical ground for devotion to liberal values was, as he says, religious love of a God who set an absolute value on every individual human being. Free speech and free inquiry concerning political and scientific questions; free consent in issues arising out of economic activities; free enjoyment of the produce won by man's own labour—the opposite of all tyranny and oppression, exploitation and robbery—these were ideals based on the fact that God loved the human individual and Christ had died for him.[16]

Accordingly, the liberal constellation of values and its conception of human nature were not derived historically from empirical research into sociological and psychological data; it was originally a matter of faith. Collingwood's point is that the Enlightenment calculated to change this by regrounding the liberal tradition to a largely rational, secularized, naturalistic terminus, one that disenfranchised and suppressed especially those beliefs and practices of Christianity calculated to evoke the passion and power of religious emotions, emotions necessary, as it turns out, to inspire and sustain those very same liberal values and ideals. Philosophically this change is represented by the difference between Locke's *Two Treatises* and Mill's *On Liberty*. Historically this difference was at first disguised by the continuity of inherited vocabulary and conceptual resemblance. In time, however, the shift manifested itself and, in Collingwood's view, contributed greatly to the destabilization of European civilization, leaving it vulnerable to powerful alien, irrational forces such as fascism and Nazism.

Second, and simultaneous with this motion of demythologizing, accordingly, there occurred a concomitant motion of disenfranchisement that also contributed to the secularization of modern European civilization. The privileged position with which the Enlightenment treated reason not only shaped a strictly symmetrical version of the world and society but at the same time conspired to disown and suppress human and especially religious emotions and what it considered to be the irrational, magical practices associated with them. But by suppressing this collective reservoir of emotional energy and religious power, argues Collingwood, rationalism ironically deprived itself of the principal source of energy whereby it might put into practice and sustain its commitment to scientific reason and liberal politics. Since religion's emotional energy and superstitious practices, according to the fallacy of Enlightenment rationalism, are situated asymmetrically in relation to the principles of scientific reason, and since as such they threaten to undermine scientific progress, they, or at least their influence, must be banished as far as possible from society. This corruption of consciousness, this propensity of the Enlightenment thinkers to disown religious emotions and the ritual practices inspiring them, commits them to the fallacy of rationalism and ultimately to its failure as a viable civilizing project. For many Enlightenment philosophers, including Kant,[17] religious emotions and rituals are irrational, harmful, and unreliable because they are not susceptible to rational formulation and tend to inspire communities to believe and act in ways contrary to reason. It is for this reason that they should be eliminated.

But what these philosophers failed to see, argues Collingwood, is that religious emotions, along with the mythological beliefs and ritual practices that inspire them, are fundamental driving forces without which the principles of scientific reason and liberal politics cannot sustain themselves in practice, cannot long survive. Religious emotions, feelings, and instincts inspire people, individually and collectively, not only to religious faith and piety but also to a specific form of life (scientific and liberal) they have chosen.[18] In *The New Leviathan*, Collingwood catalogues four kinds of emotions involved in religious experience—"hunger" and love, which he calls religious appetites, and fear and anger, which he calls religious passions.[19] These emotions are evoked by certain religious practices that empower people, both individually and collectively, to live lives of passionate conviction. They are analogous in an engine to a spark, "the explosive in the economy of that delicate internal-combustion engine, the human mind."[20] These practices of religion, its cultus and magic, aim at evoking in the community that believes them an emotional force and drive to pursue and practice its unique way of thought and life.[21] In modern European society, "the emotional force, the 'drive' or 'punch,' that once made them [principles of modern science and liberal politics] victorious," Collingwood insists, "was due to Christianity itself as a system of religious practice rich in superstitious or magical elements." In Christianity as in every other religion, these elements generate the emotions that inspire humans with "the power to obey a set of rules and thus bring into existence a specific form of life."[22] Religion's irrational element, in short, amounts to something like the "soul" or breath of civilization, the vital energy at its core that enables it to continue and to resist forces of decay.

The fallacy of Enlightenment rationalism, then, involves its tendency to disown and suppress religion's irrational, emotional dimension that is otherwise vital and necessary to the survival of a symmetrical, civilized life. "Whatever is in the nature of religious emotion, passion, faith is progressively exterminated," as Collingwood puts it, "partly by ridicule and partly by force, under the name of superstition and magic."[23] Indeed, the eighteenth and nineteenth centuries witnessed an epidemic of movements dedicated to the eradication of Christianity's influence. In England and France a movement called illuminism, the cult of *La Raison* inaugurated by French revolutionaries, Auguste Comte's cult of *L'humanite*, and individuals such as Voltaire, Hume, d'Holbach, Diderot, Gibbon, and many others spoke with a single voice in demanding in the name of reason and progress that all philosophy, all values, all social and political ideals be purged of the old and prevailing Christian influences. Their efforts largely succeeded, at least among the intellectuals, politicians, and privileged whose power and influence shape the character of a society. By disposing of much of Christianity's irrational element and the powerful emotions that inaugurated and sustained the liberal tradition in the first place the Enlightenment undermined its own system of immunity that could otherwise protect it from tyrannical and despotic tendencies.

Implicit in Collingwood's remarks about the Enlightenment's tendency to disown the irrational and ritualistic dimension of religion is his charge that those succumbing to such tendencies suffer a corruption of consciousness. A truthful, candid consciousness confesses to itself the reality and vitality of the wide variety of experiences (religious and scientific, rational and irrational, intellectual and emotional) that fundamentally, whether one likes it or not, constitute human experience individually and collectively. Untruthful or corrupt consciousness finds ways to justify suppressing one or more of those features. For Collingwood, as we have seen, it is not that the corrupt consciousness simply denies or ignores some feature of human experience; rather, it is that it dogmatically disenfranchises "certain features of its experience," shrinks from "something which it is its business to face."[24] In short, a corrupt consciousness is one that deceives itself, suppressing what is otherwise an undeniable feature of human experience.

Insofar as the Enlightenment disowned those irrational, emotional features of religion, its consciousness was corrupted and its power to discharge its function of civilizing society eclipsed. The typical Enlightenment intellectual suffered such a corruption because he disowned this vital and indispensable feature of human experience—religious affections—and did so by divorcing and isolating two otherwise mutually interdependent and inseparable aspects of Christianity; it demythologized and reinterpreted Christianity's rational, intellectual component, and it suppressed or exterminated its irrational, emotional component. This effectively destroyed the delicate balance between reason and emotion that Collingwood believes is essential to a healthy and vigorous scientific and liberal society. Lionel Rubinoff aptly summarizes his view. "To destroy the natural dialectic [between the rational and irrational, between reason and emotion] by using the rise of natural science as an excuse for disposing of religion is a mistake whose consequences are disastrous for the whole of human culture. The suppression of any form of life in favour of another was for Collingwood an irrational and pathological activity. Just as no society can be expected to survive without art so no society can prevail without religion."[25] More especially, no civilization can long survive without the power and passion provided by human emotions and religion. For along with art, they are the means by which that power is produced, preserved, and practiced. The romantic Enlightenment partly recognized this and attempted, albeit belatedly, to compensate for it.

By demythologizing Christianity's rational element and by disenfranchising the passion and power of its irrational element, the Enlightenment secularized European society and thereby deprived both science and liberal politics of the emotional drive and force necessary to practice and persevere in its way of life. Modern Europe was not the first to suffer this fate. Collingwood believed, contrary to Gibbon, that the decline of the Roman Empire also followed this pattern. It disowned important, powerful forces of its own religious heritage and in doing so sowed seeds of its own destruction. The Emperor Julian understood the empire's predicament and labored to rescue it by reviving the traditional religious beliefs and ritual practices of pagan Rome. His instincts were sound, in Collingwood's view, but his inspiration too late. Roman civilization "died because the religious passion that provided its driving force ceased to exist."[26] The "'pagan' world died because of its own failure to keep alive its own fundamental [religious] convictions."[27] Collingwood believed that something resembling this was and is happening in modern liberal civilization and that the rise of fascism and Nazism can be traced to it. To the extent to which the Enlightenment eclipsed Christianity as the ground and driving force of the liberal tradition, to that extent the liberal tradition was and is unable to sustain itself and becomes vulnerable to antagonistic forces like fascism and Nazism. Because Christianity was eclipsed, adherents of the liberal tradition, especially intellectuals and politicians, lost their sense of it "as a thing of absolute value, . . . [lost] a religious sense of its rules as things which at all costs must be obeyed." And "without a conviction that this way of life is a thing of absolute value, and that its rules must be obeyed at all costs, the rules became dead letters and the way of life a thing of the past."[28] The eclipse of Christianity by the Enlightenment, in other words, was like a virus that undermined liberalism's immune system, rendering it helpless and vulnerable to a wide variety of diseases and deaths.

Faith and Asymmetry: Neo-Paganism

What happened, then, to the powerful emotional energy and superstitious practices of Christianity that the Enlightenment disowned and suppressed? Whatever happened to them, whether they were sublimated or bracketed or simply subdued, one thing is for certain: they were not exterminated from European civilization as most Enlightenment philosophers had hoped and many expected. For psychological, emotional energy, like physical energy, is never destroyed but only transformed and transferred from one form to another. What seems to have happened, says Collingwood, is that much of this emotional energy, suppressed by the Enlightenment and sublimated in the collective consciousness, transposed and reasserted itself asymmetrically as a form of neo-paganism whose most savage manifestations in fascism and Nazism ravaged Europe's twentieth century. Collingwood regards as misleading, accordingly, attempts to explain the triumph of Nazism largely in terms of radical politics or economic forces; and he judges some of them, particularly the Marxist explanation of Nazism in terms of class conflict, to be simply wrong. What Collingwood seeks to show is how religious faith, along with other forces, played a role more fundamental in the rise of Nazism than suggested by simply acknowledging the obvious historical fact that Christianity contributed to Nazis success by its anti-Semitism, silence, and complicity. In addition to this truth, he insists that fascism and Nazism are forms of neo-pagan religion that eagerly filled the vacuum created by the Enlightenment's eclipse of Christianity. An oft quoted speech of Mussolini, for example, declares that "fascism is a religious conception in which man is seen in his immanent relationship with a superior law and with an objective Will that transcends the particular individual and raises him to conscious membership in a spiritual society."[29] Fascism and Nazism are modern forms of pagan religion comprised, on the one hand, of an ideology that supplies them with a mythological structure of belief and, on the other hand, of pagan rituals and piety that supply an emotional power and drive necessary to bring a pagan way of life into existence. What, then, is the nature of this neo-pagan religious ideology, and how does Collingwood account for its emergence in European civilization?

As a vicious reaction to the fallacy of Enlightenment rationalism, it is not surprising that neo-paganism should arise and that its blind, fanatical fideism should commit a fallacy roughly opposite to that of rationalism. This fallacy of fideism is a function of a consciousness more corrupt than any fallacy of rationalism. What is disowned and suppressed in paganism is the just and civil morality of a symmetrical world and consequently it happily positions itself asymmetrically, and even satanically, in relation to scientific reason and liberal values. In their place it substitutes a pseudo-science and pseudo-nation that are in service to the irrationality of its mythological version of the world. To believe and practice this neo-pagan mythology, as did the prophets of fascism and Nazism, is to commit the fallacy of fideism.

This fallacy, as manifest in neo-paganism, revolves around several foci. First, it presupposes that the world is constituted most profoundly by a myth in which raw, irrational faith situates itself consciously and deliberately in asymmetrical relation to reason and its fantasy of a perfectly symmetrical world. Second, it presupposes that this mythology fully interprets the world and justifies "civilizing" society asymmetrically. Third, it presupposes that certain elements of human life and faith—like human emotions, religious rituals, and superstitious practices—are essential to shaping and sustaining neo-paganism's myth of the world's asymmetry. All scientific reason, accordingly, must either conform to the shape of that myth or, what is the same thing, be exterminated. Indeed, for neo-paganism the value of its mythology lies not in its capacity for rational explanation but in its capacity to invoke passionate commitment. And so it happily practices civilization by faith alone. It inaugurates a process of remythologizing that combines two simultaneous motions, both of which Collingwood refers to as forms of "herd-worship" and "self-adoration." One motion involves "ancestor worship," the highest freedom for which is conformity of one's will to the will of the ancestral, racial community. And the other motion involves "autocrat worship," creating a cult of personality that permits the "aristocratic leader" to exploit irrational and emotional forces without which its pagan mythology cannot triumph over rationalism and sustain its way of life. Both ancestor worship and autocrat worship are forms of communal self-adoration and, says Collingwood, both characterize a paganism that is ancient and widespread in European tradition. It is around these two motions—ancestor and autocrat worship—that my analysis of neo-paganism's fallacy of fideism revolves.

Ancestor worship is an ancient practice common to most forms of paganism. Vergil's remythologization of Rome's ancestral tradition functioned in the republic and later in the empire as a justification for the "glories" that were Rome, "glories," at least, for Roman citizens. Hitler consciously and deliberately retrieves this Roman tradition of ancestor worship as vital to the shape and sustenance of his Third Reich. Negatively, says Collingwood, ancestor worship involves an individual's feelings of powerlessness before a community into which he is born but about whose character he has little or no choice. He may be a generally happy, active, and contented member of his community, but he remains subservient ancestrally and racially.[30] Positively, ancestor worship enfranchises individuals in an ancient hereditary community whose natural genius requires a cause and vision unique to its racial tradition. National Socialism, as portrayed by Hitler in *Mein Kampf*, is just such a community whose genius provides a vision and cause around which Aryans create an aristocratic ideal independent of inferior peoples and degenerate cultures.[31] "The inner seclusion of the species," Aryan superiority, Aryans as "culture-creators," Jews as "culture-destroyers," prohibitions of "blood or race mixing," eugenics, liberalism's transgression of nature's "aristocratic ideal," a cult of personality, the necessity of "thinking with the blood"—these and many more dogmas of Hitler's *Mein Kampf* together form a myth of self-adoration by and through which neo-pagan faith situates itself asymmetrically in relation to the symmetry of Enlightenment reason, and in so doing it commits the fallacy of fideism.

Collingwood makes clear that the German tendency toward ancestral worship is not, however, the same as state worship. State worship ordinarily involves the Hobbesian conception of the state as something artificial in origin and human in essence, something existing by convention. In contrast, ancestor worship or the worship of the *Volkstaate*, as Hitler puts it, involves a view in which the nation as ancestral community is in origin natural and racial and in essence divine.

Hegel's view of the state is of this sort, though he prudently admits that it is not God Himself but "*der Gang Gottes in der Welt.*"[32] It is no artificial, human artifact (i.e., the state) that is adored in ancestor worship, but the nation—the divinely ordained organic, racial community of people. Thus, Nazi Aryanism, as a form of communal self-adoration, requires that devotees offer themselves and everything they have in sacrifice not to a human institution but to the divinely ordained ancestral community.

Coupled with ancestor worship, a second movement, autocrat worship, contributed to the process of remythologizing that corrupted German consciousness. Autocrat worship is a form of piety that increasingly characterized German paganism in the late nineteenth and early twentieth centuries. It means just what the phrase suggests: adoration of the independent and unrestricted power of a supreme ruler or, in Collingwood's words, "the conjuring up of a social order based on the superstitious adoration of individual leaders."[33] Bismarck perhaps only partly typifies such a leader, but Mussolini and Hitler do so quite completely. Collingwood analyzes such autocrat worship in terms of what he calls "the propaganda of irrationalism." The strategy of the autocrat is to substitute for the liberal ideal of rational thought "the ideal of tangled, immediate, emotional thinking; for the idea of a political thinker as political leader the idea of a leader focusing and personifying the mass-emotions of his community; for the ideal of intelligent agreement with a leader's thought the idea of an emotional communion with him; and for the idea of a minority persuaded to conform the idea of unpatriotic persons . . . induced to conform by emotional means, namely, by terror."[34] Autocrat worship of this sort is, like ancestor worship, a form of self-adoration, a way for the Germans as a people to think of themselves collectively as constituting an entity more divine than human.

Collingwood further argues that especially in Germany pre-Christian paganism never entirely died out. We are apt to think that the roots of Nazi paganism lie no deeper than the nineteenth century. But influential survivals of an ancient, pre-Christian pagan religion can be traced throughout German history. Like other Protestant countries, Germany did not tolerate paganism. It officially banished pagan practices and influences and even persecuted pagans. Unofficially, however, survivals of pagan beliefs and practices "have always been extremely vigorous" in Germany, insists Collingwood.[35] For example, a tendency to disparage ideas such as political freedom, equality, and individualism and to applaud servility are, in Collingwood's view, vestiges of pagan values woven throughout the writings of influential German Christians. He singles out the German writer Thomas Haemmerlein's (more commonly known as Thomas à Kempis) *Imitatio Christi* as typical writing that "harbors" and perpetuates pagan beliefs. An entire chapter (I.II) is dedicated to belittling freedom and praising servility to one's superiors.³⁶ Moreover, even though the Reformation in general may have generated many of the values later cultivated by liberalism (e.g., freedom and individualism), the German Reformation, especially as pioneered by Luther, merely "exchanged the yoke of Rome for the yoke of the princelings." It thereby guaranteed the loyalty of the German peasants to the maxim "cuis regio eius religio," which was later used to describe those princes.³⁷ Luther's rejection of the peasants' demand for the abrogation of serfdom, then, is not unexpected; it was of a piece with *De servo arbitrio* and the ancient pagan scorn of freedom and individualism. In philosophy this pagan scorn for values of freedom and individualism is perpetuated, according to Collingwood, by Hegel, Marx, Wagner, and Nietzsche.³⁸ On this basis and more, Collingwood concludes that the new political movement, Nazism, is really not so new because it "contains ideas drawn from the survivals of an unextinguished pre-Christian religion, and derives its 'punch' from the emotional appeal of that religion."³⁹ Without denying the roots of anti-Semitism in Christianity, Collingwood insists that Nazism owed much of its success in Germany to pagan worship of the autocrat and to the autocrat's ingenuity for invoking and exploiting powerful emotional forces sublimated in the collective soul of the ancestral community. These two pagan practices, worship of ancestors and autocrats, then, inspired the process of remythologizing that in the collective German consciousness situated itself asymmetrically in relation to rationalism. Collingwood believed that these two forms of ancestor worship constituted the kind of neo-pagan religion that quickly filled the emotional and spiritual void left by the eclipse of Christianity and supplied the emotional energy and driving force needed to bring into the midst of civilized, scientific Europe a culture of irrational, racial self-adoration and at the same time a culture of self-destruction.

The question arises as to how it was possible for the collective German consciousness to simultaneously commit two fallacies, the fallacy of rationalism inherited from the Enlightenment and the fallacy of fideism inherited from pagan mythology. How could it commit itself at the same time to scientific reason and to neo-pagan irrationality? The Nazi version of paganism was able to emerge and flourish in civilized Europe, argues Collingwood, because to be German meant "to suffer from a divided consciousness,"⁴⁰ from a double-mindedness out of which there simultaneously flowed a commitment to pure reason and science and a devotion to a fanatical, antirational pagan piety. The dialectical demands of these antagonistic traditions on German consciousness obligated it at once to the worship of enlightened truth, on the one hand, and the worship of pagan passions, on the other. Enlightenment rationalism and neo-paganism fideism, incompatible though they were, were embraced and held together, insists Collingwood, by the sheer force of German will. The discoveries of the natural and social sciences fly in the face of any rationale for adopting the pagan practice of ancestor and autocrat worship. Nevertheless, Collingwood suggests that the German mind by compromise and concession managed certain accommodations that minimized the interference of one tradition with the other. For a time, the German habit of self-adoration was "so far relaxed as to permit the worship of truth as well as the worship of the German people."[41] But such a compromise is easier to manage in theory than in practice. Strains between these two contradictory habits of mind would inevitably develop to a point at which the pursuit of truth and scientific inquiry and the practice of liberal values, drained by the Enlightenment of the Christian passion and power that originally inspired them, would give way to the impassioned, fanatical pursuit of a neo-pagan mythology and way of life. All thinking and scientific inquiry would not cease, nor would universities be closed. But scientific thinking would now be enlisted in service to pagan religion and prejudices. All thought and inquiry would, as Collingwood puts it, now "redound to the greater glory of the German people."[42] Collingwood does not go very far in explaining in detail why such a divided German consciousness should arise in the first place. But one can plausibly argue, I think, that his entire theory provides the answer. On the one hand, the rational, scientific habit, forming one side of this divided consciousness, survived through the process, already described, by which the presuppositions of Christian beliefs were demythologized and secularized in such a way as to form the premises of modern science and liberal politics, while Christianity's irrational, emotional, and ritualistic elements were simply disowned and suppressed. On the other hand, the powerful irrational, emotional forces, which in their Christian context were suppressed by the Enlightenment, were nevertheless available to the German consciousness from its pagan tradition. Pools of powerful emotional forces, latent but surviving in Germany's primitive paganism, were exploited by the Nazis and re-erupted in a fury of ideological passion.

Of course the majority of people in postwar Europe were opposed to Nazism and were devoted to the principles of liberal democracy. But liberal democracy, as a stepchild of the Enlightenment, had been eviscerated of those emotional forces necessary to resist the passion and power of fascist forces that swept Europe. In England and France, where Christianity was still somewhat influential and liberalism a long and cherished practice, fascist forces were largely resisted although not without some difficulty. In Germany, however, Nazism succeeded, and not only because of economic conditions or because of the humiliation imposed on Germany by the Treaty of Versailles or because of Christian anti-Semitism. Collingwood's work brings to our attention the fact that even more basic forces were at work in history to bring about, in 1933, what Hitler called *Machtergreifung* (the seizure of power). For the Nazis contrived to tap a reservoir of religious passion that, for reasons already given, had become largely unavailable to the devotees of liberalism. In 1940 Collingwood wrote: "Fascist and Nazi activity exhibits a driving power, a psychological dynamism, which seems to be lacking from the activity of those who try to resist it. The anti-Fascists and anti-Nazis feel as if they were opposed, not to men, but to demons; and those of them who have analyzed this say with one accord that Fascism and Nazism have succeeded in invoking for their own service stores of emotional energy in their devotees which in their opponents are either latent or nonexistent."[43] But could Nazi paganism have sustained its power and carried out its atrocities had there not already been in Germany a long and deeply rooted tradition of Christian anti-Semitism? or if ecclesiastical alliances, both Protestant and Catholic, had not ensured for the Third Reich the active support of the churches? Ecclesiastical complicity with the National Socialists is well documented and familiar. We can only speculate whether, without the aid of Christian anti-Semitism and the complicity of churches, the religious ideology described by Collingwood would have been sufficient to ensure the success of Nazism. What we do know is that its success was a function of all of these forces, Enlightenment, Christian, and pagan.

The combined impact of rationalism and fideism in modern European civilization is perhaps analogous to taking improper dosages of a drug, in which a deficient dosage results in the constipation of rationalism and an excessive dosage results in the laxative of fideism. Imagine, as Kierkegaard does, a medicine that in correct dosage balances the forces of reason and emotion, thereby guaranteeing a healthy, civilized society. Imagine also a person who, despite the doctor's orders, fancies himself as exceptionally advanced and insists on taking half of the medicine only, a half dosage that as it turns out has a constipating effect. Then imagine this same person, in reaction to his constipation, taking a double dose of the medicine that as it turns out has a laxative effect. The damage inflicted by such fluctuations, of course, places his health in jeopardy. The patient needs to simply follow the doctor's orders and take the medicine in its proper dosage, reason and emotion together, in equal amounts and so ensure a return of the body, a return of the body politic, to its properly balanced and civilized health.

Compassion and Supersymmetry

If we look candidly at the history of modern Europe, we see what the convergence of these two fallacies, rationalism and fideism, has meant for the twentieth century: a savagery of such proportions as to defy human imagination. Not so easily seen is the role religion and philosophical attitudes toward religion play in establishing conditions conducive to such savagery. Who in seventeenth-century Europe could have anticipated that Enlightenment rationalism and its eclipse of Christianity would spark a neo-pagan conflagration of such vicious brutality as to threaten the very foundations of reason and civilization? These are the facts that so far in this chapter I have tried to trace, and this is the reality in whose dark shadow we still grope, a reality from which philosophers of religion must not avert their gaze. And if we do not look away we shall see that religion itself, for all its faults and failures, bears within it seeds that when cultivated contribute to a process of civilizing, rather than brutalizing, societies.

By now we are familiar with compassion as that activity through which the world's asymmetry is overcome and a supersymmetrical harmony established. Every religion worth preserving, as argued in chapter 6, is one for whom compassion is a pivotal moral category for participating in public life. It is by practicing compassion that religions contribute to the health of societies and the equilibrium of civilizations. Indeed, compassion is that primary religious experience with sufficient spiritual and moral depth to overcome the fallacies of rationalism and fideism and establish the supersymmetry needed to civilize human life. And it does so by performing two public roles, one prophetic and one pastoral. It is the Christian version of these two roles through which I shall show how compassionate supersymmetry is possible. Recall that in her song Mary's "soul rejoices" because the proud and powerful are scattered and the humble and lowly are exalted. The former reflects Christianity's prophetic role and the latter its pastoral role; together these roles constitute systolic and diastolic motions of Christian compassion in public life. We shall find that in its prophetic role Christianity demands justice, while in its pastoral role it grants care and mercy. My premise is that if religions assume responsibility for performing these two public roles, then fallacies such as Enlightenment rationalism and Nazi fideism are likely to be avoided and the glories of civilization advanced.

Compassion in its prophetic role is comparable to the philosopher's role as gadfly. For all their differences, Socrates and Jesus similarly embody this role in their respective societies and both suffer and suffer death in performing it. A prophet or prophetic community is without honor in its own country because it is called to situate itself critically in relation to the powerful and power structures (political, social, intellectual, economic) of a society. Its business is to speak out, to reveal to society the secrets, especially the secret failings, of its own heart, to make known to the powerful those self-deceptions and corruptions of consciousness about which ignorance means tyranny and injustice, savagery and death. A prophetic community, in other words, shines as a light and shines light on that vital dimension of experience its particular society is susceptible to disowning and suppressing. The prophetic community demands justice, but to do so it must first unmask the self-deception that would lead those in power to believe that theirs is already a just society. Only with light radiated by a prophetic community are those in power able to see the injustice in their midst and see the need for justice. So the prophetic aim is not simply to expose injustices (e.g., tyranny, prejudices, poverty, exploitation) of a society, which is simple enough. But its aim is first to candidly and no doubt painfully unmask to a society the corruption its consciousness suffers, to disclose a society's tendency to disown certain experiences that are otherwise vital to its health and wholeness, experiences of which poverty and prejudice are tragic symptoms. If the self-deception a society suffers is not first disclosed and admitted, the call for justice is not likely to be heard by those in positions of power and perhaps even by those marginalized by that power.

This candid prophetic self-disclosure is evident in Plato's *Apologia*, where Socrates, in defense of himself, recounts how, inspired by the Delphic oracle, he seeks to discover who in Athens is truly a philosopher, a lover of wisdom. In so doing he finds that the Athenians are generally deceived about the matter, that those whom they consider wise are really lacking in wisdom and those whom they consider foolish, namely, Socrates, are those whom the gods consider wise. Not until Socrates proclaims to the Athenians this self-deception, this corruption of consciousness, does he then proceed to cast light on the flaws in Athenian society—that they are inclined to put wealth and possession, status and honor foremost in their lives and neglect what is most important, namely, the welfare of their own souls, virtue. Indeed, Socrates is arguing that the Athenians are first and foremost unjust to themselves, preferring temporal goods, like fortune and fame, to eternal goods like virtue and justice.

The Hebrew prophets with great drama and clarity, following this same pattern, first proclaim to the people of Israel that their failures—the idolatry, immorality, poverty, and injustice in their society—are a result of a corrupt consciousness, of mistakenly believing that by offering sacrifices to the Lord with their hands and praises with their lips they are fulfilling their obligation as God's chosen. Most famously, the prophetic voice of Amos condemns those hypocrites who practice religion but do not live righteously and compassionately. The Lord despises their feast, "solemn assemblies," "burnt offerings," songs, and instruments, declares Amos. Banish all things religious from my sight, says the Lord; only "let justice roll down like waters and righteousness like an ever-flowing stream" (Amos 5:21–24). That is why "Remember" is perhaps the most frequent prophetic command of the Hebrew prophets. By forgetting, Israel disowns its spiritual identity and its moral orientation. By forgetting, it suppresses the very identity and orientation without which it loses its raison d'être. Only by remembering can Israel recover from self-deception, retrieve its identity, and reenact in its own political and social life the just and merciful compassion whereby the Lord delivers them from oppression and poverty. By forgetting and disowning their past identity, Israel did not know how to live in the present, and thus found itself practicing as policy those very treacheries (exploitation of the poor and powerless) from which God had delivered them. For the Hebrew prophets the demand for justice, then, follows naturally the imperative to remember. Upon remembering who it is, Israel can on the basis of that recollected identity reorient itself morally, reenacting the same justice in its own life that God from ancient times has enacted toward it.

Jesus also finds himself without honor in his own country because the targets of his prophetic light are those with political, economic, and religious power. As prophet and light he first exposes to them the corruption of their consciousness, the most explicit form of which is the hypocrisy of self-righteousness. Religious hypocrisy is a function of a self-deception in which people disown the truth about themselves, namely, that they are not, and of themselves cannot be, the righteous persons they mistakenly believe and portray themselves to be. In acting self-righteously, a community alienates itself from the truth about itself; it deceives itself about who and what it is. The prophet's initial business, then, is to declare to his own community the painful truth about this self-deception. For unless a community admits this deception and remembers its identity, it can never hope to orient itself according to the moral symmetry of justice, freedom, and peace. Throughout his ministry Jesus repeatedly relates prophetically to those in power. One provocative example of this is the portrait Jesus paints of a Pharisee who in the temple square proudly prays, thanking God that he is not a poor miserable sinner like so many others, including the tax collector who also prays but in a place where he cannot be seen, and prays sincerely, humbly asking God's mercy on him, a sinner (Luke 18:10–14). The Pharisee is deceived about himself, disowns his true identity, stands asymmetrically in relation to himself, and is thus unable to orient himself morally. The light of compassion that Jesus and all prophets shine is a light that illuminates this fundamental human deception on which an individual and individual community stands in relation to itself. And only then is a community in a position to orient itself morally and to following the prophetic demand for justice and peace.

Concomitantly with its prophetic role in society is Christianity's pastoral role, rooted in the soil of compassion and comparable to the philosopher's role as midwife. Socrates and Jesus both perform this role, by situating themselves compassionately in relation to the society's marginalized and disenfranchised, in relation to those who are powerless politically, socially, intellectually, and economically. A pastoral community's business as midwife is to grant mercy and care for all people but especially those who suffer some kind of physical, psychological, emotional, social, intellectual, or spiritual difficulty. It is a community, in other words, which like salt heals wounds and preserves the health and wholeness of a society. In contrast to demanding justice in its prophetic role, Christianity in its pastoral role grants mercy and care. The Christian community, unlike secular communities, does not first ask whether the recipient of its care merits or deserves it. For that would be to disown and suppress its own identity, that would be to corrupt its consciousness by laboring under the illusion that it is a community that merits the mercy and care it receives from God. In truth the Christian community's self-identity is a function of the unmerited mercy and care with which God in Christ has redeemed it, and it is this kind of merciful care that its pastoral role in society requires of it.

Although when we think of Socrates we more often think of him in his role as Athenian gadfly, he frequently fulfills, in relation to his fellow citizens, the role of midwife, of caring for the welfare of the Athenian soul, as Plato puts it in the *Apologia*. Socrates' primary concern seems to be more for the intellectual, moral, and spiritual welfare of the Athenians than for their physical, economic, and psychological welfare, at least as portrayed in Plato's dialogues. In the *Crito*, for example, Crito raises the question as to whether Socrates should escape from prison and save himself from death. Whereas Crito's concern is purely instrumental, Socrates' concern is moral and spiritual. He asks on what basis we should decide whether escaping from prison is the moral thing to do. And in his role as midwife and by means of his infamous questioning Socrates leads Crito to see for himself what the virtuous person should do. As midwife, Socrates demonstrates a pastoral concern for Crito's welfare and the welfare of all who care to converse with him.

Although the Hebrew prophets are perhaps better known for their prophetic role of demanding justice, they likewise demonstrate a pastoral care, especially for the oppressed and marginalized. Hosea, for example, is portrayed as persistent in his care for adulterous Israel, who although it has desecrated itself is nevertheless still the object of God's compassion and mercy. The Psalmists, as much as any of the biblical writers, manifest a profound sense of pastoral care for the poor and disenfranchised of society. God and God's people are to advocate for the poor (9:9–10; 34:6; 86:1–2, 7), support the needy (107:41; 109:31; 146:5–9), liberate the oppressed (10:17; 69:32–33), and comfort the afflicted, sorrowful, lowly, widows, and orphans (25:16; 68:6; 74:21; 147:6). Again, as with the prophetic role, the frequent biblical command to "remember" is provocative, for it requires of a community the same pastoral concern in society that God in the past has shown toward it. So Israel is instructed, for example, to care for foreigners and strangers in its land just as God cared for them when they were foreigners and strangers in Egypt (Exodus 22:21; 23:9–11; Deuteronomy 10:19; Psalms 146:9). By remembering, a community recalls its identity as those who have received God's care and mercy and therefore a community who on the basis of that identity orients itself morally with the same care and mercy toward those in society who are in need physically, psychologically, socially, morally, and spiritually.

Compassionate care, in other words, is the way God and God's people overcome those various conditions in society that are situated asymmetrically in relation to the desired symmetry and health.

The prophetic role of Jesus' public ministry is likewise balanced by the continuous pastoral care he demonstrates to a wide variety of society's marginalized, a care that is both inclusive and holistic. It is inclusive in that Jesus shows merciful care toward members of all strata of society. He cares for Nicodemus and Zaccheus, elite members of the Israeli society; he cares for the average woman, man, and child, and feeds them, for example, when they go hungry; and he cares passionately for those who are disenfranchised from the social, political, economic, and religious institutions of society. In short, Jesus shows compassion for the poor, the needy, the self-righteous religious, the irreligious, prostitutes, prisoners, politicians, thieves, murderers, tax collectors, soldiers, priests, foreigners, Romans, Samaritans, and so on. The mercy and compassion with which Jesus cares for this diverse population is not contingent on whether the recipients merit care. By the social criteria of his day many do not. One of the unique dimensions of Jesus' pastoral role is that his care is unconditional and unmerited and therefore a gift of equal mercy to all in his society. Consider, for example, Jesus' treatment of the woman caught in the act of adultery (John 8). By law she deserves to die; and yet Jesus shows pastoral care for her not only by protecting her from her accusers and from death but by granting her the mercy and renewal of forgiveness. Along with demanding justice, the Christian community is, therefore, obligated to follow Christ's pattern of granting mercy and care in public life. By so doing, by caring for even the least and marginalized of society, it cares for Christ himself (Matthew 25:31–46). The pastoral care Jesus practices, however, is not only inclusive but also holistic. Robert Kysar, in *Called to Care*, shows how the merciful care of Jesus is granted to the whole person, to her physical, emotional, economic, social, and political as well as spiritual well-being.[44] Jesus heals the sick and afflicted, he casts out demons, he forgives the guilty, he cares for needs of the poor and hungry, he befriends social outcasts and strangers, he feasts with the irreligious and prostitutes and tax collectors, and he cares for Roman soldiers. So also should be the care of Christian communities that claim to follow his pattern of life. The care they grant the society in which they find themselves should be as inclusive and holistic, as unmerited and merciful a gift to all as that gift which they themselves have received from God in Christ.

Looking candidly at the history of modern Europe, we are confronted by the stark and sturdy fact that Christianity often has failed in its role as compassionate community; it often fails to situate itself prophetically and pastorally in relation to society and civilization. It is partly because of this failure that the fallacies of rationalism and fideism were able to emerge and thrive in modern Christian Europe.

What prophetic light did shine was apparently too dim to illuminate the corruption of consciousness under which both Enlightenment rationalism and Nazi neo-paganism flourished. Theologians and philosophers routinely failed to brightly shine Christianity's prophetic light on rationalism, for example, and its irrational repudiation of religion's vital and invigorating role in civilizing societies. Instead of prophetically exposing this self-deception and its dangers, most Christian theologians and philosophers scrambled like frightened supplicants before the altar of rationalism, eagerly offering sacrifices to the idol of science. And what they sacrificed was the one thing without which reason withers and dies, namely, "the wholesome flowing waters of emotion, which alone fertilizes all human activity. . . ."[45] The collaborative failure of enlightened Christian thinkers was not their desire to interpret Christianity in accordance with the principles of reason, nor their desire to bring Christianity up to date intellectually and morally. Their failure, simply put, was committing the fallacy of rationalism: suppressing emotions and failing to prophetically expose this corruption of consciousness. Their failure, ironically, was the passionate, irrational, superstitious worship of the idol of reason alone.

The ramifications of this failure and fallacy in the twentieth century, as is well known, were magnificent. Churches in Germany and throughout Europe largely disowned and suppressed a sense of responsibility for those suffering Nazi racism and brutality. Jews, gypsies, gays, and Catholics were eliminated in large numbers. Even from North America ships of immigrant Jews were turned away to deposit their human cargo in Europe to face Hitler's final solution. And where was the church? Where was Christianity? Where were Christian prophets and pastors and professors? Who would demand justice and who would grant mercy? Most church leaders and theologians, suffering from divided allegiances, submitted to the mythological irrationalism demanded of them by the Nazis, while at the same time submitting to the rationalism demanded of them in their scholarly work by their Enlightenment heritage. Most abandoned any prophetic and pastoral sense of Christian compassion in public life. Most abandoned the prophetic and pastoral roles that Christ himself had instituted and practiced in the public life of his own society. There were a few notable, courageous exceptions: the Confessing Church, Deitrich Bonhoeffer, Karl Barth, the Barmen Confession, who demanded justice and granted care in the midst of horrendous evil, and whose prophetic voice and pastoral care still inspire Christians today.

If prophets fail to shine light on the fallacy of rationalism, if they fail to demand that human emotions and religious affections be properly and fairly reenfranchised as vital and indispensable to the health of a civilized society, then we can be sure that societies in our own day will be susceptible to the fallacy of fideism and forms of neo-paganism whose savage irrationalism will erode the illusion of a contemporary world that is civilized. Capitalism, the Enlightenment's economic project, for example, is a function of the same fallacy of rationalism and the corruption of consciousness it presupposes. Disowning the intersubjectivity of compassion whereby humans care for one another economically, worshipping rational economic principles as if they are natural and alone sufficient to guide markets and distribute goods, constitutes a self-deception to which Adam Smith and many other enlightened Christians to this day blissfully but speciously succumb. The history of modern Europe has proven beyond doubt, I think, that if we allow for the tyranny of reason (the fallacy of rationalism) then we establish conditions that may very well trigger a reactionary neo-pagan undertow. The antidote is for Christianity to practice its prophetic and pastoral roles. And if it does not, then, we should not be surprised. We should not be surprised that if Christianity can persuade itself to collaborate with the fallacy of rationalism, then Christianity can also, as indeed it did, persuade itself to collaborate with the fallacy of fideism and the irrationality of neo-pagan religions like Nazism. Nor should we be surprised at the persistence of these two fallacies and their ongoing potential for ravaging civilized life on a global scale. We should not be surprised, for example, that in reaction to rationalism's globally domineering idol of capitalism a form of vicious neo-paganism reemerges whose myths and rituals are able to invoke a latent reservoir of globally sublimated developing-world passion of such power as to be able to decimate those societies erected on the cool, calculated but fallacious rationality of capitalism.

From Corruption to Compassion

The decay of Western civilization is not fundamentally a matter of violence and immorality, although these are tragic symptoms. It is not fundamentally the result of indulging beastly instincts or betraying scientific reason. Nor is it the result of a withering array of philosophies and religions. These sturdy facts are symptoms of decay that are rooted much more deeply in the human soul and its infidelity of mind. Throughout this book I have addressed, directly and indirectly, the question, What does "fidelity of mind" mean? I have tried to answer with my own renovated version of the ancient philosophical adage *credo ut intelligam*. I have argued that a civilization's health and harmony, its supersymmetry as it were, requires in simultaneous and equal measure the veracity of reason and the vitality of faith. Although distinguishable, they are nevertheless inseparable and interdependent aspects of a single whole that survives only as a totality. The vitality of the one depends on the vitality of the other; the decline of one precipitates the decline of the other.[46] Their primary combined function is civilizing societies.[47] And practicing religion is a primitive and primary way in which reason and emotion weave into the fabric of society sentiments specifically tailored for and to the purpose of civilizing it. It is true that at times a society may favor one factor, rational or irrational, over the other; but the truly stable, civilized society works for a balance of the two.

By religions practicing compassion in its prophetic and pastoral manifestations, then, the fallacies of rationalism and fideism are surmounted, as are the horrendous evil and suffering resulting from them. But religions in general and Christianity in particular very often fail the societies in which they find themselves, largely because of the corruption of consciousness, because they permit themselves to be seduced by the fallacies of rationalism and fideism, forsaking the prophetic and pastoral roles that compassion otherwise empowers them to practice. This seduction of Christianity continues today insofar as it sanctions, sanitizes, and tries to sanctify global capitalism, for example, whose roots are deeply planted in the fallacy of the same rationalism that was helpless to resist the propaganda of irrationalism preached by the Nazis. To answer the question as to how Christianity comes to suppress an experience (God's loving compassion) without which it loses its spiritual identity and moral orientation would be to repeat the argument and paradigm already set forth in this chapter. It does so, on the one hand, by accommodating itself to the forces of rationalism. These forces are calculated to demythologize religious beliefs and disenfranchise religious emotions from society, thereby secularizing it. Secularization, however, eviscerates a society of the spiritual and psychological power necessary to inspire it to practice and sustain its civilized way of life. And Christianity typically fails, on the other hand, by accommodating forces of neo-pagan fideism whereby a society devotes itself to ancestral and autocrat worship. This remythologization at the same time unleashes those spiritual and psychological forces sublimated by secularization, which reassert themselves in a society with such brutal savagery that the very foundations of civilization are threatened. One can scarcely imagine a greater failure on the part of Christianity, a failure to sustain the very tradition that it had civilized in the first place. What hope there is for Christianity is that its failure is a matter of its own self-deception, the corruption of its own consciousness. And it is thus a matter within its power to redeem and transform. Christianity's corruption is to disown, for the sake of accommodating rationalism's secular civilization, those religious practices and emotional forces without which reason and civilization ironically cannot long survive.

Contemporary philosophers of religion contribute to the fallacy of fideism and the vitality of various forms of neo-paganism to the extent that they insist on speaking as ventriloquists, speaking "in such a way that it is impossible to identify who is speaking," to the extent they commit the fallacy of rationalism, shrouding their "I" in the disguise of a third person, abstract "I."[48] The remedy for these corruptions of consciousness, the remedy for these fallacies of rationalism and fideism, is fidelity of mind. For the Christian philosopher, fidelity of mind means a single-minded commitment to practice in public what it preaches in private: that the loving compassion that God in Christ mercifully grants to humanity is the same loving compassion that, in the form of prophetic voice and pastoral care, Christianity must practice in public, in society, in global community. "Peoples rich in religious energy can overcome all obstacles and attain any height in the scale of civilization. Peoples that have reached the top of the hill by the wise use of religious energy may then decide to do without it," says Collingwood; "they can still move, but they can only move downhill, and when they get to the bottom they stop."[49] Philosophers of religion often contribute to this descent, it seems to me, by committing in the substance of their own writing and teaching the same fallacy of rationalism committed by Enlightenment thinkers. Too often we think and write before the altar of reason alone, disowning the local dialects of faith and our faith traditions, disowning the ritual practices that invoke religious passions sufficiently powerful to put into practice the asymmetrical as well as symmetrical beliefs that are vital for civilizing a society. To philosophers of religion who want not the simple fallacious symmetry of rationalism nor the simple fallacious asymmetry of fideism, I offer fidelity of mind, reason and faith, intellect and emotion inseparably. And I offer religion as primary steward of that fidelity. Religion, accordingly, is not a luxury but a necessity, an experience vital to the well-being of civilizations. Just as a healthy civilization must encourage robust scientific, philosophical, and artistic communities, so too it must encourage robust religious communities. And just as civilization need not, indeed, must not, favor one community of scientists or artists over another, so too it need and must not favor one religion over another while encouraging citizens to speak and practice the dialects of their own local traditions. In Collingwood's view, it is important that our civilization never again deceive itself in this matter. If it does, it will again sow within itself seeds of destruction that may grow into any kind of collective disorder, any kind of folly and irrationality, any kind of savagery. Religion's first public business is the health of society, to be society's medicine for the worst illness of mind, the corruption of consciousness.

Rationalism and fideism are corruptions commonly suffered by the Western intellectual tradition. As fallacies they are corrosive not just of mind and philosophy but, as I have tried to make clear, of society and civilization as well. That is why in the beginning of this book I insisted that "fidelity of mind" is a matter of some urgency for philosophers. For the effects of any collective betrayal of mind, whether a betrayal of faith or reason, ripple far beyond those originating it. Religious passions inspired by ritual practices (faith) are as vital to the health of society as is the practice of formulating beliefs rationally (reason), and vice versa. To practice both habits of mind simultaneously is the challenge of any philosopher and scientist, any theologian and minister, any society interested in survival. The power and patience required of any mind if it is to persevere and flourish in faith and reason, however, explain why natural (fallen) human instincts often pursue the path of least resistance by favoring one over the other. The cost of indulging these instincts in modern Europe, culminating in the Holocaust of the twentieth century, is one of the great tragedies of human history. Rationalists who expect the world to be primarily a matter of simple symmetry and scientific rationality are as deceived as fideists who expect it to be primarily a matter of asymmetry and religious faith. But the waters of the human spirit are calmed and civilized neither by the high tide of rationalism (modernism) nor by the undertow of fideism (postmodernism). Nor are they calmed by the suspended animation of these two forces equally. For philosophers who want not simple reason or simple faith but who want to practice fidelity of mind and want to know what fidelity of mind can mean, compassion supplies an answer. For not only does compassion supply specific answers to specific questions traditionally treated by philosophers of religion, as I have tried to show throughout; not only does it unmask the self-deceptions underlying the fallacies (of rationalism and fideism) to which some fall prey; but compassion requires the practice of both habits of mind, faith and reason, without which societies are susceptible to decay and corruption but with which societies civilize themselves and flourish.

Notes

1. Collingwood died in 1943 and would not have known the full extent of the Holocaust. From what he writes in *The New Leviathan* about German barbarism, however, he would not have been surprised at its occurrence, although he would have been surely horrified at its brutality.

2. R. G. Collingwood, *An Autobiography* (London: Oxford University Press, 1939), 167.

3. R. G. Collingwood, "Fascism and Nazism," *Philosophy* 15 (1940): 168–176.

4. I use "irrational" here and throughout this chapter advisedly. Until recently it was a common assumption and certainly the assumption of Enlightenment philosophers that human emotions are raw, irrational forces indifferent to if not often opposed to the principles of science and reason and unreliable as moral guides. Throughout this chapter, then, I use "irrational" to refer to the Enlightenment belief that human emotions are contrary to reason and unreliable as moral guides. This view of the emotions as simply irrational is almost universally rejected today. Research in psychology, sociology, biology, physiology, neurology, not to mention philosophy, has established that emotions are in some sense cognitive experiences, a view that Collingwood seems to support in his later writings, like *The New Leviathan*. If the reader has been even half awake in reading thus far in this book, she or he will know that its author shares this cognitive interpretation of human emotions.

5. Collingwood, "Fascism and Nazism," 169.

6. R. G. Collingwood, "Reason Is Faith Cultivating Itself," in *Faith and Reason: Essays in the Philosophy of Religion by R. G. Collingwood*, ed. Lionel Rubinoff (Chicago: Quadrangle Books, 1968), 119.

7. See F. M. Cornford, *From Religion to Philosophy* (New York: Harper & Row, 1957), passim.

8. Collingwood, "Fascism and Nazism," 169.

9. Ibid.

10. R. G. Collingwood, *An Essay on Metaphysics* (Chicago: Henry Regnery, 1972), 219–227, 248–257. Collingwood points out that the first two of these four beliefs were inherited by Christianity from Greek thought, while the second two are uniquely Judeo-Christian contributions. Together, these two traditions and these four absolute presuppositions produce and shape what we know as modern Western civilization.

11. See Collingwood, *An Essay on Metaphysics*, 201–207; "Fascism and Nazism," passim; *The New Leviathan* (Oxford: Clarendon Press, 1942), 18, 42–44; and *The Idea of History* (Oxford: Clarendon Press, 1946), 255–256.

12. R. G. Collingwood, *The Idea of History* (Oxford: Clarendon Press, 1946), 255–256.

13. Collingwood, "Fascism and Nazism."

14. The case for the historical roots of modern science and liberal politics can and has been made. Founders of modern science like Kepler, Galileo, and Newton, and of liberalism, like Locke and Rousseau, undeniably were driven by the desire to know the laws governing God's natural and social creations. But it is also true that modern science and liberal politics long endured resistance and even hostility from Christian thinkers and institutions, both Catholic and Protestant. Very often Christianity bitterly opposed laws advocating toleration and pluralism and only reversed itself when it lost control of governments and the power to do what it wished. Very often, only ex post facto did Christianity come to interpret liberal values and modern science as logical reflections of its own version of the world.

15. The dogmas of civil religion, according to Rousseau, include "the existence of a might, intelligent, and beneficent Divinity, possessed of foresight and providence, the life to come, the happiness of the just, the punishment of the wicked, the sanctity of the social contract and the laws." See N. L. Torrey, ed., *Les Philosophes: The Philosophers of the Enlightenment and Modern Democracy* (New York: Capricorn Books, 1960), 160.

16. Collingwood, "Fascism and Nazism," 170–171; cf. *The New Leviathan*, 13.5–13.53.

17. Although Kant believes emotions such as love can have no primary place in guiding moral decision making, he does grant love and other emotions a greater role in moral life than many scholars acknowledge. See my discussion of this matter in *Fidelity of Heart: An Ethic of Christian Virtue* (New York: Oxford University Press, 2001), 42–45.

18. Collingwood, "Fascism and Nazism," 169, 175.

19. Collingwood, *The New Leviathan*, VIII and X.

20. Collingwood, "Fascism and Nazism," 175–176.

21. See Collingwood's *Principles of Art* (Oxford: Clarendon Press, 1938), 65–77, 109–111.

22. Collingwood, "Fascism and Nazism," 174.

23. Ibid., 169.
24. R. G. Collingwood, *The Principles of Art* (Oxford Clarendon Press, 1938), 216–221, 282–285.
25. Lionel Rubinoff, *Collingwood and the Reform of Metaphysics: A Study in the Philosophy of Mind* (Toronto, Ont.: University of Toronto Press, 1970), 89.
26. Collingwood, "Fascism and Nazism," 168.
27. Collingwood, *An Essay on Metaphysics*, 225; cf. 220, 227n.
28. Collingwood, "Fascism and Nazism," 168.
29. Quoted in *Communism, Fascism, and Democracy: The Theoretical Foundations*, ed. Carl Cohen (New York: Random House, 1962), 330.
30. Collingwood, *The New Leviathan*, 33, 35–36.
31. Carl Cohen, ed., *Communism, Fascism, and Democracy: The Theoretical Foundations* (New York: Random House, 1962), 378–380.
32. Collingwood, *The New Leviathan*, 33, 38–42.
33. Collingwood, "Fascism and Nazism," 173.
34. Collingwood, *An Essay on Metaphysics*, 135.
35. Collingwood, "Fascism and Nazism," 175.
36. Collingwood, *The New Leviathan*, 33.50–51.
37. Ibid., 33.51.
38. Ibid., 33.72–99.
39. Collingwood, "Fascism and Nazism," 175.
40. Collingwood, *The New Leviathan*, 33.73.
41. Ibid., 33.65.
42. Ibid., 33.61.
43. Collingwood, "Fascism and Nazism," 171–172.
44. Robert Kysar, *Called to Care: Biblical Images for Social Ministry* (Minneapolis, Minn.: Fortress Press, 1991), see pages 31–44.
45. Collingwood, *The Principles of Art*, 335.
46. Collingwood, *The New Leviathan*, 41.31.
47. Ibid., 41.4–41.55.
48. *Søren Kierkegaard's Journals and Papers*, Papers, ed. and trans. Howard V. Hong and Edna H. Hong (Indianapolis: Indiana University Press, 1975), 4, 125.
49. Ibid., 176.

Bibliography

Adams, Marilyn McCord. "Problems of Evil: More Advice to Christian Philosophers." *Faith and Philosophy* 5, 2 (April 1988): 121–43.
Anderson, Pamela Sue. *A Feminist Philosophy of Religion*. Oxford: Blackwell, 1998.
Apczynski, John. "Belief in God, Proper Basicality, and Rationality." *Journal of the American Academy of Religion* 60, 2 (Summer 1992): 301–312.
Arthur, Chris. "A Revolution in Religious Consciousness." *Bulletin* 29, 1 (February 2000).
Barclay, William. *And He Had Compassion: The Miracles of Jesus*. Valley Forge, Penn.: Judson Press, 1992.
Bilynskyj, Steven. *God, Nature, and the Concept of Miracle*. Ph.D. Dissertation, University of Notre Dame, 1982, 117–46.
Blomberg, Craig. *Matthew*, in *The New American Commentary* 22. Nashville, Tenn.: Broadman Press, 1992.
Blum, Lawrence. "Compassion." *Explaining Emotions*. Edited by Amelie Rorty. Berkeley: University of California Press, 1980.
Burrell, David. "Religious Belief and Rationality." *Rationality and Religious Belief*. Edited by C. F. Delaney. Notre Dame, Ind.: University of Notre Dame Press, 1979.
Caird, G. B. *Principalities and Powers: A Study in Pauline Theology*. London: Oxford University Press, 1956.
Carus, Paul. *The History of the Devil and the Idea of Evil: From the Earliest Times to the Present Day*. La Salle, Ill.: Open Court, 1974.
Clack, Brian R. *An Introduction to Wittgenstein's Philosophy of Religion*. Edinburgh, Scotland: Edinburgh University Press, 1999.
Close, Frank. *Lucifer's Legacy: The Meaning of Asymmetry*. London: Oxford University Press, 2000.
Cohen, Carl, ed. *Communism, Fascism, and Democracy: The Theoretical Foundations*. New York: Random House, 1962.

Collingwood, R. G. *An Essay on Metaphysics*. Chicago: Henery Regnery, 1972.
———. "Faith and Reason." *Faith and Reason: Essays in the Philosophy of Religion by R. G. Collingwood*. Edited by Lionel Rubinoff. Chicago: Quadrangle Books, 1968.
———. "Fascism and Nazism." *Philosophy* 15 (1940): 168–76.
———. *The Idea of History*. Oxford: Clarendon Press, 1946.
———. *The New Leviathan*. Oxford: Clarendon Press, 1942.
———. *The Principles of Art*. Oxford: Clarendon Press, 1938.
———. "Reason Is Faith Cultivating Itself." *Faith and Reason: Essays in the Philosophy of Religion by R. G. Collingwood*. Edited by Lionel Rubinoff. Chicago: Quadrangle Books, 1968.
———. *Religion and Philosophy*. London: Macmillan, 1916.
———. *Speculum Mentis*. Oxford: Clarendon Press, 1924.
Cornford, F. M. *From Religion to Philosophy*. New York: Harper & Row, 1957.
Craig, W. L. *The Historical Argument for the Resurrection of Jesus During the Deist Controversy*. Lewiston, N.Y.: Edwin Mellon Press, 1985.
Craig, W. L., and Quentin Smith. *Theism, Atheism, and Big Bang Cosmology*. Oxford: Clarendon Press, 1993.
Dalai Lama. *Ethics for a New Millennium*. New York: Riverhead Books, 1999.
Davies, Brian. *Thinking About God*. London: Geoffrey Chapman, 1985.
Davies, Paul. *God and the New Physics*. New York: Simon and Schuster. 1984.
———. *The Cosmic Blueprint*. New York: Simon and Schuster, 1988.
Descartes, Rene. *Discourse on Method*. Translated by John Veitch. La Salle, Ill.: Open Court, 1962.
———. *Philosophical Works of Descartes*. Translated by E. S. Haldane and G. R. T. Ross. New York: Dover, 1934.
Edwards, Jonathan. *Religious Affections*. Portland, Ore.: Multnomah Press, 1984.
Everitt, Nicholas. "The Impossiblity of the Miracles." *Religious Studies* 23 (1987): 347–49.
Farley, Wendy. *Tragic Vision and Divine Compassion: A Contemporary Theodicy*. Louisville, Ky.: Westminster John Knox Press, 1990.
Fiering, Norman. "Irresistible Compassion: An Aspect of Eighteenth-Century Sympathy and Humanitarianism." *Journal of the History of Ideas* 37, 2 (1976): 195–218.
Fuller, Reginald H. *Interpreting the Miracles*. Philadelphia, Pa.: Westminster Press, 1963.
Gilman, James E. *Fidelity of Heart: An Ethic of Christian Virtue*. New York: Oxford University Press, 2001.
Goetz, Stewart C. "Belief in God Is Not Properly Basic." *Religious Studies* 19 (1983): 475–84.
Goodman, Nelson. *Ways of Worldmaking*. Indianapolis, Ind.: Hackett Publishing, 1978.
Greenspan, Patricia. *Emotions and Reasons: An Inquiry into Emotional Justification*. New York: Routledge, 1988.
Harrison, Peter. "Newtonian Science, Miracles, and the Laws of Nature." *Journal of the History of Ideas* 56 (1995): 531–53.
Heim, S. Mark. *Salvations: Truth and Difference in Religion*. Maryknoll, N.Y.: Orbis Books, 1997.
Hick, John. *Evil and the God of Love*. New York: Harper & Row, 1966.
———. *An Interpretation of Religion*. New Haven, Conn.: Yale University Press, 1989.

Hume, David. *Enquiry Concerning Human Understanding*, Section X. (New York: Collier & Son, 1910).
Inbody, Tyron. *The Transforming God.* Louisville, Ky.: Westminster John Knox Press, 1997.
Jammer, Max. *Einstein and Religion.* Princeton, N.J.: Princeton University Press, 1999.
Keller, James. "A Moral Argument Against Miracles." *Faith and Philosophy* 12 (1995): 54–78.
Kierkegaard, Søren. *Søren Kierkegaard's Journals and Papers* 1–4. Edited and translated by Howard Hong and Edna Hong. Indianapolis: Indiana University Press, 1975.
———. *Training in Christianity.* Translated by Walter Lowrie. Princeton, N.J.: Princeton University Press, 1952.
———. *Upbuilding Discourse in Various Spirits.* Edited and translated by Howard Hong and Edna Hong. Princeton, N.J.: Princeton University Press, 1993.
———. *Works of Love: Some Christian Reflections in the Form of Discourses.* Translated by Howard Hong and Edna Hong. New York: Harper & Row, 1962.
Knitter, Paul. *One Earth Many Religions: Multifaith Dialogue and Global Responsibility.* Maryknoll, N.Y.: Orbis Books, 1996.
Kysar, Robert. *Called to Care: Biblical Images for Social Ministry.* Minneapolis, Minn.: Fortress Press, 1991.
Larmer, Robert. "Miracles and the Laws of Nature." *Dialogue* (Canada) 24 (1985): 227–28
Lauritzen, Paul. "Emotions and Religious Ethics." *Journal of Religious Ethics* 16, 2 (1988): 307–324.
Lewis, C. S. *The Screwtape Letters.* New York: Simon and Schuster, 1996.
Lowe, E. J. "Miracles and the Laws of Nature." *Religious Studies* 23 (June, 1987): 263–78.
Mackie, J. L. *The Miracle of Theism.* Oxford: Oxford University Press, 1982.
McCleod, Mark. "The Analogy Argument for the Proper Basicality of Belief in God." *International Journal for the Philosophy of Religion* 21 (1987): 19.
McKenzie, David. "Miracles Are Not Immoral: A Response to James Keller's Moral Argument Against Miracles." *Religious Studies* 35 (1999): 73–88.
Mill, J. S. *A System of Logic.* London: Longmans, Green, 1949.
Mitchell, Basil. *The Justification of Religious Belief.* New York: Seabury Press, 1973.
Nielsen, Kai. "Wittgenstein's Fideism." *Philosophy* 42 (July 1967) 205–6.
Noddings, Nel. *Caring: A Feminine Approach to Ethics and Moral Education.* Berkeley: University of California Press, 1984.
Nussbaum, Martha. *Cultivating Humanity: A Classical Defense of Reform in Liberal Education.* Cambridge, Mass.: Harvard University Press, 1997.
———. *Love's Knowledge: Essays on Philosophy and Literature.* New York: Oxford University Press, 1990.
Olson, Alan, ed. *Disguises of the Demonic: Contemporary Perspectives on the Power of Evil.* New York: Association Press, 1975.
Peacocke, Arthur. *Paths from Science Towards God: The End of All Our Exploring.* Oxford: Oneworld Publications, 2001.
Plantinga, Alvin. "Is Belief in God Rational?" *Rationality and Religious Belief.* Edited by C. F. Delaney. Notre Dame, Ind.: University of Notre Dame Press, 1979.
———. "The Reformed Objection to Natural Theology." *Proceedings of the American Catholic Philosophical Association* 54 (1980).
Pojman, Louis P. *Philosophy of Religion: An Anthology.* Belmont, Calif.: Wadsworth, 1987.

Polkinghorne, John. *Belief in God in an Age of Science.* New Haven, Conn.: Yale University Press. 1998.
Prior, William J. "Compassion: A Critique of Moral Rationalism." *Philosophy and Theology* 2 (Winter 1987): 173–91.
Roberts, Robert C. "Emotions as Access to Religious Truths." *Faith and Philosophy* 9, 1 (January 1992): 83–94.
Rubinoff, Lionel. *Collingwood and the Reform of Metaphysics: A Study in the Philosophy of Mind.* Toronto, Ont.: University of Toronto Press, 1970.
Russell, Jeffrey Burton. *The Devil: Perceptions of Evil from Antiquity to Primitive Christianity.* Ithaca, N.Y.: Cornell University Press, 1977.
Schaaffs, Werner. *Theology, Physics, and Miracles.* Translated by Richard Renfield. Washington, D.C.: Canon Press, 1974.
Schubert, Frank D. "Thomas F. Torrence: The Case for a Theological Science." *Encounter* 45 (1984): 133.
Scruton, Roger. "Emotion, Practical Knowledge and Common Culture." *Explaining Emotions.* Edited by Amelie Rorty. Berkeley: University of California Press, 1985.
Smith, John. "Faith, Belief, and the Problem of Rationality." *Rationality and Relgious Belief.* Edited by C. F. Delaney. Notre Dame, Ind.: University of Notre Dame Press, 1979.
Sokol, Moshe Z. "The Anatomy of Reason, Revealed Morality, and Jewish Law." *Religious Studies* 22 (1986): 423–37.
Solomon, Robert. *The Passions.* Notre Dame, Ind.: University of Notre Dame Press, 1976.
Stith, Richard. "Generosity: A Duty without a Right." *Journal of Value Inquiry* 25, 3 (1991): 203.
Swinburne, Richard. *The Existence of God.* Oxford: Clarendon Press, 1979.
Wink, Walter. *Engaging the Powers: Discernment and Resistance in a World of Domination.* Philadelphia, Pa.: Fortress Press, 1992.
———. *Naming the Powers: The Language of Power in the New Testament.* Philadelphia, Pa.: Fortress Press, 1984.
———. *Unmasking the Powers: The Invisible Forces That Determine Human Existence.* Philadelphia, Pa.: Fortress Press, 1986.
Witte, John, Jr., and Ralph C. Martin, eds. *Sharing the Book: Religious Perspectives on the Rights and Wrongs of Proselytism.* Maryknoll, N.Y.: Orbis Books, 1999.
Wittgenstein, Ludwig. *Philosophical Investigations.* Translated by G. E. M. Anscombe. New York: Macmillan, 1958.

Index

Absolute presuppositions, 48–51, 55
Adams, Marilyn McCord, 68, 70
Anselm, 40, 47, 55
asymmetry, 5, 12, 16, 17, 22–24, 27–28, 30,35, 41–44, 45, 48–51, 53–55, 55–59, 70, 71–72, 79, 81, 83–86, 111–12, 168
Augustine, St., 6, 13, 19, 81, 145, 160
Ayer, A.J., 49

Blum, Lawrenece, 135–36
Bohr, Niels, 25, 29
Burrell, David, 21, 47, 53

compassion, 13, 30, 32–33, 59–62, 82, 83, 84–91, 94, 11–12, 131–33, 134–55, 181–82, 183
Collingwood, R.G., 8, 21, 26, 29, 41, 45, 46, 48–50, 53, 55–59, 161–63, 166–68, 169–74, 183
corruption of consciousness, 29–30
Craig, W.L., 43, 100, 102
cumulative case, 20–22, 51–52, 63, 108

Davies, Paul, 24–26, 31, 60, 97, 101
Descartes, Rene, 6, 17, 19, 32, 45, 46–47

Edwards, Jonathan, 126–127
Einstein, Albert, 19, 29–30, 61, 62
Enlightenment, 9, 29–30, 34, 129, 160–62, 162–68, 174–75, 178, 183
evil, 35, 68–70, 72, 74, 85–86, 93–94; horrendous, 67, 68–69, 72–73, 74, 79–80, 90, 93–94

faith, 8, 9, 12, 15–16, 19–22, 26–28, 31, 40–41, 45–46, 55–59, 142, 145, 160, 168
Farley, Wendy, 83, 88–90, 93
fallacy of fideism, 9, 47, 170–171, 180, 181–83
fallacy of rationalism, 9, 47, 160, 182
fideism, 5, 8, 9, 16, 28, 55, 174–75, 183–84
Fuller, Reginald, 102, 112, 113–14, 117

Goetz, Stewart, 40, 46
Good Samaritan, 135–36, 153–55

Hawkings, Stephen, 43
Hegel, Friedrich, 7, 13, 19, 171
Heim, Mark, 124, 141, 153

Index

Heisenberg, Werner, 25
Hick, John, 8, 69, 124
Hitler, Adolf, 170–171, 180
Hume, David: Humean, 5, 6, 7, 19, 40, 68, 97–99, 101, 108, 110, 135, 161

Inbody, Tyron, 81–82
intersubjectivity, 127–28, 129–30

Jesus, 3, 15, 39, 88, 91, 92, 93, 107, 111, 113–17, 123, 128, 131–32, 138, 140–41, 142, 144, 145, 148–49, 151–54, 175, 177–78, 179–80
Job, 67–68, 70–71, 74–75, 79, 83, 85–89, 93, 94

Kant, Emmanuel, 7, 13, 17, 19, 22, 28, 30, 34, 45, 46, 59, 60, 160, 161
Kierkegaard, Soren, 5, 6, 10, 13, 26, 39, 59, 60, 131, 132, 146, 148, 154, 174
King, Jr., Martin Luther, 139
Knitter, Paul, 124–25, 133

Lauritzen, Paul, 126
Lessing, Gotthold, 149–50
Locke, John, 7, 13, 19, 161, 164

McGill, Arthur C., 73–74, 79
mercy, 92–93, 116–17
Mill, J.S., 100–102
miracle, 28, 35, 44, 45, 50
Mitchell, Basil, 20–21, 51

Nazism, 160–61, 168–69, 170–74, 179–80
neo–paganism, 160–61, 169, 172, 180–81, 182

Nielsen, Kai, 6, 40
Nussbaum, Martha, 126, 131, 148

Otto, Rudolph, 161

Paul, St., 5, 15, 35, 59–60, 91, 114, 142, 153
Plantinga, Alvin, 6, 40, 68–69

Rationalism, 6, 8, 9, 16, 28, 159, 164, 179–81, 183–84
reason, 8, 17, 19, 31, 40–41, 55–59, 160, 161–62; prospective, 21–2, 53–54, 62, 109
retrospective, 21–22, 41, 53–54, 109

Santayana, George, 130
Satan, 28, 67–68, 71–75, 79, 81, 83, 93–94
Scruton, Roger, 126
Socrates, 175–76, 178
Standard model, 19, 56
Stith, Richard, 91–92
supersymmetry, 16, 17, 30–32, 34–35, 59–62, 83, 84, 91–93, 111–12, 150, 174–75, 181
SUSY, *see supersymmetry*.
symmetry, 5, 12, 16, 17, 18–22, 23, 24, 26, 28, 30–32, 35, 40–44, 47, 51, 55–59, 112, 117, 161–62

truth: practical, 33–34; 145–151

uncertainty principle, 24–25

Wink, Walter, 50, 73–78
Wittgenstein, Ludwig, 6, 9, 19, 26

About the Author

James E. Gilman is professor of philosophy and religion at Mary Baldwin College in Staunton, Virginia. His recent publications include *Fidelity of Heart: An Ethic of Christian Virtue* (Oxford) and "Whose God, Which Religion: Compassion Normative for Interreligious Cooperation" in *Journal of Ecumenical Studies*. He is a volunteer mediator for a local nonprofit, a mentor in the mental health community, and a deacon in the Episcopal Church USA. His children, Ian and Caitrin, are who he loves best.

www.ingramcontent.com/pod-product-compliance
Lightning Source LLC
Chambersburg PA
CBHW021849300426
44115CB00005B/86